# The Programmer's Survival Guide

Selected titles from the YOURDON PRESS COMPUTING SERIES
Ed Yourdon, *Advisor*

# THE PROGRAMMER'S SURVIVAL GUIDE
## Career Strategies for Computer Professionals

JANET RUHL

Foreword by
EDWARD YOURDON

**YOURDON PRESS**
Prentice Hall Building
*Englewood Cliffs, New Jersey 07632*

*Library of Congress Cataloging-in-Publication Data*

RUHL, JANET. (date)
  The programmer's survival guide : career strategies for computer professionals / Janet Ruhl.
    p.  cm. — (Yourdon Press computing series)
  Includes index
  ISBN 0-13-730375-0
  1. Programming (Electronic computers)  Vocational guidance.
I. Title. II. Series.
QA76.25.R84  1989
005.1'023'73  dc19

Editorial/production supervision
and interior design: BARBARA MARTTINE
Cover design: LUNDGREN GRAPHICS, LTD.
Manufacturing buyer: MARY ANN GLORIANDE

The following are registered and/or trademarks: XPEDITER (Application Development Systems); ADR DATACOM/DB, ROSCOE (Applied Data Research, Inc.); PC/DACS (Applied System Technologies); dBASE III (Ashton-Tate); Unix (AT&T); PACBASE (CGI Systems, Inc.); MANTIS (Cincom Systems); Abend-AID, File-AID (Compuware Corp.); Life-Comm, Life-70 (The Continuum Company); IDMS, IDMS/R, ADSO, DML, IDD (Cullinet Software, Inc.); NOMAD (D&B Computing); HOGAN (Hogan Systems, Inc.); GCOS (Honeywell, Inc.); FOCUS (Information Builders, Inc.); IBM, VSAM, MVS/SP, DOS/VSE, VM/CMS, TSO, CICS, IMS, DB2, BMS, DMS, IMS/DC, PROFS, SPF/PDF, REXX, XEDIT, EXEC, IEB-GENER, SDF, ADF, MAPICS, System/34, System/36, System/38, 43XX Series, 309X Series, 9370, Query by Example (International Business Machines Corp.); Recorder (Language Technology); Lotus 1–2–3 (Lotus Development Corp.); On Line File Utility (MacKinney Systems); VSUM, InterTest RAMIS (on-Line Software International); ORACLE (Oracle Corp.); Panvalet (Pansophic Systems, Inc.); Gen-A-Rate (Programming Resources); PC-Write (Quicksoft); SAS (SAS Institute); ADABAS (Software AG Systems); SyncSort (Syncsort, Inc.)

10  9  8  7  6  5  4  3  2

ISBN  0-13-730375-0

PRENTICE-HALL INTERNATIONAL (UK) LIMITED, *London*
PRENTICE-HALL OF AUSTRALIA PTY. LIMITED, *Sydney*
PRENTICE-HALL CANADA INC., *Toronto*
PRENTICE-HALL HISPANOAMERICANA, S.A., *Mexico*
PRENTICE-HALL OF INDIA PRIVATE LIMITED, *New Delhi*
PRENTICE-HALL OF JAPAN, INC., *Tokyo*
SIMON & SCHUSTER ASIA PTE. LTD., *Singapore*
EDITORA PRENTICE-HALL DO BRASIL, LTDA., *Rio de Janeiro*

# Contents

How do you get to be a paid programmer? Academic requirements. What if your credentials are poor? Making the most of CO-OP programs. Your interview for the first job.

Beginner's mistakes and how to avoid them. What programmers really do and why. Understanding the business world.

Building a long-term career in the corporation as a technical programmer. Going into management. The forces that push technical people into management against their will. How far can you go in DP management?

When and why you should change jobs. When you should not. Why you may need to use a headhunter and how to get the best service. Alternatives to head hunters.

PART TWO
Noncorporate Career Paths
for Programmers

Do consultants really make $50 an hour? The benefits and pitfalls of consulting. Are you ready for consulting? Foreign consultants in the U.S. and their special problems.

The realities behind the latest American Dream. What kind of software can you develop. How do you do it. How can you improve your ability to succeed as a software developer?

You can teach without an advanced degree. What it takes to make big bucks selling programmer services.

Wanna sleep with a beeper or would you rather party?    How different kinds of corporate cultures manifest themselves for programmers.

What do you say when the interviewer asks "How Much?" Determining the going rate.    Hidden factors that affect salary.    Salary ceilings.

A handy review to prepare yourself for the heady interview situation. Chapter references are included.

# Foreword

If I had had Janet Ruhl's *The Programmer's Survival Guide* available to me in 1964, it would have changed my life. I had just finished the first half of my senior year at MIT and discovered by accident that I had enough credits to graduate. Rather than spending an idle second semester taking basketweaving courses, I decided that I simply wouldn't show up at school and would get a full-time job instead.

After some initial interviews, I found that I had three choices: a full-time systems programming job at DEC, where I had spent the previous summer working as a part-time student programmer; a scientific programming job at MIT's Instrumentation Lab, where software for the Apollo space missions was being developed; or a junior-level programming position at IBM's Poughkeepsie complex.

There was nobody I could talk to about career choices, and no book like Janet's that I could consult. Most important, I didn't realize that I was making a *career* choice, and that my first job might well have an enormous impact on subsequent career options. In fact, none of the advice that Janet offers in *The Programmer's Survival Guide* ever occurred to me. I turned down the offer from IBM, because they told me I would have to go through six months of training before I would be allowed to write any programs. ("But I've already done programming!" I told them. "I even wrote an assembler for DEC!" It made no impression upon the gnomes in Poughkeepsie.) I turned down the job offer from the Instrumentation Lab, because they told me that two other people would read every line of code I wrote, in order to ensure that it was correct. ("What!?" I exclaimed. "Someone else is going to look at *my* code? Not on your life!"). I took the full-time job offer from DEC, and lived happily ever after...but what if I had gone instead to IBM? Where would I be now?

A college student who decides to go to medical school has a pretty good idea of what his or her professional career will be like for the next several years, and can find several role models to investigate. And a student who opts for law school knows that there is a good chance of spending several years as an associate in a law firm before becoming a partner; by watching popular TV Shows, he or she can at least get a glimmer of what life is like *after* becoming a partner. The same is true for accounting students who look forward to a lifelong career as a partner in a Big Eight accounting firm.

But what about programming students? What role models do we have? What career plans can we show them? In most universities and in most data processing organizations, these subjects are totally ignored. Instead, we focus on the *technology* of software engineering, database management, and telecommunications.

In my case, I was lucky; I made several job changes and career changes that turned out to be successful despite my naivete. Janet Ruhl has been equally successful in a career path that included IBM and EDS before becoming an independent consultant. But along the way, she and I have both seen burned-out programmers; programmers stuck in dead-end jobs; programmers who felt that the only way to improve their career was to become a manager, even though they hated supervising people; and programmers who decided to become a consultant or software entrepreneur without understanding the risks involved.

Obviously, a book can't guarantee a successful career. But if it makes the novice programmer think about important career issues, and if it warns him or her about the major traps and obstacles along the career path, it can be enormously valuable. The *Programmer's Survival Guide* does just that. It discusses the advantages and disadvantages of working for an IBM shop, as well as a mainframe versus a minicomputer or PC shop. It discusses the impact of programming languages and operating systems on the programmer's career. It deals with the issues of maintenance programming versus new development projects, as well as the kind of application environment (insurance, banking, etc.) in which the programming work is being done. Perhaps most important, it discusses the "corporate culture" in which programming work is done—distinguishing between the crisis-mode "macho" organizations, and the passive, low-key organizations where there is never any pressure and never any excitement. And it's all written by someone who has "been there," and who has the scars to prove it.

If there are still programming jobs in the mid-1990s when my children finish school, and if my children should rashly decide to pursue a programming career like their old man, I would exert my last bit of parental authority and insist that they read Janet Ruhl's *The Programmer's Survival Guide*. They might not thank me, but they would certainly thank Janet by the time they finished reading the book.

EDWARD YOURDON

# Acknowledgments

This book could not have been written had it not been for the help of the many programmers who have shared their stories with me in the places I've had the privilege to work. There is not room enough to list all their names, but they know who they are. I would particularly like to thank John Taber and Pete Opstrup, two young old-timers who at different stages of my programming career took me under their wings and taught me the basics of survival as a programmer, long before I realized that I needed to learn them.

I would also like to express my appreciation to teachers at Nashville State Technical Institute, in Nashville, Tennesee, who first got me excited about programming, and then made me attend 10 hours a week—per course—of required computer lab, so that I learned how to program well.

I cannot begin to list all the things my parents, Fred and Minerva Brown, have done to encourage me as a writer, but I will note here that they are responsible for introducing into our household my *own* computer, the Leading Edge, Model D computer on which I prepared this manuscript.

I owe a debt of thanks to Edward Yourdon for giving me his encouragement and help in publishing this work and for providing detailed comments and suggestions on my original manuscript. I thank him as well for his his many efforts in the cause of encouraging writers on computer-related topics.

Finally I would like to thank my family. I owe a lot to the children, Joanna and David, for taking naps when they were not sleepy so I could work on this book, and even more to my husband Larry, a terrific programmer in his own right, as well as a composer of intelligent and humorous electronic music, who is able to keep his sense of humor while living with someone who loves to give advice.

# Introduction

Other books can teach you how to program computers. The purpose of this book is to teach you how to be a successful computer programmer. According to the U.S. Department of Labor, Bureau of Labor Statistics almost one million people currently make their careers as computer programmers and systems analysts. Another 60,000 a year are graduating from college courses designed to turn them into programmers.[1]

Yet because this field is so new the person who is thinking about entering it has very few people he can look to as role models. Most of the "old-timers" you will meet in business data processing have

---

[1] United States Department of Labor, Bureau of Labor Statistics, Employment and Earnings, January, 1988. Census Department estimates are that in 1987, 527,000 people were employed as programmers, and an additional 447,000 as Systems Analysts and Computer Scientists. BLS statistics indicate that in the academic year 1985-1986 10,704 associates degrees, 41,889 bachelor's degrees, 8,700 master's degrees and 344 Ph. D's were granted in computer information sciences majors.

worked in the field for an average of ten years! Among those who have gone on to management the average number of years in the field only rises to fourteen according to *Datamation's* 1986 "Salary Survey."[2] And the experience of many of these "old-timers" cannot in many cases be duplicated today. They were pioneers, but the profession of computer programming has begun to mature past its pioneering phase.

The only way for most people entering a programming career to find out how to go about it properly has been by trial and error. Unfortunately, only when it was too late to do much about it have all too many programmers figured out what steps they should have taken early in their careers. In the world of mainframe programming what a programmer does in his first five years may well dictate what he can do for the next thirty.

I've made my living as a computer programmer since 1980. I entered the field in my early thirties, looking for a way to make a living after having pursued an academic career in the fields of anthropology and history as well as making a small name for myself as a professional musician. I added a two-year degree in Business Data Processing to my almost complete Ph.D. by attending an excellent two-year college, Nashville State Technical Institute, in Nashville, Tennessee. At graduation I was lucky enough to be hired by the IBM Corporation as an applications programmer at one of their manufacturing plants.

I worked for three and a half years at IBM, first as a manufacturing applications programmer on a large IMS system, and then, through a series of almost random events, got involved with IBM's PROFS office systems/electronic mail system. I worked first implementing PROFS in our plant, then I developed some utilities for the product, and eventually I was recruited to join the team of programmers IBM had assembled in Dallas to turn PROFS into a Program Product.

I left IBM eventually because I wanted to be able to devote more time to my daughter than was possible working a full-time schedule, and took a part-time job with Electronic Data Systems in Dallas as a tech support programmer working on a patient care system that ran

---

[2] Parker Hodges *"Datamation's* Annual Salary Survey," September 15, 1986 pp. 72-87.

on networked micro- and minicomputers. When my husband received an attractive job offer in Hartford, EDS transferred me to an insurance applications group there where I worked as an insurance applications programmer specializing in Assembler language code problems.

For the last few years I have split my time between tending two obstreperous children and working stints as an independent consultant, programming on a contract basis at several local insurance companies.

In the course of my travels I've met and observed a great number of working programmers in a variety of environments. I've met people who started out as programmers and went on to found successful software development and programming service businesses. I've known others who have left programming to become corporate managers. I've watched other programmers evolve into technical gurus. And sadly, I've met a lot of bright, hard-working people who after five or more years on the job are totally burned out.

The idea for this book grew out of the many conversations I've had with programmers I've met, especially while working as a consultant. Just about everywhere I've gone I've been struck with the number of intelligent, skilled programmers I've encountered, many with more years of experience on the job than I have, who have told me how frustrated they felt with their careers, and asked me, a virtual stranger, what I thought they could do to recapture the excitement that they used to find in programming for a living.

In these conversations I was struck by how great a role these people had let random chance play in their professional lives and how little they seemed to know about the field that they were in. Often these people had skills that were in great demand on the open market but had no idea of their own worth, like the man who had worked his way up from operations to a job as an IMS specialist, but whose salary after almost 10 years was considerably below $20,000 in 1981. When he shrugged his shoulders and said, "I know I should do something, but where could I get another IMS job?" I almost fell out of my chair. Although he was in the only IMS shop in his town he could easily have made $15,000 a year more in a nearby city!

I've seen people with B.S. degrees from expensive name brand universities go to work doing the dullest kind of maintenance programming, only to quit after a year, sure that programming was not for them. I've also seen talented people stay in jobs that they hated for years, simply because they were phobic about job hunting and preferred to stick with the job that the college placement office had found them rather than look for something new.

So much of the frustration I've seen among my coworkers is unnecessary. All of these people had good skills and many much better than good. They were working in a field that offers unprecedented mobility and opportunity. Their problem, as I saw it was that these technical people had never learned how to think about the organizations and the profession they were in.

At a certain point I sat back and asked myself what it was that I knew that so many people seemed to be missing. While I had never considered myself an authority on business data processing, and regretted quite a number of naive mistakes I had made at different points in my career, I had managed to put myself in a position where I had only to make a few phone calls to be offered jobs at the kind of salary levels that had been unattainable for women, no matter how qualified, only a few years ago. And going beyond the issue of money, I had been able to put myself in a position where I am routinely called and offered jobs doing precisely the kind of work I enjoy most--no trivial accomplishment.

In between contract assignments I began to make notes for this book. At the same time my husband, who had followed me into programming, was testing out in his career the principles we had identified through trial and error in my career development. Although our original credentials were very different, by avoiding many of the mistakes I had made he was able to progress very quickly in his own career, lending credence to the fact that maybe we were on to something.

Between the two of us we have worked in thirteen different programming shops and gotten to know somewhere around 200 programmers. We have also followed a fairly typical American tradition and relocated every two or three years. As a result, we have participated in the data processing community in not one, but five different cities in four different geographical sections of the country, and have job hunted in yet another two. It is because of this broad exposure that I have come to believe that much of what I have observed is true not in just one company or one city, but for a large number of business programmers around the nation.

The patterns I've seen repeated have led me to conclude that the first five years of a programmer's career are a critical period. The opportunities that you need to have to succeed as a programmer and to keep your options open for your future usually can be most easily gotten during these first years. After this critical period it is much harder to improve your credentials and pick up the things you missed in the earlier period. The reason for this is that in programming the training you need to have to get ahead is available only from large corporate employers. You cannot teach yourself mainframe programming at home in your spare time. You can't learn very much about it at college either—not the stuff that is precisely what you need to know to increase your value to an employer or to yourself. No, the stuff a programmer needs to learn can only be learned through a combination of company-sponsored courses not available to the general public and hard-won, day-to-day experience working with large business mainframe systems.

It is only by carefully selecting the jobs you take early in your career that you can ensure that you get the training you need for the career direction you want to follow. Often by the time a programmer figures out what it is that he would like to work on it is too late. He is simply at too high a salary level and too far along in his career to have an employer give him the training he needs to change course.

With this in mind it seemed that a career-planning book intended for programmers and would-be programmers would have to do two things.

First, it would have to make clear the range of programming career paths that were open to people experienced in business programming. The goal here would be to help the reader get some idea of what he could expect if he pursued a career within a corporation or if he took a more independent or entrepreneurial route. Particular attention would be paid to the requirements needed for pursuing the different career options.

Next, it would have to show the programmer how to choose jobs that would maximize his ability to follow the career path he had chosen.

This, then, is the form I have given this book. The first section sketches out the various career paths that are most commonly trodden. I have avoided going into great detail about particular careers in this section because my aim was to present a more general picture of the broad categories that are open, not to tell you about other people's wonderful, or not-so-wonderful jobs.

The second part of the book does give you a lot of details about the real working programmer's world. In this section I have given you eight different factors with which you can analyze a given programming job, whether it is one you currently have or one you are considering taking. Using these factors I suggest how you can best position yourself to pursue the career avenues that appeal to you.

At the end of the book you will find a list of twenty-five sets of questions that you might want to ask the interviewer at a job interview for a programming job. These questions correspond to various points made throughout the book. You might want to browse through them before reading the book and then return to them later to help you focus on the points that would be of most interest to you in pursuing your chosen career path.

In the course of writing this book I have tried to stick to certain principles. First of all I have limited myself to discussing the things I know. Lord knows there are enough books out there purporting to tell you about a programming career written by people who have never written a line of code. This book therefore focuses on business data processing (often referred to as DP), rather than on engineering and scientific programming careers. Nevertheless much of the advice in this book will be useful to anyone pursuing any career as a programmer in the world of American industry. The other area I have limited my discussion of is PC programming. Because personal computers have captured the public imagination, there is already a disproportionate amount of writing about PC programming available. Therefore you can read about the careers of successful PC programmers elsewhere. Then too, the world of PCs is in such flux that anything I write now will be out of date in a year or two. I have therefore limited my discussion of PC programming to covering the subjects of PC software development and PC language programming, emphasizing those areas where PC programming is pursued in connection with mainframe business programming or by mainframe programmers.

In many cases I've been able to find statistics to back up what started out as intuitive observations. Where possible I've included them in my text. However in some cases I don't think the statistics will ever be available. Who for instance has ever counted the number of Assembly language programmers who refuse to use normal English spelling because it is not logical? No one to my knowledge. But I've known enough folks who fit this description that I feel justified in including my observation that this is a fairly typical Assembler programmer trait.

I've included many such observations throughout the book, some trivial and some more important. If your experience contradicts what I've stated then let me know. I would enjoy hearing from you. If my opinions bother you, and I admit I have some strong opinions, then you are free to ignore them. My book is intended as a guide but no guide is infallible. I would hate to start receiving mail that said "I did just what you said in Chapter 10, and now I just got fired!"

This book is intended to have the same effect as a long chat with a couple of knowledgeable DP professionals. Take from it what is useful to you, and leave the rest.

I originally intended to write this book for students of computer programming and working programmers who were wondering what steps they could take to improve their situations. As I talked with people about the book I was struck by how many people outside the field were curious about what it was that programmers did. In the hopes of making this book useful to such readers, I have tried to keep my language as nontechnical as possible and have occasionally spelled out concepts that trained programmers would consider basic. I have also resisted the temptation that all programmers encounter of telling anecdotes that require three pages of detailed technical discussion to set up the punch line. You will find a brief, irreverent glossary of data processing terms at the end of the book.

If you are thinking about becoming a programmer I hope this book can enable you to enter the field with realistic expectations and a strategy that gets you where you want to be in ten years. If you are already working as a programmer, I hope this book helps you sort out those features of your experience that are unique from those that are the common fate of programmers everywhere. Finally, if you are just a curious bystander, or perhaps a programmer's spouse, relative, or friend, I hope this book gives you some idea of what it is that programmers deal with in this world, and what all those odd looking acronyms in the Sunday classified section are all about.

## A Word on Terminology

Like many writers I have had to decide what to do about the English convention that uses the word "he" when "he or she" would be more appropriate. This problem is particularly bothersome when writing about programmers since so many programmers at every level are women. Unable to take on reforming the English language at the same time as I illuminated the world of computer programming, I have reluctantly stuck with using "he" where a third person singular pronoun was required. Just keep in mind from chapter to chapter that an awful lot of the "he's" you see are really "she's"!

I must also clarify my use of the word "programmer." I have always used this word proudly to describe what I do for a living. At IBM where I received my training, "programmer" was a term of great respect and one applied to people at very senior levels.

In my travels, though, I have discovered that many companies use the term "programmer" to refer to the least-skilled kind of worker who modifies computer programs: humble dogsbodies who slavishly code in response to detailed specifications provided by higher-status personnel called "Systems Analyst" or "Programmer Analyst". In these companies calling someone a programmer is almost an insult.

For the purposes of this book I have decided to continue to use the term "programmer" to cover the spectrum of people whose jobs include systems analysis, systems design, program development, coding, testing, and maintenance. I do so with the understanding that I am including in the term "programmer" all the other glorified titles you might use for the same thing.

| Quantity | Title/Author | ISBN | Price | Total $ |
|---|---|---|---|---|
| _____ | Building Controls Into Structured Systems; Brill | 013-086059-X | $35.00 | _____ |
| _____ | C Notes: Guide to C Programming; Zahn | 013-109778-4 | $21.95 | _____ |
| _____ | Classics in Software Engineering; Yourdon | 013-135179-6 | $39.00 | _____ |
| _____ | Concise Notes on Software Engineering; DeMarco | 013-167073-3 | $21.00 | _____ |
| _____ | Controlling Software Projects; DeMarco | 013-171711-1 | $39.00 | _____ |
| _____ | Creating Effective Software; King | 013-189242-8 | $33.00 | _____ |
| _____ | Crunch Mode; Boddie | 013-194960-8 | $29.00 | _____ |
| _____ | Current Practices in Software Development; King | 013-195678-7 | $34.00 | _____ |
| _____ | Data Factory; Roeske | 013-196759-2 | $23.00 | _____ |
| _____ | Developing Structured Systems; Dickinson | 013-205147-8 | $34.00 | _____ |
| _____ | Design of On-Line Computer Systems; Yourdon | 013-201301-0 | $48.00 | _____ |
| _____ | Essential Systems Analysis; McMenamin/Palmer | 013-287905-0 | $35.00 | _____ |
| _____ | Expert System Technology; Keller | 013-295577-6 | $28.95 | _____ |
| _____ | Concepts of Information Modeling; Flavin | 013-335589-6 | $27.00 | _____ |
| _____ | Game Plan for System Development; Frantzen/McEvoy | 013-346156-4 | $30.00 | _____ |
| _____ | Intuition to Implementation; MacDonald | 013-502196-0 | $24.00 | _____ |
| _____ | Managing Structured Techniques; Yourdon | 013-551037-6 | $33.00 | _____ |
| _____ | Managing the System Life Cycle 2/e; Yourdon | 013-551045-7 | $35.00 | _____ |
| _____ | People & Project Management; Thomsett | 013-655747-3 | $23.00 | _____ |
| _____ | Politics of Projects; Block | 013-685553-9 | $24.00 | _____ |
| _____ | Practice of Structured Analysis; Keller | 013-693987-2 | $28.00 | _____ |
| _____ | Program It Right; Benton/Weekes | 013-729005-5 | $23.00 | _____ |
| _____ | Software Design: Methods & Techniques; Peters | 013-821828-5 | $33.00 | _____ |
| _____ | Structured Analysis; Weinberg | 013-854414-X | $44.00 | _____ |
| _____ | Structured Analysis & System Specifications; DeMarco | 013-854380-1 | $44.00 | _____ |
| _____ | Structured Approach to Building Programs: BASIC; Wells | 013-854076-4 | $23.00 | _____ |
| _____ | Structured Approach to Building Programs: COBOL; Wells | 013-854084-5 | $23.00 | _____ |
| _____ | Structured Approach to Building Programs: Pascal; Wells | 013-851536-0 | $23.00 | _____ |
| _____ | Structured Design; Yourdon/Constantine | 013-854471-9 | $49.00 | _____ |
| _____ | Structured Development Real-Time Systems, Combined; Ward/Mellor | 013-854654-1 | $75.00 | _____ |
| _____ | Structured Development Real-Time Systems, Vol. 1; Ward/Mellor | 013-854787-4 | $33.00 | _____ |
| _____ | Structured Development Real-Time Systems, Vol. II; Ward/Mellor | 013-854795-5 | $33.00 | _____ |
| _____ | Structured Development Real-Time Systems, Vol. III; Ward/Mellor | 013-854803-X | $33.00 | _____ |
| _____ | Structured Systems Development; Orr | 013-855149-9 | $33.00 | _____ |
| _____ | Structured Walkthroughs 3/e; Yourdon | 013-855248-7 | $24.00 | _____ |
| _____ | System Development Without Pain; Ward | 013-881392-2 | $33.00 | _____ |
| _____ | Teams in Information System Development; Semprivivo | 013-896721-0 | $29.00 | _____ |
| _____ | Techniques of EDP Project Management; Brill | 013-900358-4 | $33.00 | _____ |
| _____ | Techniques of Program Structure & Design; Yourdon | 013-901702-X | $44.00 | _____ |
| _____ | Up and Running; Hanson | 013-937558-9 | $32.00 | _____ |
| _____ | Using the Structured Techniques; Weaver | 013-940263-2 | $27.00 | _____ |
| _____ | Writing of the Revolution; Yourdon | 013-970708-5 | $38.00 | _____ |
| _____ | Practical Guide to Structured Systems 2/e; Page-Jones | 013-690769-5 | $35.00 | _____ |

**Total $** _____

**Discount (if appropriate)** _____

**New Total $** _____

# AND TAKE ADVANTAGE OF THESE SPECIAL OFFERS!

**a.)** When ordering 3 or 4 copies (of the same or different titles), take 10% off the total list price (excluding sales tax, where applicable).

**b.)** When ordering 5 to 20 copies (of the same or different titles), take 15% off the total list price (excluding sales tax, where applicable).

**c.)** To receive a greater discount when ordering 20 or more copies, call or write:

Special Sales Department
College Marketing
Prentice Hall
Englewood Cliffs, NJ 07632
201-592-2498

**SAVE!**

If payment accompanies order, plus your state's sales tax where applicable, Prentice Hall pays postage and handling charges. Same return privilege refund guaranteed. Please do not mail in cash.

☐ **PAYMENT ENCLOSED**—shipping and handling to be paid by publisher (please include your state's tax where applicable).

☐ **SEND BOOKS ON 15-DAY TRIAL BASIS** & bill me (with small charge for shipping and handling).

Name _____

Address _____

City _____ State _____ Zip _____

I prefer to charge my   ☐ Visa   ☐ MasterCard
Card Number _____ Expiration Date_____

Signature _____
*All prices listed are subject to change without notice.*

**Mail your order to:** Prentice Hall, Book Distribution Center, Route 59 at
Brook Hill Drive, West Nyack, NY 10995

Dept. 1                                                              D-OFYP-FW(1)

Career Paths for Programmers

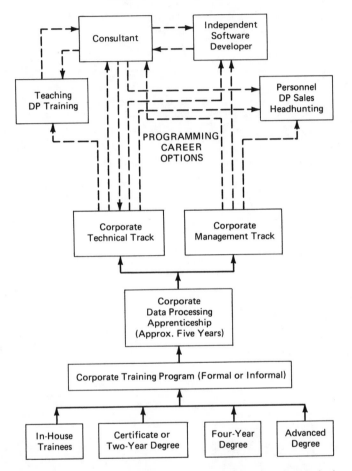

**Figure 1** A view of the programming career ladder. Starting at the bottom, the solid lines lead up through the required stages of the "DP apprenticeship." The dashed lines and the boxes on the upper portion of the page represent career options open to the experienced programmer.

# 1
# *Getting Started*

There is only one way to break into business mainframe programming and that is to get hired as a programmer by a company that has a mainframe. A PC enthusiast might be able to start off a career that turns him into a millionaire software developer in his bedroom, hunched over a machine that he bought with money from his paper route. But to acquire the lowest level of experience as a mainframe programmer you need to work on systems that cost millions of dollars—where a single terminal in a network that includes a thousand terminals costs as much as the hobbyist's PC.

You need to sit in front of one of those terminals. If you hope to have a career that is related to business data processing you need to spend anywhere from three to seven years working for a company that is large enough to be able to pay for a mainframe system and can afford to pay your salary while you learn how to put that system to work.

What qualities must you have to appeal to the people in the companies that have the jobs you need?

If you want to be a doctor, you go to medical school. If you want to be an accountant you get a four-year degree in accounting and then work to pass the CPA exam. Lawyers must go to special law schools after they finish their college careers and then pass the bar exam. These are professions that have been around for a while. As competition for jobs in these lucrative fields grew more intense, the people working in them erected stringent qualification procedures. No matter how much medicine you know today you will go to jail if you claim to be a physician but haven't passed the necessary exams.

Computer programming, in contrast, is such a new field that no such clearly defined qualifying process exists for it. Many a proud college graduate with a shiny new Computer Science degree is appalled to discover that he is working for people whose only academic qualification is six months at the kind of private technical institute that advertises on matchbooks. I suspect that a certain number of highly trained people do inestimable damage to their careers by failing to relate to the fact that the boss worked his way into his job, with its complete control over the neophyte's career, with no more qualifications than a high school degree, a stint in the military, or the persistence to spend a year or two in the operations output area ripping paper out of a printer.

Computer programming as a career came out of nowhere. From the late 1960s on, American industry, spurred on by the possibilities opened up by the power of IBM's 360 and 370 series of mainframe computers (and the persuasiveness of its sales force), rushed into computerizing its most vital functions. First banks and insurance companies committed the heart of their businesses to computerized systems. Then manufacturers computerized their accounting, payroll, and inventory systems. As more mainframes were installed, software products were developed that extended their capabilities. These in turn suggested a whole new generation of applications to businessmen who were becoming convinced that they were part of an "information revolution."

The result of this was an insatiable demand for programmers in a world where a handful of colleges had computer science courses and these were entirely for engineers.

Every computer system that industry installed needed people to tend it, in numbers far greater than industry had ever expected.

To fill this need business first turned to people who had been exposed to the nascent technology in the military. Many of the oldest old-timers you will encounter in the field got their start in programming simply because they had some electronics exposure in the military of the sixties. If you work with one of these gentlemen you will sooner or later be regaled with tales of the birth of the computer age. One man, now in his late forties, liked to tell new people about the first insurance system he worked on sometime, I believe, in the early sixties. This was a first-generation system, a system that predated the invention of the operating system. Operating systems are the programs in all modern computers that manage the systems devices, allowing a program access to files and devices such as the printer. Since his computer lacked this piece of software, this gentleman's job was to sit at the system console and key in the hexadecimal addresses in storage where programs should run and information about which devices should be allocated to the program. Then he would load in punched cards containing the object code, "let 'er rip", and send the output to the appropriate printer. It could take all night to run a single program. The system was far less powerful than the PC now on his desk.

Others who began in this early period made their living wiring accounting machines, which were devices halfway between computers and the older generations of office accounting machinery. Programming one of these involved dealing with a Medusa-like tangle of wires which the programmer plugged into different sockets to achieve different effects.

In these early years a large number of programmers moved up out of the operations area. They started out doing the most menial tasks such as loading and tending printers. Often they had very long hair and short academic histories. If they showed up regularly and demonstrated some competence, their companies invested in training them for more sophisticated programming jobs.

In these early years hardware vendors, not universities, provided the training that was the basis for a programming career. When businesses recruited college students for programming they usually took those with degrees in mathematics, and in the process introduced into the business world of the sixties and early seventies a generation of women who would otherwise have faced a lifetime of teaching high school math.

For a while no one really noticed business programmers. While computer engineering majors from schools like MIT commanded what were at the time princely salaries, the programmers working on insurance or billing applications were treated like any other group of technicians. They received modest salaries many of which remained below $10,000-a-year until the later part of the 1970s.

But as the seventies progressed, the need for programmers became acute, especially for the DP-intensive insurance and banking industries which by then employed thousands of programmers. These companies traditionally paid low wages and could not compete for the few college graduates emerging from the few colleges that were teaching computer science. Consequently, these companies looked at their other departments for people they could train as programmers, picking people out of areas that used the computer systems and from related areas like technical writing. When these people were insufficient to fill their needs they turned to the larger community, offering anyone who could get a high score on programmer aptitude tests, such as the Data Processing Aptitude Test (DPAT), the opportunity to enter an intensive programmer training program.

English majors, piano teachers, and middle-aged widows who had been getting by selling real estate answered the call. The training courses were comprehensive and intensive: in some companies the participants were informed that they would have jobs at the end of the course only if they achieved certain grade levels. Many old-timers remember these training courses as times of sheer personal terror. However, if the trainee survived the course, he or she entered the work force with a solid grounding in programming fundamentals, including more experience with assembly language than many recent college graduates now command. By now many of these people have entered the ranks of management.

In 1980 the media discovered the programming shortage and trumpeted the news of the $20,000-a-year salaries being paid to new hires. Computer programmers were suddenly being paid as much as engineers and a lot more than people starting out in most other fields.

The programming shortage was real. I can remember overhearing two college students bragging over lunch in the cafeteria of the

University of Massachusetts. They were computer science majors and were comparing notes on the four or five companies that had flown them to headquarters, wined and dined them, and made them enormous offers even though they were only maintaining C averages in their courses.

Suddenly it seemed as if every college was offering computer science courses. Computer science became a fad and students stood in line for days to register for required courses the way that, in other eras, they had crowded into phone booths.

As the flood of people grasping Computer Science and Information Science degrees began, companies could suddenly afford to become more selective about the qualifications of the programmers they hired. By 1987 an estimated 60,000 graduates were competing for some 25,000 open positions. Except in rare cases it is now obligatory to have attained at least a two-year junior or technical college degree to enter the programming field. In areas where there are fewer large mainframe shops, a four-year computer science or business data processing degree and a good grade point average are required. The person who wants to work for a prestige company like IBM or AT&T will need a four-year degree with impeccable grades and perhaps even a master's degree just to get interviewed.

But that person should be aware that the person interviewing him at those companies very likely has no such credentials himself! At one point at IBM I was chatting with my manager, my team leader, and the local technical guru about a friend who had been turned down for an interview. My manager pointed out that with the current guidelines he had to follow, not a single person in the room would have been granted an interview for a programming job. And this was only three years after I had begun my career in the company!

If you are a highly qualified graduate coming into the business world for the first time you would do well to realize just how shiny and new your credentials are, because, not surprisingly, many older experienced people who grew up with the business data processing business itself and did all their learning on the job find cocky new college grads obnoxious in the extreme. A new hire fresh out of college babbling about "algorithms" and announcing that the local database could have benefited from the index structure he invented for his senior project, grates on the nerves of an experienced professional who may not be quite sure what an algorithm is but can remember hardcoding patches in machine language in the days of his youth.

The wise college-trained programmer will treat these old-timers with tremendous respect. The real work of programming is about 5 percent theory and 95 percent trivia. The old-timers know the trivia, and when the new hire finds himself completely baffled his salvation often lies in some detail that the old-timer has stored away in the back of his mind.

Also, the wise beginning programmer—especially one with a prestige degree—will make no assumptions about the training of the managers he works for. Many very successful DP managers come from families that would find it very hard to send a child to college today.

As I mentioned before, there is currently no commonly accepted qualification in data processing that would correspond to the CPA exam or the bar. There have been attempts to come up with one. The programmer or systems analyst with five years of experience can take a five-part exam called the CDP exam which was created by the Institute for the Certification of Computer Professionals. But no one ever seems to ask about this certification when you apply for jobs later in your career, so I suspect that awareness and acceptance of this certification program are limited.

As the data processing profession matures it is likely that snobbism will grow and certification barriers will be erected to maintain exclusivity and salary levels among programmers. For the time being, the person entering the field still finds himself entering a career whose practitioners range from the extremes of yuppie graduates of expensive colleges to working-class folks with gumption.

If you happen to be a working-class type with gumption you have probably figured out by now that breaking into DP is not going to be the piece of cake it once was. The good news is that it is still possible.

In the following pages I will briefly describe the different levels of qualification that you could use to enter mainframe programming and try to suggest the strategies which would be the best for you at each level.

## Four-Year College Degree in Computer Science with Good Grades

If you have a four-year college degree in computer science or one of the many other synonyms such as "information science" or "business data processing," you are a lucky dog. But I hope you realize that it will take more than luck to build a good career. You can safely assume that you will get some kind of entry level mainframe programming job. The challenge, however, is to make sure you get the job that will put you in the best position possible for the future you want to build for yourself. This means you need to develop a good understanding of what long-term career possibilities exist for mainframe programmers. Furthermore, you need to have insight into your own strengths and weaknesses so that the long-term career path you choose for yourself is one that you are temperamentally and intellectually suited for. Finally, you must be able to see through the heady haze of the interview situation to the reality of the jobs that are offered to you. Only then will you be as excited by your career ten years down the line as you are when you receive your diploma.

If you are in this situation you are in the ideal situation to use the information contained in this book. In particular you should pay attention to the chapters on job selection so that you can make the best of the opportunities open to you.

The time to start your job search is in your sophomore year, right after you declare your major, because that is the time you should begin looking into summer co-op programs. Many companies with large DP installations bring in a great number of college students each summer to work as programmer trainees for periods of two to three months. The work you do in these positions varies. Some trainees rearrange the program listings on the racks in the departmental library. But others write programs for new systems, and some do maintenance and enhancements for large production systems. If you do a good job in a summer co-op position you are almost assured of being hired by the company when you graduate. And you are likely to get top dollar too, since the hiring manager can demonstrate your worth by pointing to the work you did for him.

And this is not all the good news about co-op positions. Many companies will hire promising college co-ops to work on a part-time schedule during the school year. If you are paying your own college costs this can make the difference between hot dogs and steak. Furthermore, if you graduate college having worked for a year under this arrangement you enter the work force as an experienced programmer, and can demand a corresponding boost in pay. Obviously, the student who is serious about his future will take advantage of an opportunity like this.

Surprisingly, a great many students don't. I have more than once worked alongside college co-ops who informed me that they were majoring in other aspects of business and had no interest in pursuing a programming career. They only took the co-op positions, they said, for the money. I assume that these people only got the jobs because they didn't face competition from devoted would-be programmers.

If you plan to try for a co-op position you should bring the same discrimination to that job search as you would to the search for a position after graduation, since, as I have said, the co-op position can easily turn into one of these. Why waste your energy establishing your reputation as a co-op in a company you would never want to return to?

### Dealing with Corporate Recruiters

As a four-year student you will probably be hired into your first job as a result of an interview arranged by your college placement office. Typically, corporate recruiters will come to your campus throughout the year to hold interviews. You should start looking at the bulletin boards in the placement office as soon as you know you want to be a programmer in the business world—in fact, even before you decide exactly what kind of programmer you intend to be. What you should be doing is finding out what companies regularly interview, and presumably hire, students from your college. You should be paying careful attention to their interview announcements, especially to what qualifications they require of applicants. You should also be aware of the kinds of positions they are offering.

Then you should try to talk with older students who have interviewed with these companies. Find out what kinds of questions they were asked and what kinds of jobs they were offered. Talk to people who worked as co-ops in these companies too. Treat this as the most important research project of your college career, because it is. You will have to stay in your first full-time job for at least a year and probably two before you can even think of changing companies. If you don't do this research before you interview, the job you fall into may well represent wasted time you can never really get back. The best careers start off with the programmer hitting the ground running in a job that offers great training coupled with the opportunity to rack up accomplishments. The effort you expend finding the right first job can mean the difference between a lifetime of career satisfaction or burn out in five years.

Once you have chosen the companies you would like to work for, you have only just begun. You have to find the right positions within those companies: this is no simple task. Far too many college graduates land, almost randomly, in one of the handful of positions that recruiters are interviewing for the week that they get around to signing up for interviews at the campus placement office. They trust that the same forces that have carried them through high school and college giving them the best of everything because of their good grades and good test scores will give them good jobs. It ain't so. Schools are devoted to aiding their students' personal development. Corporations are devoted only to making a profit, and their interest in the student is only in how quickly he can contribute to that profit. Recruiters come to college campuses to fill open positions. Some of these are terrific and some of them are dead ends. The recruiters fill them with whoever they find that meet the qualifications set by the hiring managers. To the recruiter there are no "bad jobs." He hopes to fill them all, and he doesn't save the best ones for the most deserving students.

It is up to you, therefore, to learn to identify what constitutes a "good job." The second part of this book will provide you with some tools with which to penetrate a recruiter's salesmanship. The most important thing for you to realize now is that you need these tools.

One word of warning though about preliminary interviews with recruiters from out-of-town companies. Many companies will let any management-level person interview college students if they happen to be going to another part of the country for business or personal reasons. Often these people will interview people for jobs unrelated to their own fields of expertise. Their job, as far as I can tell, is to make sure that the applicant has a nice suit and can speak English.

When their trip is done they relay resumes and brief reports to corporate recruiting offices that take it from there.

Do your best to make a good impression on these people, of course, but don't take too seriously anything they might say, positive or negative. When I applied to IBM for my first job in 1980, I had interviews with two IBM managers, both of whom, I believe, were visiting children at a local university. The first manager who came from IBM's Burlington, Vermont, plant took one look at my resume, grunted that he couldn't imagine a single job at Burlington that I would be qualified for and spent the rest of the interview complaining to me that the salt on the Vermont roads was destroying his car. The second manager was from Poughkeepsie. He declared that he was very impressed by my humanities background and that several of his best people had backgrounds very like mine. He expressed the desire that I would give him a call when I came up to Poughkeepsie as he thought I would like to meet his wife whose background was similar.

Did I ever get to Poughkeepsie? Only on visits from Burlington where I was subsequently hired. I never even got a Poughkeepsie interview! It turned out that the man with the rusty car was an engineering manager whose job never brought him into contact with any of the plant's business programmers. Nevertheless, his report got me a follow-up interview.

Other people tell similar stories. I also urge you to reapply to a company that may reject you the first time. Openings come and go in many departments. Six months after you first apply you may encounter entirely different people both at corporate recruiting and in hiring departments. If you know that a company can give you what you need to build your career—and that they hire people with your level of qualifications—be persistent.

### Two-Year Graduates and Four-Year Grads with Poor Grades

If you fall into this category you know already that you will have a harder time breaking into mainframe programming. Certain companies simply will not interview you. If you do get hired you can expect to be brought in at a considerably lower salary than a four-year grad with a 3.5 cumulative average. However, if you are realistic and do some research you can get a job that offers you training and future prospects that are just as good as those received by the top 10 percent. You may also find that in three or four years you are making the same salaries they are.

You chances hinge greatly on the economic strength of your local economy. If things are booming and people are getting $6.50 an hour flipping burgers at fast food restaurants, the chances are that your area will need programmers. In that case recruiters will also be interviewing students at junior colleges. They will probably be from local banks and insurance companies which run yearly trainee classes in the summer, but you will also see people from local manufacturing firms who have had good experiences hiring people from your school.

In a good market, four-year students with "ho-hum" resumes may also get quality interviews.

However, if you are in this situation you cannot afford to be as picky about your first job as you might wish to be. If you have a choice between two jobs, evaluate them using the criteria in the second part of this book, but be reasonable. The time for you to concentrate on getting the perfect job will be in a year or two when you have some experience and no one will look very hard at your college record. The only thing that you have to be careful about is that you get a mainframe programming job, not a glorified operator's job or a job programming a stand-alone PC for a small company. In the first case it will take you years to become a "real" programmer: in the second case you will find that it is extremely difficult if not impossible to move into mainframe programming from PC programming, although going the other way—from mainframe to PC—is quite easy.

If your local economy is not in great shape you have several alternatives. You can be brave and move to a part of the country where conditions are better, or you can stay in your current geographical area and be extremely persistent. If you do the latter, plan to spend six months on your job hunt. Expect to encounter a lot of rejection. Interview for any mainframe job you can get.

Do not go to employment agencies. Respectable headhunters will tell you flat out that they only place experienced people. Less reputable ones will ask you to pay a hefty placement fee. The fee can range up to $4,000. In return for this they will send you out to interviews that you could have found for yourself if you had done a very small amount of research. Most likely they will try to talk you into taking a job in an entirely different area where they have an opening. One friend of mine when desperate asked an employment agency to find him a job as a programmer or computer operator only to be sent on an interview for a job as a machine tool operator.

What you have working in your favor in a bad market is this: the majority of people who went to school with you and have the same credentials as you will give up fairly quickly. There will be a big burst of job hunters in the spring, but by August or September many people will either have found jobs or have stopped looking. If you have been making regular phone calls to local DP managers and recruiting departments by now they know who you are and may even be impressed by your persistence. (By regular I mean once a month, any more often constitutes a nuisance!) Sometimes they will interview you for an open position you otherwise wouldn't get to see just to get you off their backs. Most won't of course, but it only takes one!

As an illustration of what you might have to go through I'd like to tell the story of a friend of mine who graduated from a two-year college in the Dallas area just as the Dallas economy was coming apart. That year not a single employer held interviews at his school. The local banks that had traditionally hired people at his level canceled their annual training programs because they were cutting back staff. Undaunted, this young man went to the public library and compiled a list of 204 companies in the area large enough to possibly have DP departments. He then began calling every single one and asking to speak to a DP manager.

This calling resulted in his getting three interviews over a period of five months. One interview was with a manager who had no open positions. One interview actually resulted in a job offer that was withdrawn two days later because the manager who made the offer did not realize that his company would not hire anyone who did not have a four-year degree.

Things were looking pretty bleak for my friend. Four months had passed and he had not even been able to find a job as a computer operator, when a follow-up call to a friendly a personnel department secretary who had previously remarked that a trainee class would be forming but she didn't know when, revealed that the class was indeed being formed—but that personnel had already selected the people to be interviewed for the new openings. This intrepid soul reminded personnel of the many calls he had made, which he documented with the date he had made them and what he had been told at the time. He was grudgingly allowed to join the interviewees for the training class and given a grueling exam which he passed with flying colors. This time he got the job!

There is more to this story though. A mere ten months later this individual, who had even been rejected for operations entry-level jobs, was recruited by an out-of-town headhunting firm for a programming position in another part of the country. He got paid relocation to the tune of almost $10,000 and a hefty raise in his new job. Why? Because he was now considered to be an experienced programmer! And managers were desperate to hire anyone with experience.

This tale may seem a bit extreme, but I know of an ex-typist and an ex-waitress with no qualifications beyond a lot of spunk and a six-month certificate program at a for-profit business school who have used similar strategies to break into mainframe programming, and are now well on the way to having good careers. Their secret, too, was to be persistent: each spent about five months pursuing an entry-level job.

## No Academic Credentials at All

The days are gone when a person with only a high-school degree could routinely expect to be trained from scratch in data processing by large corporations. The only way open to such an individual is a long and increasingly chancy one. If you can manage to get hired into an entry-level operations job doing the most menial tasks like tending the printer, you many, some three or four years down the line, be sent to the company's in-house programmer training course.

However, many two-year schools now graduate people with certificates or degrees in computer operations and you will be competing with them for the entry-level positions in this field. Although this used to be a heavily traveled pathway in the 1960s and 70s, I would advise against trying it. Even if you manage to make it into a programming department, you will enter with a job title and class that indicates your lowly origins in operations. This will likely be accompanied by a pathetic salary. Typically you will have a technician job class and there will be several promotions to pass through before you reach the professional job class that the college graduates begin at. This is true even if you are doing the job as well as they are.

If you are considering this path, or if you have already started out on it, your best bet is to take courses at your local college or junior college. If you are currently employed, your employer may pay for them and there is a good chance that the company will move you into a college trainee slot when you graduate even if your grades are nothing to look at, since they already know you are a hard worker and you have demonstrated your loyalty to the company.

Another difficult career path leads up to programming from clerical positions. Many women in traditional "pink collar ghettos" are being exposed to word processing systems now. A certain percentage of them are discovering that they have a real knack for working with computers. Often when they express an interest in pursuing the computer angle further they are told that they can take the first step by taking "paraprogrammer" or "program librarian" jobs. These jobs are low status technician grade jobs in which the worker's prime responsibility is usually to copy files, fill in forms, run canned procedures to manage files in the department's computerized library system, and update documentation, both on paper and on-line. These are usually jobs in which you can expect to work very hard, since programming departments usually have enormous amounts of this kind of work to be done. These jobs may, over a very long period of time, lead to becoming a real programmer but only after years of scut work which add nothing to your eventual skills as a programmer. If you get interested in programming and are currently working in a secretarial capacity do the smart thing: get yourself some college training so that you can qualify for the real entry-level programmer jobs.

## Retreads

"Retreads" is the term I use for people who have good credentials and work experience in some other field entirely unrelated to business mainframe programming. I'm a retread myself. Many retreads are school teachers who would like to have an income that lets them live on more than toast. Many are trained musicians who can't even currently afford toast but have heard that musicians are known to have a very good aptitude for programming. In the science/engineering field many retreads are hardware engineers for whom there is no longer any work in the hardware area.

At one time, five or ten years ago, it was easier for these people to break in and there are a lot of them currently working in the industry, but prospective retreads suffer from the abundance of college computer science graduates now emerging.

If you already have a four-year college degree you can adopt a different strategy than a person who doesn't, no matter what your degree was in.

But I cannot stress strongly enough that, for the retread especially, strategies that would work very well in one part of the country will fail miserably in another.

As a retread what you need to determine is what is the minimum credential that will combine with your existing degree and accomplishments to get you into an interview. In some areas attending a junior college and getting an associates degree in business data processing will be enough to qualify you for interviews. In others attending a six-month course at a for-profit school like CPI (Computer Processing Institute) can give you enough training, coupled with a classy four-year degree in something else, to get you started. However, in other parts of the country either of these strategies would be a waste of time.

What you need to do before you invest in any training is talk to recruiters and managers at local companies and ask them directly what kind of credential they would have to see in order to give you an interview. Talk to several companies and pay attention to what they say. Where I lived, recruiters at the largest insurance company said that they would recommend attending the local technical college because its graduates got better, practical hands-on training than the graduates of the expensive four-year school I had been considering. My two-year degree cost me $75 a quarter and led, as I have mentioned, directly to a job with IBM.

Conversely however, several years ago in Dallas, Electronic Data Systems (EDS), the huge data processing service company, had no interest in hiring graduates of two-year colleges. That company preferred to hire liberal arts majors especially those with majors in music or anthropology who had almost no computer experience and to train them in its own in-house programs.

In Dallas programmers treated for-profit schools as a joke, classing them with the radio broadcasting and modeling schools that advertise on the radio. In Hartford, a city with a disproportionate number of programmers in its population because of the DP-intensive nature of the insurance industry, a great number of working programmers, especially those with degrees in other fields got their training at for-profit schools. So once again you will have to do some research to determine what goes on in your area.

---

Whatever your background or credentials, in the long run there is one final factor that really determines whether you will be able to break into and succeed in mainframe programming. It is this: Do you love to program computers? Do you, deep down, find that learning the ins and outs of software programs and debugging code is fun?

I've worked with a woman who had a master's degree in advanced mathematics who washed out of programming in two years in spite of a terrific college record. The reason was simple. She hated debugging. When the system she was working on "broke" it offended her. She had trouble dealing with disorder, which is the state in which most computer systems exist most of the time, and when a nonprogramming low-level administrative job offered itself she fled into it without a look back.

I suspect we will see a lot more of this sort of thing as people continue to enter the field, drawn not by real interest but by the rumors of big bucks to be made. I feel sorry for the high-school students who are pushed toward computers by parents fearful for their economic futures. Many of them would be happier—and more successful—doing other things.

Whatever it takes to break into mainframe programming, the person who is going to succeed at it as a long-term career is the person who loves to code and debug, who finds computer software so interesting that he browses through manuals during lunch time. This person will have to choose his jobs wisely and learn how to function in a business environment created by business people whose characteristics are very different from his own. But with good planning that follows the principles set out in this book, such a person can find himself in the enviable position of doing something he loves, and doing it very well, with all the financial and personal rewards that that can bring.

# 2
## Your First Job

A great number of computer science graduates are shocked to discover what it is that "real" programmers do all day. This is largely because most college computer science curriculums have been developed by people who have little or no experience of programming in the business world. College curricula are often designed by people with backgrounds heavy in theoretical mathematics who were drafted to teach computer science courses because of the shortage of people with Ph.Ds in computer science willing to work for what the universities can pay. Their computer science curricula include courses on database theory and compiler design and they challenge students with courses where they write their own operating systems. There is no question that coursework like this gives the student a grasp of the underlying structure of the software world that he will be working in. Such work is also interesting and intellectually challenging. But it bears little relationship to what it is that business programmers do to earn their living in the real world. Unless you go to work for one of a handful of vendor firms it is very unlikely that you will ever write a compiler in the business environment. Nor will you write an operating system. The computer systems in use in large business applications need to be easily learned and easily maintained and that means that the vast majority of them use off-the-shelf software for system functions like operating systems and compilers which they buy from well-known vendors with a history of good product support.

It has been my experience that when companies do attempt to develop their own systems software, the result is often a nightmare: a poorly documented system where all too often the vital facts needed for ongoing maintenance are stored in the brain of the one or two geniuses who cooked it up. Homemade system software does exist in the business DP world, but as I will explain later in chapter 11, becoming involved with it can spell real career suicide for the student just out of college.

Business programmers do design databases, but only after having achieved many years of on-the-job training. And the databases that they design are usually built using off-the-shelf vendor database management systems packages, again in the interests of maintainability. The theoretical discussions of database classes bear little relationship to the task before a business database designer. His task is rarely to design an index structure or select a database form. More likely his task is to take an existing vendor database management system, whose quirks he has already mastered, and use his exhaustive knowledge of the applications that will use his database to design a file structure that will do the most for the many applications programs that will use the database. The most valuable asset such a database designer brings to the job is his experience with earlier systems, especially the disasters and embarrassments he experienced with them. "Performance" and "Data Integrity" are not just words underlined in a textbook to the experienced programmer who has faced an irate customer whose entire day of transactions has disappeared, or the systems analyst faced with a "daily cycle" that takes two days to complete!

What this means is that the student coming out of college has very little likelihood of doing most of the things he studied in school and should be aware of this. He will not analyze and design major systems. If you are told in an interview that you will be designing major systems software or that you will be designing a new applications system you can assume that either you are being lied to in order to attract you to an otherwise awful job or that you are dealing with lunatics.

What you should hope to find yourself doing on your first job(s) in the corporate environment is watching real, as opposed to theoretical, computer systems in action. What you can expect to be given to do are small, clearly defined programming tasks, which will give you the opportunity to wallow in existing programs, slog through manuals, and slowly put together the picture of a large complex business computer system.

## Reading Code

In college you learned how to write programs. In your first year as a programmer you are going to learn to do something much harder: You are going to learn how to read programs—programs written by other people. It is this skill above all others that will set you apart from your coworkers, because the person who can read and understand existing code is the person who can make changes that don't abend in the middle of the night or crash the on-line system in production. The person who can read other people's code is the one who gets the reputation for competence, which is the key to all subsequent career moves.

You may be lucky. The system you begin on may have been written in the last five years by enlightened disciples of structured coding methodology supported by a management that demanded they take the time to get it right. In that case reading the programs that make up your system will simply be a question of flopping through your listings and following the program logic.

If, on the other hand, you start working on a more typical system, what you will find will be quite different.

In this case your normal reaction after your first encounter with production code will probably be fear. The chances are that the stuff you are looking at was written fifteen years ago by someone who was showing off and who was proud of the fact that no one but himself could figure out what he was doing. I have personally encountered code where the explanatory comments were written in Italian. I have also seen a program in which the field named "FOUR" was assigned the value "3" somewhere in the program execution logic. Imagine what this does to the simple COBOL statement "ADD FOUR TO COUNT1."

And this is only the beginning. The chances are that the original program has been changed fifteen or twenty times since it was written, by people who made no notes anywhere explaining what the changes were supposed to accomplish. If there are comments, they will usually be so cryptic as to be useless anyway. Why, you wonder, is there a special paragraph to execute if the customer number is 43211706? This, dear neophyte, is called hardcoding, and it is what desperate programmers do late at night when a job keeps blowing off at a specific customer record and the programmer can't figure out why. He puts in code to ignore the problem record and the program (maybe) continues. But what about this, why is there a special routine that only gets executed in April of a leap year? Good question, and one that you can ignore only if you don't have to make a change that involves that paragraph!

If you have been thinking of yourself as a "supertechie" assembler language programmer, your first brush with real assembler language code can be unnerving. The listing is over an inch thick, not a few pages like the ones you wrote in school. And where are the field names? All you see are offsets off of registers and DSECTS.

There is no shortcut in these cases. You cannot leaf through this stuff and get the gist of it. What you have to do—and this is true for the old-timer as well as the neophyte—is read every single line slowly, jot down all the field values as they get changed, and follow every single subroutine call. And then, slowly, the code will begin to make sense.

This is far from the vision that most new programmers have of themselves at work. It has no glamour to it at all. It is not elegant. But by humbly immersing yourself in the programs that make up the system you have been assigned to, you prepare yourself to walk on water at some future time in your career. Your attention to a detail will bear fruit when you are the only one able to find the solution to some show-stopper of a system failure that has stumped your boss. Then you begin to emerge from the crowd.

### Magical Manuals

Wedged on a shelf somewhere in your department are some thirty or forty manuals, probably in very institutional metal holders.

Chances are they are covered with dust because no one has looked at them in ages. I hope you are not allergic to dust, because if you are serious about your career as a programmer, the minute you get a free moment you are going to go over to that rack and commence to read through every manual you can find that describes a software product you have access to.

Manuals are not always well written, especially the IBM manuals designed before 1981 when IBM started a campaign to improve their more obscure offerings. But manuals tell you how to get things done, and getting things done is how you advance your career. Learn the features of your language that weren't covered in class. Learn how your file access method works so that you can think in systems terms when you get weird errors in testing. If your system has an interpreter language, learn its features. You can use this to automate the repetitive tasks you have to do in the test environment, and even sometimes create snazzy utilities for your user very quickly.

If you want to be an on-line programmer and are stuck in a batch system, read the on-line software manuals. Find out how the on-line software works. Then if an opportunity presents itself to work on something on-line you can jump in and be productive fast.

A lot of programmers waste a lot of time waiting to be sent to courses for things they could learn by reading the manuals that are sitting on a neighbor's desk. Most people don't mind your borrowing their manuals if you return them. If you see something interesting, borrow it!

And don't be put off if the manual for something you really would like to learn seems incomprehensible and assumes that you know things you don't. Often if you just keep reading you will find paragraphs later on in the book that illuminate what stumped you earlier. It is not that you are stupid; the books are badly written.

After some time spent soaking up random information a funny thing will happen. People will start to come and ask you questions when they get stuck. You won't know the answer right off, but you will have some vague memory of having seen something somewhere that might be useful and you will root around in your pile of books until you come up with the little fact about your software that offers a solution—a solution that the person asking the question could have looked up just as well as you did, but didn't. Pretty soon the word will get out that you know everything! You don't, of course, but you do know how to find things out. Many people never get this far. Once you begin to build up this kind of "guru" reputation you are really on your way!

### Avoiding Beginners' Mistakes

There are a couple of behaviors that scream out "new guy in town!" It is natural that you will display some of them, after all you *are* the new guy in town! But with some foresight you can prevent yourself from making the more flagrant errors that new people are prone to.

In almost every case these errors come from a new person's lack of appreciation of the complexity of the environment that they have entered. Often, too, they occur because the new programmer, fresh from school, is used to working as a lone individual and not as part of a team. He is not used to thinking what the effect of his actions will be on the many other people who are working on the same system as he is.

It is this unawareness that leads new people to edit system files shared by many other programmers and forget to mention it; or leads them to move their own untested modules into the department's test system, again without mentioning it. In many "test" environments there are programs that are shared by all programmers currently doing testing—programs that may be considered "test" programs because they are not the actual production programs run to do the company's business but which twenty or thirty programmers use to enable them to build a framework in which to do further testing. If you mess with one of these debugged "test" programs you can easily ruin many other programmers' entire day of testing. Final "parallel" test runs, which are supposed to have perfect output, can, for example, show up with junk all over them. Worse, the programmers who unwittingly use your modification of a testing module often waste a lot of time debugging your code, thinking that the errors they see are coming from their own changes not yours.

Take the time to have your test environment explained to you in detail and when you are in any doubt about whether you can modify something—ASK! Attempting to appear smart by not asking "dumb questions" usually just results in your doing something far dumber—screwing things up for your coworkers.

Another typical mistake that new programmers make is to write tricky code that cannot be understood by ordinary programmers. Seeing an opportunity to use something they picked up in school, they use a little-known technique (the more devious the better) that a teacher or more likely a lab assistant showed them. This devious solution solves an immediate problem, and the person rushes it into production without writing an explanation of what he did, because he knows he did a great job and assumes that no one will ever have to fix his code. Two years later something changes in the system and his nifty code ceases to work. Perhaps he used some undocumented feature of a software product that no longer works under the latest release of the operating system. Perhaps he "faked out the system" by doing something tricky to a system control block somewhere that the vendor just changed. Whatever the reason, such displays of brilliance always result in time-wasting and frustrating work for other people.

No matter how smart you are, the code you write will always need work someday. Write it so the dumbest guy in the world can understand what you did. Believe me the worst possible experience is having to give an immediate lifesaving fix to tricky code that you simply can't follow, and then realizing that you wrote it yourself a few years back!

There is another common mistake made by brash young programmers. They comment loudly on the deficiencies of the old programs they have been given to maintain. "Look at this," they crow. "The documentation stinks! Talk about spaghetti logic! I could have written this whole routine in six lines! Who wrote this garbage?"

The answer, all too often, is "the current boss." This is especially prone to happen when the new programmer doesn't recognize the boss's maiden name.

Even if the author is not in a position to slow down your career there is never any excuse for insulting the people with whom you work. But beyond that there are often very good reasons behind the writing of what looks like "bad" code. The code in question may have been written in response to hardware or software limitations that have been remedied in intervening years. The code may have been developed before standards that are now commonly taught to all fledgling programmers were even thought of. After all, those standards only could develop after a large enough body of work had been developed and maintained that the need for the standards became apparent.

Finally, the code you are looking at might have been gorgeous when it was first developed but since then has been subjected to a host of enhancements and fixes applied by harried maintenance programmers who preferred to remain anonymous. The developer whose name is in the documentation at the head of the program is often the only person whose name can be found, even though only slight vestiges of his actual work remain.

The wise programmer will therefore keep his exclamations of disgust to himself and share them only with members of his immediate family. You can be sure that a certain percentage of the code you are writing right now will embarrass you in years to come.

Sometimes our brash programmer doesn't stop at just commenting about old code either. He takes it upon himself to improve it—without consulting his boss first. He lavishes time on rewriting routines that already work in order to make them more efficient. Since his own salaried time is usually worth a whole lot more to the company than the nanoseconds he saves, this kind of behavior marks our new programmer in the eyes of management as someone who is not yet aware of the rules of the business game. Even worse, all too often in improving the program's efficiency our new programmer fails to grasp some obscure function the sloppy code was performing so that the program, at some future time, fails.

Another set of problems occurs because new programmers fail to understand the sanctity that surrounds the company's production systems and the elaborate safeguards that must protect them. Most places have a test environment that consists of libraries and files the programmers can pretty much do what they want with, and a production system that does the company's work.

Production is a very big deal. In a factory where each day the line turns out half a million dollars' worth of product, bringing the warehouse system to its knees has major implications.

If an on-line system that processes customer orders stops processing them for more than a few minutes, hundreds of employees are suddenly being paid to sit around and shoot the bull—and a vice-president is going to want to know why.

Because of the importance of production systems most installations have rigid procedures in place to ensure that any new versions of programs that are moved into production are thoroughly tested. Unfortunately, new programmers often don't understand the need for this and see the procedures as obstacles keeping them from making their target dates on an assignment and looking good. The rigmarole involved in moving stuff into production is irritating. It involves collecting signatures and filling in forms. It is only after a programmer has been called in at 2 A.M. because the module with his latest change in it abended the production system (i.e., stopped it dead in its tracks) that many programmers develop a healthy respect for the testing process. Especially since it is always some extremely stupid, niggling detail that causes the furor.

The experienced programmer has learned that there is no such thing as a "minor" change. Something as minor as going in at the last moment and changing a comment can cause a program to bomb. The experienced programmer gets serious about testing, paranoid even, and is in no hurry ever to move anything into production, because he would much rather fix programs at his terminal in the morning, than at the data center late at night.

## Who Is the Boss?

After you begin work the person who hired you will introduce you to someone he identifies as your team leader or maybe your manager. The terms may differ, but his function does not. This person, and no other, is in direct control of your career.

It is very important to understand the team leader's role. As important as learning all the technical details that go into making you a good programmer is learning the business realities of the environment you have stumbled into. In fact, a cynical person would probably say that if you master the details of maneuvering in the business environment you can probably slack off as regards the technical stuff and still get promoted before anyone else in your trainee group. They might be right.

Businesses in America generally are organized in a hierarchical fashion with each person reporting to a single superior. Your team leader therefore is the only person who has authority over you. He will be the person who assigns and evaluates your work. He will tell you what specifically he expects you to accomplish and assign deadlines for your work. You will report any accomplishments to him and at the end of a predefined period he will conduct some sort of

A Typical Organization Chart
(Only the Path to One Function is Shown)

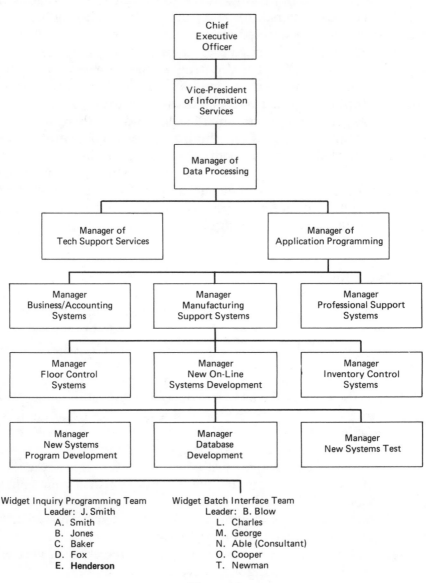

Widget Inquiry Programming Team
Leader: J. Smith
A. Smith
B. Jones
C. Baker
D. Fox
E. **Henderson**

Widget Batch Interface Team
Leader: B. Blow
L. Charles
M. George
N. Able (Consultant)
O. Cooper
T. Newman

**Figure 2**

appraisal, formal or informal, and report its result to his boss. If he says that you are doing a great job the word will be passed on and you may get a raise or a promotion. If he says you stink, nothing you can do or say can undo the damage, no matter how much respect your coworkers have for you.

Obviously your relationship with this individual is of prime importance to your career. If you find yourself in an ambiguous situation, which occurs sometimes, and are not sure who really is your boss, do whatever you possibly can to get a clear answer. I have seen a situation where a person was told to take technical guidance from a so-called "team leader" but was informed that another, less-visible person would be in charge of administrative details, such as vacation time. When the "team leader" got into a clash with the administrative person the programmer did what the "team leader" wanted, only to discover too late that the administrative person was not only his only boss but was preparing to fire him for doing what the team leader, not the administrator, had suggested.

Your boss may be the nicest person in the world, eat lunch with you, and dance around at company parties with a lampshade on his head. Don't drop your guard. Your boss is not your buddy and the main thrust of your relationship with him must be aimed at receiving the highest possible rating from him when evaluation time comes.

The irony for you in this situation is that the person with this kind of power over you is actually situated at the very lowest administrative level in the management hierarchy. He is not very important in the business scheme of things, even though he is of great importance to you.

To demonstrate this look at figure 2. Figure 2 is a typical organization chart of the type used by managers to represent their view of the company. Organization charts depict the flow of authority from the top of the organization downward. In the example given, E. Henderson is a programmer working under team leader J. Shmoe on a development team designing, testing, and coding a Widget On-Line Inquiry System. Note how many levels of management separate the team leader from the three highest levels of the corporation, which are the executive levels where most important decision making occurs. Note that on this chart the programmers are the end of the line. Their names don't even appear on the chart in boxes; this is true no matter what their technical level or their salary. In actual practice the names of the programmers in the various departments would not appear at all on an organization chart used by upper management. These names are usually only put into the version of the chart distributed to programmers after a departmental reorganization. You should be sure to get a copy of the organization chart mapping your department and familiarize yourself with your company's management's view of how what you do fits in.

The team leader who is your direct superior is usually a programmer who has just taken the first step toward a management career. He has just moved from a position where his technical skills were of the most importance to one where he is expected to demonstrate leadership and organization ability.

Unfortunately for you, people vary widely in the facility with which they can make this shift. Your team leader may be able to select just the tasks to help you develop your own systems knowledge and make the maximum contribution to the work at hand. Or he may have real difficulty delegating work and may simply try to do, himself, the work he is supposed to give to you.

In the worst case a team leader may go so far as to mark on the program listing the very line where a change should be made and write out what the change should be. In a case like this you need to control your feelings and do the best job you possibly can. Your task is to assure an insecure team leader that you won't totally screw things up for him if he gives you some responsibility.

If you have been exclusively a supertechie in college you owe it to yourself now to do some hurry-up reading about management. You need to understand what it is that the people who are in charge of you think it is that they are doing. As you will find out, there is a very structured ritual going on around you in the business world, and if you intend to have anything approaching a career you must understand it, no matter how foolish or irrelevant it appears to be. The penalty for ignoring it is career stagnation.

We will talk about management again in the next chapter, but for the new hire the important thing to understand is that your team leader is your intersection with the company, and your only one. Therefore you will further your career inestimably if, when you encounter problems with your team leader, you do *not* do any of the following:

- Ignore what he told you to do because it is stupid and do what you think is the correct thing instead.
- Go to his manager and complain about his behavior.
- Announce loudly at the lunch table that he is a real turkey.

In the business world the basic ground rule is that you relate only to your immediate supervisor. You should violate this rule only if you are so desperate that you are prepared to quit.

If you have problems with your team leader there are several things you can do. If the problem is not something major you can sometimes wait it out. Businesses often reorganize and you might find yourself with a new, easier-to-deal-with team leader in a few weeks. If any rumors of change are in the air, wait and see what happens.

If you are really stuck, you should take refuge in memos. Document in writing to your team leader what he has required you to do and then document that you have done it. Make suggestions, politely, in print. Always approach your memo writing in the most positive tone possible—you don't want to be seen as a troublemaker, but you do want to make sure that in case of a conflict you have a paper trail that demonstrates the correctness of your actions, or the fact that you did what you did at his direction, in spite of your better judgment. If you confront a team leader in a polite way with this kind of evidence sometimes you can head off trouble.

If you are not getting enough responsibility, be aggressive in pointing out the good work you have done and present the team leader with what you would like to be given for your next assignment. Give him a couple of choices so that he has to give you something you want. Most of all understand that if you are having problems with him it is often because he is having a hard time doing his job and is probably very anxious. Try to present yourself as someone helping him achieve departmental goals, not as someone just looking out for himself, and you might be able to turn the situation around.

## Learn from Old-Timers

The final thing that you should do in your first year on the job is get to know as many people as you can. By this I don't mean socially, although that is always nice. What I mean is that you should learn what it is that the people around you know. You will never be able to know everything about an applications system, the software environment, or a company's business. What you can do is figure out whom you can ask about what. Universally you will find, when you enter a new company, that certain people will present themselves to you as the experts. Universally too, you will also discover that most of these loudmouths are the very last people to go to when you have real problems to solve.

You must identify who it is in the systems area that really understands the business part of your application. This person can tell you which individual to go to in the user group when you need a business issue clarified. Next, find the person who is Mr. (or Ms.) Manual—the person who knows all the little-known features of the software your company has installed. Find the "oldest living programmer." This is the person who was there twenty years ago when the very first program was installed and knows the history of the system. Often he can explain the seemingly unbelievably stupid things in your system by telling you the political situations that swirled around a project's developmental phase.

Be friendly, humble and nonexploitative to these people. If you treat them as valued resources and bother them only when you really cannot find an answer on your own you will be able to get answers in tricky situations that stymie other programmers, because you will know who to go to for help.

Another rule-of-thumb to keep in mind when you enter a new environment: It's a good idea to avoid classing yourself with any particular group of people when you enter a new job situation. You simply cannot tell until you have been in a company for a while what is going on all around you. Eat lunch with different groups of people every day until you have a clearer picture of what is going on. If you identify yourself too strongly with any group you may later discover that you have unwittingly taken some kind of political position in your department that could limit your career growth.

------

Your first year should be an exciting worthwhile time. By its end you should feel confident in dealing with the technical details of your environment, and you should have begun to see the business issues you will have to confront as your career develops. You probably have changed a few of your original ideas about what you would enjoy doing in the business world, and it is likely that you have a several future possibilities roughed out for career development. If you are lucky you have even been able to pull off some technical feat that has given you a local reputation, and managers will soon be striving to get you on their teams because of what a good worker you are. Now it's time, in the next chapter, to look at the divergent pathways that will begin to open up to the programmer at the end of his first year.

# 3
## *Making Choices—*
## *Corporate Career Options*

By the end of your first year of working as a programmer you should have begun to figure out the rudiments of what is going on around you. You have gotten your bearings and perhaps begun to make a name for yourself. If you plan to continue your career in the corporate environment and do not intend to leave the corporation for a more entrepreneurial career, you will have to come to terms with a major decision very soon—whether you want to remain a technical person or whether instead you want to set your course toward becoming a manager.

Most of us became programmers because programming computers was something that interested us, and we were pleased to discover that our programming skills were valued in the marketplace. It therefore comes as an unpleasant surprise to discover, after a few years of earning our livings as programmers, that many of the people we work for see no better way to reward us for the good technical work we've done than to make sure we never get to do it again! The reality in many, if not all, companies is that there are very strong forces pushing people who demonstrate intelligence and competence away from technical work and into management. Most programmers come into the work force vaguely aware that management is a career option open to them but determined not to take it, convinced that the kind of people they know themselves to be would not be happy in an environment of memos and meetings. Many of these people a few years later reluctantly join the herd competing for entry-level management jobs, convinced that there is no other way to get their career (and income) moving again, and kicking themselves for not having directed their efforts toward management earlier in their careers.

Becoming a manager is not really the only viable career path open to ambitious programmers in the corporate world; it is merely the simplest and most lucrative! In the pages that follow we will look at the technical career paths that programmers follow in the corporate world and the strategies you can use to keep a technical career humming. Then we will look in depth at management. We will consider the fundamental tensions that exist between the needs and thought patterns of executives and the realities of computer systems. We will look at what kind of career you can expect in DP management and examine, finally, some of the pitfalls management brings.

## Technical Paths—Applications Programming Expert

It seems that the simplest career path open to a programming professional should be the one leading to becoming an applications expert; after all, most programmers start out as applications programmers. By definition an applications expert is a programmer who has worked with an application or a family of applications for enough years that he or she has mastered both the application's many details from a business perspective and the details of the programs in the computer system that the application uses. For example, a programmer who began working in a pensions administration environment and who wanted to become a pensions application specialist would gradually, through working on different portions of several pensions systems, learn how pension contributions are credited to different funds, how pension withdrawals are made from these same funds, how tax law changes have affected pension transactions, how pension fund investments are tracked, and how pension administrators prefer to keep their records. After a few years this person would be able to hold an intelligent conversation with a manager from the pension administration departments on topics like legislative changes to 401K plans and IRA's, as well as the company's document retention standards and client reporting requirements. On top of all this, the applications expert would know what programs in the company's system performed each of the above functions and what technical limitations the system might embody that would require future programming efforts to correct.

When the company decided to revamp the computer systems used by the pension administration areas, it would be this person who would probably be given the job of developing the specifications for the new system. His task would be to take his level of knowledge about the business aspects of pension administration and his ability to understand what the users wanted when they described some new feature, and design a new set of programs that could provide the new features at a cost the users could afford.

Obviously such a person would need to have a solid understanding of the technical aspects of the system too, but most likely they would probably have only a middling interest in technical matters. The heavy technical decisions would probably be made in conjunction with people from a technical support department associated with the pension systems who would review the application expert's plans and specifications. Usually an applications expert has a very clear idea of the limits of his own technical knowledge and has built up a strong relationship with people in the more bits and bytes areas of the company who usually have a compensating lack of interest in business concerns.

This sounds like a great job. Here we finally get to design systems from scratch. This is a very visible job and should lead to some kind of recognition for the applications expert.

The problem is that companies very infrequently develop systems that call for the technical expert's vast experience. Most of the time applications areas confine themselves to making modest changes in existing systems, which incorporate small changes in the way that the company does business. A major development project is a very expensive and highly risky undertaking for management. Many development projects waste thousands of corporate dollars before being rejected as infeasible. Many more development projects languish for a while and then are canceled when upper management changes direction. There just aren't that many opportunities to do really exciting work at the applications level.

Thus, for the large number of people who would like to stay applications programmers, corporate life can become very drab. The long-term applications programmer can expect to work for years on the same systems, making a change here and a change there, installing a vendor package, or copying his system in order to create a new clone system. After a while he will know most of what there is to know about the system and the feeling of excitement that comes from learning new things will be gone.

The other problem that the application expert faces is simply the fact that no matter how good he is at his job, if a new system does actually get designed, no matter how brilliantly he designs it, the person within the organization who will get the lion's share of the credit for the success of the project is the project's manager—not the system designer. Businessmen generally assume that the programmers did as good a job as they did because of the excellent quality of the management that they had! Thus when the project "goes live" and the corporate bigwigs assemble at the awards banquet the hardworking applications expert often is chagrined to hear the corporate vice-president attribute the success of the project to "Bob and Sally" who are second- and third-level managers, rather than to the person whose intellectual child the system was.

The applications expert who does distinguish himself on a project is usually rewarded by being invited into the lowest rung of management. If he does not take this "promotion" he faces the risk of being viewed by his own management as being sadly lacking in ambition since he just wants to stay "in a rut" doing the same old thing and not improving himself—i.e., leaving programming to become a manager.

After a couple of years of bucking this system most applications experts allow themselves to be washed into the lower administrative levels of the company. Often they move in and out of low-level management and staff positions.

I have met only a few people who were strong enough to stay applications experts and still keep their career momentum growing. The key for these people seems to have been a combination of terrific programming skills, the kind that simply cannot be faked, and an ability to pick projects that are highly visible and likely to succeed. These successful applications experts also seem to have outgoing personalities of the kind that made them extremely popular people on a personal level, the kind of people who remember the first names of all their coworker's children. Finally, and not surprisingly, these people, while not wanting to go into management themselves, usually understood what it was that managers did and were able to interact with managers in a businesslike way to get what they wanted. I suspect that part of these people's success derives from the fact that it is very clear to anyone in management that these people could easily succeed in management if they wanted to and that their decision to stay in technical roles was not a reflection of some inadequacy or failure.

There are many other people who are applications experts in less happy situations who change jobs every few years looking for some place where they can recover the excitement. Others have simply accepted salary levels that have topped out and a comfortable job that they know how to do and can do well. These people are happy with their role in their companies, content to see younger people steam by on their way up the corporate ladder, and satisfied with their cost-of-living salary increases. If you can accept these things and draw a feeling of satisfaction from being a solid applications programmer then this might be a reasonable career path for you to follow.

## Technical Support and Systems Programming

There are many kinds of systems programmers. By definition systems programmers are the ones who take care of the software environment that the application programmers use to develop user applications. In practice there are two main kinds of systems programmers. The first kind is made up of people who probably started out way-back-when as operators, usually with no college training. They became experts in things like JCL and disk pack management and eventually were sent to training schools to learn how to install the new software products provided by vendors and how to apply the fixes that the vendors send out. These programmers do very vital work but have a fairly low status due to their origins in operations, and their work environment often has a rather blue-collar tinge to it. By the time a person coming from the operations area has put in enough years to demonstrate his worthiness for training he is usually a long-term employee and not likely to move around to other companies.

The other kind of systems programmer is more of an aristocrat in the business DP world. Usually this person comes out of an applications area where he has demonstrated unusual technical ability and typically has gone from being an applications programmer using a software product to being the person who troubleshoots that software for other applications programmers when they are at their wits' end. The people who solve CICS problems for on-line programmers fall into this category as do database specialists in tech support areas. Other tech support people work at help desks where they are a resource for applications programmers stumped by failing programs. These people usually are adept at reading and interpreting system dumps and have been given advanced formal classes in subjects like MVS internals, CICS internals, and database management systems.

The highly successful tech support programmer can become an expert in subjects like building computer networks and evaluating software packages for purchase by the company. Some become experts in evaluating hardware options too. Yet others get training in software tuning, the fine art of improving system performance. However what tech support system programmers usually do not get to do is develop or code programs. Most of their life is spent exclusively dealing with vendor software.

This can be a gratifying career path for a technically oriented person. These positions command great respect. I have seen whole rooms full of programmers fall into a respectful silence when the CICS maven entered, followed by acolytes, to look at a system dump. The salaries paid these systems programmers are usually higher than those for applications programmers at what are supposed to be the same job classes.

The main problem with this career path is that it is so hard to break into. The training that systems programmers receive, which enables them to support popular software packages, may increase their value on the job market tremendously, and employers often do not give people this kind of training until they have put in a lot of years demonstrating loyalty to the company.

Often, too, there are many different kinds of tech support units in a company, requiring widely different skill levels. Some may turn

out to be dead ends requiring and providing little technical expertise, as in help desks that mainly support end-user groups.

Other people have encountered technical support jobs where
their role was to do nothing more than increase the red tape that applications areas had to deal with and where the prevailing attitude
was that the technical support areas were defending "their stuff" (the
system) from all those darn programmers who kept messing it up.
Sad to say such attitudes do occur. After all, if applications programmers wouldn't keep adding their programs to the system it might
just work!

The only consideration that should make you think twice about
taking this career path is if you would like to keep the consulting option open. Although there are occasionally high-paying contracts
available to systems heavies, the vast majority of open consulting
positions are for applications people. Your high level of technical
skills might therefore make it difficult to support yourself contracting if you want to contract half the year and hang out in the woods
the rest of the time.

If you do decide to become a systems programmer you should
be very careful that the expertise you garner is the kind of expertise
that is marketable outside your present company. Keep current with
articles in the trade press—by knowing what trends are occurring in
the software world you will have some idea whether the software
you're mastering is the software that will be in demand in the future.

## Using your DP Apprenticeship to Prepare for a Strong Nonmanagement Career

The person who has completed his first year in DP and is thinking
about how to position himself for a technical career that doesn't run
aground needs to do the following:

- build technical skills
- build visibility within the company
- understand management's role and its goals

Any company with a large investment in computer systems is
forced to keep a few good programmers around who can solve the

problems that, left untended, can bring those computer systems to a complete stop. No matter how many management directives demand that head count be kept low and staff be cut back there will always be a need for truly good programmers until the day they close up the building for the last time and everyone goes home.

Programming skill cannot be faked. You cannot bullshit a program into working right. A manager may overstate his results. A salesman may slide around the truth, but a programmer brought in to solve a computer problem has to find its source or the problem remains. Because of this if you want to be valuable to a company as a technical person you have to be a very good one. It is possible to build a career without learning anything more than what you picked up in your first year training program. I've seen people do this. But the career you build is mediocre. There are in every installation a few people without whom everything would grind to a halt. Management is usually smart enough to recognize this and to do what is necessary to keep these people happy.

To build a strong technical career you must learn as much as you can about the systems of the company you work for. On the other hand you must strive at the same time to keep your technical skills general enough so that if your company should hit bad times, or if it should merge with another company and cause your job to be eliminated, you could find a job of a like caliber in another company. You do this by making sure that you stay current and by making sure that your resume demonstrates that you are familiar with a few of the software products that are industry standards for database management, on-line, or fourth-generation language development, which are discussed in depth later in this book.

The next thing you must pay attention to in the formative years of your career is building visibility within the companies you work for. It is not enough to accomplish things in this world, you must make sure that the people who run things know that you are accomplishing things. One way to do this is to document interesting things you find when you are working on the system. If you solve a pesky problem, particularly one that other people have encountered before, write up a short, clear memo describing the problem and the solution and buck it around the department, making sure that it passes by your manager. If you see a potential problem it is often a good idea to write that up as a suggestion to management. For example one person I know noticed that an on-line database was filling up more rapidly than had been anticipated, wrote a memo pinpointing the exact week when all available disk space would be full and then suggested a simple way of staging older, less useful information off of the database.

By doing things like this you help management appreciate the work that you do and ensure that it will be rewarded.

Finally, just because you have decided to be a "techie" doesn't mean that you don't have to understand management. In the corporate world managers control the flow of resources. They get to pick what jobs you are assigned and even decide what kind of terminal you have on your desk. As long as you are in the business world you must understand what managers think about and what fears drive them. You must be able to show them your worth in their own terms.

One programmer I know who is truly a supertechie, with awe-inspiring mastery of assembly language programming and operating system logic, found himself receiving consistently mediocre performance reviews. One manager finally explained that as he was now a senior-level person he was supposed to be providing "leadership." Management didn't know that this individual had personally solved all of the technical show-stopping problems of not only his own but several other departments for the past several years because it had never occurred to him to mention it. All management saw was his gray locks bent over program listings in his office, or a bunch of people looking like they were having a gabfest in his office. The solution he found for getting better performance appraisals and thus improved opportunities within his company was to define what he was already doing—showing newer people how to approach and solve difficult debugging problems in a complex environment—as providing "technical leadership." By adding up the number of times a month that he had taken a newer person through this process, he was able to show in the quantifiable terms that management loves best that he had indeed been leading ten or twelve people very effectively. This person had to understand the value system of the people writing his appraisals who unfortunately, having very sketchy technical skills of their own, did not have enough technical knowledge to appreciate the value of the service he was providing to his project. It is important to notice that the solution for him was not to deny that the most valuable thing he could contribute was leadership. He just had to demonstrate that "leadership" could take a new form! That is the way that managers think.

If you can build up your skills, let management know what you've done for them lately, and communicate with management on their, not your, terms then you can eventually fill the role of "DP Guru." As such you will be treated with considerable respect and earn a reasonable livelihood with much better job security than many of the managers, whom you will see come and go. When people come in to be interviewed for jobs, fresh from college, you will often be trotted out and exhibited proudly as proof that in your company there really is a technical career path that works. And, if it doesn't, you will always be able to find a job somewhere else.

## Why Management Doesn't Like Programmers

In every business I have ever worked in no matter how much lip service was paid to the importance of technical people, the simple fact remains that managers get the nice offices, managers get the big salaries, and managers get most of the corporate perks. In American business it is management that gets to give out the rewards, and not surprisingly, the skills that management rewards most highly are precisely those that management itself has—and those are definitely not technical skills. No amount of railing and protesting is going to change this. It is something that all technical people must come to grips with in the business world.

Because confronting the diverging management/technical paths is usually the most traumatic event in the career of the programmer, I want to go into some depth to explain just why it is that business does not value the technician for what he is but instead forces him to leave his technical skills behind if he wants to advance. In order to do this we need to examine the role that the programmer plays in a business as seen not by the programmer himself but by the business types who pay his salary. The following analysis might seem a little jaundiced to a person unfamiliar with the way that businesses manage their technical operations, but I assure you that any working programmer has seen these patterns repeated every place he has worked. A survey of *Computerworld* readers found that a whopping one out of three cited "ineffective or poor management" as the most frustrating aspect of their job, putting this factor way ahead of any other cause of complaint! [1]

The fundamental truth that anyone who ventures into a corporate environment needs to understand is that all rewards in the corporate world stem from the degree to which you are helping the company make a quick buck.

Companies are evaluated annually on their ability to make a profit. The more instrumental you personally are in making that profit, the better you will be rewarded. Here we encounter the two features of this system that work against you, the quality programmer, in reaping your reward.

The first is that the whole computer operation in almost every company is just a chunk of overhead and does not contribute directly to profits.

The second is that there are no rewards in business for any but short-term successes. There is no benefit to management in sacrificing short-term for long-term goals. System design, implementation, and maintenance, on the other hand, must be approached from a long-term perspective if they are not to result in an endless drain on corporate resources. Let's look at these points further.

*Computers are Overhead*

This fact should be engraved over the doorways of all data processing offices in large gold letters: Computer programming is overhead expense. Except for a small number of companies that make their profits selling computer programs and programming services, the programming of computers is not directly contributing to the profitability of the corporation.

The company makes its money from sales. The customer writes a check to the XYZ Corporation in return for widgets, or widget cleaning, or insurance for his existing widgets. He may even pay for advice on how to best use his widgets. But he does not directly pay for the computer systems that the XYZ Corporation uses internally to track its widget production, design new widgets, estimate widget costs, pay its staff, or send out invoices. The company could go right on selling widgets without even having a computer system if it had

---

[1]*Computerworld*, "Dataview, Fostering Frustration," February 8, 1988, p. 67.

to. It has put those systems in in the hope that by doing so it could cut down on its other overhead costs, usually salaries, and be able to keep more of the widget sales dollar as profit.

Because computer programming is overhead all good managers want to keep it as controlled as possible. The problem, unfortunately, is that computer systems are almost uncontrollable.

The management that blithely decides to bring in a system that is supposed to make things easier usually finds itself several years down the line supporting an ever-growing DP budget, forced to constantly upgrade its hardware, and worst of all, dependent on a steady stream of quirky, unbusinesslike computer programmers who quit whenever they are offered indecently better salaries by competitors, have little interest in widgets, and are the only people who can keep the darn systems working. *From a senior management perspective computers are a hard to manage pain in the neck.*

Let's look at the programming life cycle from the perspective of management.

Most of the major decisions that lead to the development of new computer systems in large companies are made by extremely nontechnical upper management types who don't want to go overboard on costly computer systems but are swayed by the press releases that they read in the business press and the blandishments of very effective vendor salesmen. They read glowing descriptions of their competitors' new systems and don't want to be left behind—not realizing that the articles don't mention the spiraling costs and misplaced efforts that often lay behind the system being touted.

Salesmen from hardware, software, and turnkey vendor firms assure the nervous executive that although his new system has high start-up costs, in the long run his costs will come down. Once the system is installed, the computer, aided by a couple of lowly operatives, will be able to do the work previously done by legions of better-paid staff. Computers don't get pensions and computers don't unionize. (I hasten to note that no salesman would be so crude as to come out and say that his system will let the company fire a roomful of blue-haired old ladies—he just lets the manager draw his own conclusions.)

Often salesmen will go out of their way to assure the hesitant executive that he will not be dependent on programmers. Murmuring buzzwords like "fourth-generation language" and "artificial intelligence" the salesman bears tales of a wonderful future in which computers will program themselves: conversing with the (executive) user like well-raised children.

Meanwhile it is true that the company will need to have a few programmers around, but the salesmen assure him that is only until the system is installed.

Ah, that's a wonderful word—*installed*—suggesting as it does the kind of stability usually associated with plumbing fixtures.

Senior managers make all the major decisions about the new system and then, somewhat belatedly, bring in the lower-level grunts who are going to have to write the programs that get the system to do what the various hardware and software salesmen told the executives it could do.

As a note to all this in a vendor environment a typical "in" joke is "How can you tell when a salesman isn't lying?" The answer is, "His lips aren't moving."

Salesmen usually will promise that computer systems will do whatever it is that the customer wants. If the system cannot currently accommodate the requirement, the salesman announces that the next release of the product he is selling has just that feature—and then writes frenzied letters back to the company's development departments demanding that the feature be integrated into the next release—usually without ever consulting with the vendor development people who have to pull it off.

Yet in spite of the fact that senior management rarely gives the grunt-level technical people real input into selection of the system and the high-level design process, a surprising number of competent DP teams are able to deliver what it is that management ordered. After an impressive programming effort the system is put in place and starts to run.

It is as this point that upper management expects to be able to cut down on programming resources and start realizing the cost savings that the computer system was brought in to achieve.

And it is now that management discovers it has become a software junkie.

*Why a Computer System Is Not Like a Bathtub*

The problem that management faces is that an installed computer system is a lot more complex than an installed bathtub.

Your average bathtub is designed to do one thing. That one thing is what is expected of it by anyone who might want to use it. Once installed it does that thing until, perhaps, its owner achieves yuppie status and has it pulled out and replaced with a Jacuzzi.

No one shows up one morning and tells you that the building code has changed and all bathtubs have to have built-in can openers. Nor does the average homeowner expect his bathtub to easily convert into a swimming pool to which he can invite the neighborhood kids.

Your installed computer system shares with a bathtub a certain rigidity. Although its rigidity is not evident to the naked eye, the components of a program are welded together in a very specific way to perform the very specific functions that the original designers expected the system to perform.

The problem is that the owner of the computer system is constantly demanding that changes be made to the system which were never foreseen by the original designers and correspond functionally to the built-in can opener in the bath. Worse, government regulations and legal requirements can suddenly change and force a business to add that new function to the system.

Finally, to go to our swimming pool analogy, as businesses grow their original systems become inadequate for their needs, but businesses resist throwing out existing systems that work in favor of starting from scratch to produce the larger completely redesigned systems that would accommodate their needs.

As a result many large corporations have the entire neighborhood squeezed in their bathtubs now. Many manufacturing and insurance systems that run today were originally written in the late 1950s or early 1960s and have been run through a series of conversions from one generation of computer to another. Programs designed to function in computers that had less capacity than today's desktop computer now run on multimillion dollar super machines— but they do it with logic and design that would not even be appropriate for a desktop system.

I can think of one system running right now in which subroutines are called every time it is necessary to add or subtract a decimal number. Why? Because the second-generation computer the code was originally developed on did not have a decimal instruction set as all mainframes since the mid-1960s have had.

I know of programs which laboriously spool their own print files because the early DOS system on which they were developed only could print one file at a time. The fact that this program runs on an MVS/XA computer that can write thousands of files out at once is irrelevant. The code was converted but never rewritten.

Other companies do their daily business with programs that were converted from assembly language to COBOL using line-by-line conversion. One line of assembly code becomes one line of COBOL. Registers become fields named R3 and R4 and table processing becomes a bizarre parody as the programs, now supposedly COBOL, simulate the old register-incrementing and branching logic of the low-level language.

The reason for all this is, of course, to keep costs down. This is a short-term goal. The long-term price that management pays for the refusal to spend money on its installed systems is that the systems eventually become so confusing and difficult to maintain that they resemble Rube Goldberg machines. The bathtub not only has a built-in can opener, it turns on the furnace and pitches baseballs. Unfortunately when a system this complex gets joggled only the slightest bit, whole sections come crashing down. Eventually these elderly systems require the most assiduous programmer attention. These systems are also the hardest to recruit programmers to, since very few competent people yearn to do maintenance in what is perceived to be a dead-end situation.

### How the Dream of a Programmer-Free System Leads to Ruin

The bad news for upper management is that a system is *never* entirely finished. When your business changes, your computer systems must change too. There is no easy way around it. And changing a computer system correctly is an expensive proposition requiring skilled personnel, especially programmers—the very same programmers that the executive hoped would fade away once his system was installed.

The hope that programmers can be eliminated has been behind many programming products introduced in the past few years, but what managers don't often see is that there is a trade-off. Today you can get by without programmers a lot better than you could fifteen years ago by using technologies like fourth-generation languages, but you then have to work within the confines of your programmer-replacement software. This means that your systems won't always work exactly the way that you would like them to, which introduces a whole new level of frustration. Still, executives usually will fall for any technology or product that promises to eliminate their escalating programmer costs.

The frenzied attempt to eliminate programmers has led to some of the more expensive debacles I've observed in industry. One strategy that was fashionable for a time was so-called "parameterized programming." The idea here was that since some program elements are known to be prone to change you put any item that could possibly change, like report lines or formulas, into tables kept in files, that can be edited, instead of in the programs themselves. Then, the usual logic goes, you don't need programmers to make your changes, just low-level (low-paid) operatives to fix up your tables.

The problem is that by time you get all your tables set up to handle the complexity of a real, live system your tables are so confusing that it takes a highly skilled programmer to figure out which table to tweak to achieve a desired change. In one such debacle at a major insurance company a parameterized program that was supposed to be programmable by clerk-level people eventually required the services of seventeen outside contract consultants each billing somewhere around $40 per hour to straighten it out.

Another programmer-eliminating approach upper management has read about in magazines and adopted, to its sorrow, is getting an outside vendor to do its systems work. Lured by the idea of fixed costs the executives decide to buy a package to computerize some function. The usual sequel to this is that three or four years later the original package, after absorbing an incredible amount of in-house time, is revealed as incapable of providing some subset of the functions that simply have to be performed by the system. In-house people are ordered to "fix up the package"; and eventually the package becomes the unrecognizable kernel of a huge system developed in-house—a system that has had its design stage fatally crippled by having to build on the foundation of the albatross package.

Part of the problem is that people who have the set of skills that characterize upper management are precisely those least likely to be able to understand the realities of dealing with computer systems. An executive generally prides himself on seeing the big picture and not getting hung up in details. Unfortunately a computer system is the ultimate cluster of details. Managers need to be flexible and always able to change course. Computer systems are rigid.

Executives need to learn more about the nature of computer programming in order to understand that that if some process their business carries out is dependent on a complex computer system there is no painless way that that process can change quickly and inexpensively.

The popularity of PC packages among executives makes it harder to get this point across. Managers compare their sleek PC tools to their mainframe record processing systems, whose complexity is hidden from view, and falsely think that the low cost of these PC programs demonstrates that it is easy write powerful programs cheaply. What they don't realize is the simplicity, from a programming standpoint, of these PC tools, compared with the mainframe programs that must, with little human intervention, manipulate the data in millions of highly complex records, according to rules that are unique to their own business.

### Shooting the Messenger Who Brings the Bad News

There is another reason upper management has developed an aversion for programmers. A manager who puts a poorly designed, badly tested system in place "on schedule" receives an immediate award for having met his targets. No one looks at the system's next ten years of miserable performance in relation to that initial reward. Usually the managers responsible for a system are rotated away from the system after it goes live and given new development projects to work on. Since most of the problems in a poorly designed system do not show up until you stress it or attempt to modify it, the person who encourages slipshod work is almost never connected with the damage his policies cause.

Indeed, the manager who attempts to develop a system rigorously applying the principles of structured methodology is viewed by his bosses as being obstructionist. Why is he demanding a year for the project when other managers got their whole system in in three months?

As a result, any intelligent person who has any hopes of rising in management realizes very soon that he must produce something, anything, that could possibly be interpreted as satisfying the system requirements as soon as possible and as cheaply as possible. If the system eats money for the rest of its life it is not coming out of his budget.

But programmers always try to spoil things.

Typically, when a major change is needed, upper management takes the broad view of the situation and makes what it considers to be the brilliant business decisions needed to implement the change. Since no one with detailed knowledge of the computer system involved participates in high-level management colloquies (remember, they're usually not welcome because they get too hung up in details), it is only weeks or months later that the unfortunate programmer assigned the task gets to evaluate the change at the highly detailed level at which the change must be implemented. It is his unpleasant task more often than not to explain that the task will take far more resources in terms of money and time than the company can afford.

As an example of this, one group I worked with was handed the assignment of rewriting about 120,000 lines of outstandingly devious operating system-type assembly language code in six months. Management understood correctly that if the code was rewritten in a high-level language it would be easy to maintain, but had no idea of the amount of effort needed to convert that amount of highly complex code. Three levels of management passed the word down without demur. None of them had ever read or written a line of code in their lives. The four programmers who were assigned the task were left with the unappetizing job of announcing that it could not be done. To start with no one around had the foggiest idea of how those 120,000 lines of code worked. It would take time just to analyze the programs' current functions. Besides that, of the four programmers assigned the task only one had any experience working with assembly language code. The rest were COBOL programmers.

When told there was a problem management offered to increase the size of the team. The programmers had to explain that the situation was analogous to thinking that if one pregnant woman could produce a baby in nine months then nine women should be able to produce a baby in one.

The high point of this project for me was my interview with a high-level manager who listened to my explanation of the technical problems involved and then exclaimed in exasperation, "You programmers! You always want everything to be perfect. In management we have to learn to compromise!"

As any programmer knows, you can't compromise with code. Anything not coded correctly will fail. The program will not do what it is supposed to do. Management typically cannot understand why if a certain situation occurs only 1 percent of the time the programmer must include processing for that situation and test it as thoroughly as for the situation that occurs 99 percent of the time.

The tragic events that led to the explosion of the space shuttle Challenger dramatically exemplify the difference between management's approach and the technician's approach. Management, wanting to look good and achieve their (and the president's) schedules, went with the percentages. The engineers knew that this could kill, but not having the decision-making power in the organization were powerless to prevent disaster.

Any working programmer's blood runs cold when he imagines the scenes that will be played out between programmers working on the so-called Star Wars defense system (SDI) and the managers who will be hurrying them through their projects. As currently described, SDI involves computer systems that can never be fully tested. Its failure could mean the utter destruction of life on earth, as nuclear missiles speed past laser beams that were only programmed to intercept them at 99 percent accuracy, devastating the planet. The politicians who are championing SDI are, of course, even less sophisticated about computer programming than business managers.

But even if your programming jobs do not involve matters of life and death, you will constantly play out the same conflict with management.

Your job will be to destroy their schedules and bollix up their planning. You will have to tell them that they have to spend far more money than they want just to keep their operations afloat. You will be rigorously excluded from the decision-making process but your career will rise or fall based on the wisdom of those management decisions.

Is it any wonder that after a few years of dealing with this, many technical people reach a state of utter frustration?

A large number of technically strong people enter management in the hope that by doing so they can exert control over their careers and over the way that the technical side of things is managed. "I was tired of having jerks tell me what to do," is the typical explanation from one techie turned manager. Unfortunately in order to remain in management the manager must shift into the short-term result mode and play the game as it is played. All too often within a few months the once-competent technical person appears, through weird alchemy, to have been transformed into just the jerk he used to loathe.

I have no easy answers for how to improve the situation. It goes way beyond any individual and is rooted in the basic assumptions with which American business operates. The best you can do is be aware of the inevitability of the conflict so that you can avoid being chopped up in the meat grinder of the conflict at its worst.

## What Do DP Managers Do?

Leaving behind our philosophical ruminations about the management/technician conflict, I'd like to turn now to the question of what you should expect to find if you decide to pursue the path that leads to DP management.

You may find it helpful to refer back to the organization chart in Figure 2 on page 26 as we discuss the various levels of management. However, you should remember that the chart in the illustration shows only one of various ways that the management of the DP function could be structured.

Typically your first managerial role will be that of team leader. The team leader is expected to function as part programmer and part administrator. The amount of each role given the team leader varies widely from company to company. Usually the team leader has responsibility for setting up schedules. The team leader must tell his management how long a specific task will take to accomplish, and if he is to get any further in management he must be correct! The team leader's other responsibility is to dole out the work that his team has been assigned. He assigns tasks to each programmer in his group, keeps tabs on how they are proceeding with the tasks, and assists them in getting help when they get stuck. A good team leader does not necessarily help by solving technical problems, but becomes a resource directory instead, pointing the programmer to other individuals within the technical organization who can help him. In most cases the team leader is responsible for giving the programmers under his direction their periodic evaluations.

These evaluations are like a report card, and in most organizations bear a direct relationship to the size of the programmer's next raise. It's hard for many new hires to believe, but it is ultimately only the team leader who judges their work—not other managers, and not the user for whom the programmer has done the work. The team leader is also responsible for getting additional special recognition for his team members such as bonuses and awards.

Usually but not always the team leader's managerial role stops short of controlling a budget.

Most team leaders remain at the team leader level for a year of two. If they distinguish themselves they may go on to the next level of management—if a position opens up. It is at this level that they are usually given a small budget to control. If you've been paying attention you should notice that we have just hit money. The control over money, not people, is what characterizes real management. The DP manager who has control of a chunk of corporate dollars is now, for the first time, really a manger, albeit at the lowest level.

This manager usually has two major responsibilities: to interface with similar levels of management in the departments that are the users of the department's programming services and to control the production of the work that he and the user managers decide should be undertaken. For example such a manager might have responsibility for the DP side of a function such as accounts receivable systems. He meets constantly with managers at his level from the accounting department who manage the clerks who handle outstanding accounts. They will present him with lists of problems that their subordinates need to have solved. These will range from the trivial—a strange message appeared on an input screen for example, to the important—the balances are wrong on Thursday's batch run totals. They will also periodically come up with requests for new system functions: Wouldn't it be nice if there was a way to display the summary results from the batch run on an on-line screen the next day.

The manager takes valid requests to his team leaders and asks them to determine what is causing the problems the users are experiencing, and to estimate how long it will take to fix the problems. If new functions are requested he will go to the team leaders and ask them to estimate how much work will be needed to provide the new function.

At a later meeting the manager will report back to the user managers what it will take to service their requests in terms of company resources, time, and money. Remember the DP manager's whole department is usually an overhead expense to these same operational areas that are his user group.

If the user managers give him the go-ahead, the manager then tries to juggle his existing budget for programmers and hardware resources to accommodate the users' requests. This means moving people out of lower priority tasks or hiring new people. It is this level of manager who will usually interview you and make the salary offer when you are interviewed by a company, although once you are hired it is not this manager but his subordinate, the team leader, who will control your career from thence forward.

If the manager cannot accomplish what has been requested with his current resources he must then prioritize the work requests he has been given and compromise with the user group to accomplish what will be of the most use to them or else he must go to his manager, yet a higher level, and make a very good case for increasing his budget to allow him to hire more people.

When a department is working on a project that is all new development, the manager's role is not all that different at this level. The only difference is that he must do much more negotiating with user group managers on the subject of what can and cannot be delivered, and when, and he faces a more complex task in drawing up schedules and following them since the development environment is much more unpredictable than the more stable enhancement/maintenance environment.

You should expect to stay at this departmental level of management for three to five years—or possibly forever. Past this level there are fewer and fewer managerial levels open and the competition is more intense. The next higher level of manager is usually a functional, rather than departmental level. This manager is in charge of the managers of a group of related departments. His job is to relate to the user area managers at his level, to set major priorities for the whole function, and most important, to control the money which will become the various departments' budgets. This level of management concerns itself with what are called "policy issues." At this point we are steaming away from details at a furious rate and entering the realm of buzzwords and management fads. Managers at this level are the ones who hold meetings to announce that from now on all programmers will make "quality test procedures" their watchwords. They are the ones, too, who get excited about programmer productivity aids. Often too they send managers and programmers to expensive seminars on structured program development. Less often do they allow the managers beneath them to submit schedules that reflect what they learned in those seminars.

In many companies this level of management spends a lot of time rearranging the departments under their control, performing the corporate rite of reorganization. Rarely does a person at this level have any technical knowledge at all. In many cases it has been so many years since a person at this level did any technical work of any type that his knowledge of the current technology comes only from talking with people who use it, not from using it himself. I have had the task of teaching a functional manager how to log on at a terminal. When he had been a programmer, all program development had been done by keypunching cards.

Unfortunately, this is the lowest level of DP professional who ever gets to talk with corporate vice-presidents and the other executives who make the major policy decisions affecting DP.

Beyond this level there may be one or more levels of management that control all DP functions, including computer operations and system support. The actual reporting structure at this level in the hierarchy varies widely. In some companies the DP management eventually reports to a user area manager, for example a manager in charge of all accounting functions. In others DP management is a separate organization up to the vice-presidential level. Eventually you reach the end of the DP leg of the organization chart. For a DP manager to cross out of the DP management chain and into the broader corporate management world is quite difficult in most organizations. If you intend to enter DP management you should realize that the chances are not very good that you will ever be vice-president of anything other than data processing and that you will almost never be considered for a CEO slot.

This again is because DP is usually overhead. The real movers and shakers in business tend to come from the revenue-producing areas which are sales and, increasingly, finance. Companies reward best those who are given credit for making the most money for them, and all that most DP managers can do is cost money, or at best save money. Only in those industries most dependent on computer systems such as banking and financial services is there any hint that this might be changing, as computer systems become more and more what the company is actually selling.

If you are entering DP management under the impression that you are on a fast track to the executive suite I would suggest that you save your pennies and invest in an M.B.A. from one of the nation's three or four top business schools. Doing it coming up the DP management ladder is definitely doing it the hard way.

And don't be misled by articles in the business press touting the "Data Processing" background of newly appointed VIP's. Robert Crandall, CEO of American Airlines, for example, did move into his current role after being vice-president of Data Processing at TWA. However, if you look at his resume you will see that his background included an M.B.A. from the prestigious Wharton School, one of the nation's top business graduate schools, not years spent as a programmer. John Reed, the chairman of Citicorp and another executive with DP credentials, received an engineering degree from M.I.T., but again, this was supplemented by a degree in Industrial Management from M.I.T's Sloan School of Management.[2] The very few programmers who have become company presidents have generally done so by starting their own companies, not by rising through the ranks. And even they often find themselves edged out of the companies they have founded, as businessmen with substantial stakes in the company move in following the company's first burst of success.

DP management will be satisfying to you if you can accept its inherently limited scope and if you enjoy the combination of administrating and politicking. I always feel like laughing when new hires announce that they want to go into management because they "like working with people." Managers don't work with people, they work with money. They don't socialize, they control. Far better to say you would like to go into management because you like working with lists and schedules! You need to understand the game of business to succeed in management and you need to understand real leadership, which entails getting people to give your their best stuff in exchange for the least possible return.

[2]*Fortune*, July 23, 1984, p. 6., and *Who's Who In America*, Chicago: Marquis, 1987.

The manager that the company will reward for being the best is rarely the one people like working for the best. The final judgment on your managerial worth will always be made not on how happy your workers are but on how much you could get done by your department for the least amount of money. As long as your employees don't quit in a group you will often be rewarded for the kind of "people skills" that earn you dislike from those below.

If you are seriously interested in a management career read everything you can get your hands on about business and management and learn to play within the rules of the business game.

One last piece of advice for the new programmer: Don't make any major pronouncements you might later regret. If you make the point repeatedly that you would rather eat a live mouse than enter management, the chances are good that the opportunity will pass you by. Try to remember that people change as they grow older. The management functions that appear stodgy and dull at age 22 often have a certain appeal at 35. The politicking that offends you in your youth may exert a certain fascination as you enter middle age. And most important, the challenge of keeping technically current that lends excitement to a young career may become an exhausting burden to the older person who has mastered several technologies only to see them become obsolete. If you are going to remain in the corporate world you should never rule out the managerial alternative as a future possibility.

### Management's Big Pitfall

Any logical person who examines a hierarchical organizational chart can see that as you go up the chart there are fewer and fewer boxes. Managers are expected to move up the management ladder, but there are decreasing numbers of slots for them to go to. If only one of the twenty-five departmental managers in a company can make it to DP Manager, what happens to the rest?

The answer to this depends a lot on the nature of the company you work for and its corporate culture. At one extreme companies like IBM assure a person who does not distinguish himself in the lower rungs of management an ongoing, if not brilliant career, letting him return to a technical position or fill any one of a large number of "staff" and "planning" positions where he has no direct managerial powers but has a management-level job class. Other companies are not so respectful of the individual.

In these companies a fit of belt tightening can result in the sudden layoffs of large numbers of middle-level managers. If you slipped your last dates or if your project turned out to be more expensive than upper management had expected you could suddenly find yourself pounding the pavement.

And it is not necessary to fail as a manager to loose your job. When two companies merge middle management positions are often eliminated in one of them, often quite suddenly. A sudden downturn in the economy can result in projects being canceled to save money. If projects are canceled project management is an unnecessary frill. Technical people caught in such situations usually have little difficulty finding new jobs, but a middle-level manager who has lost his technical skills is valuable primarily for his knowledge of his particular company and the way that it does business. Such a person, particularly if he is in his later years, can find the job-search process a harrowing one.

The so-called golden parachutes you read about are not given out at the levels of management that most DP managers attain. At best you might get a few months severance pay, but this is little when you consider the lost pension opportunities and the years left in which you need to support yourself.

When planning a career in management you cannot assume that you will be one of the lucky few who make it to the top. The wise thing to do would be to always have some contingency plans in the back of your mind to cover what you would do if you needed a new job. Keep up your contacts with people outside your company. Try to anticipate the kinds of business situations that might lead to your company's cutting back drastically on staff and if you see one coming try to get a new job somewhere else before it hits. Finally, as a last resort, consider entrepreneurial alternatives that would use your business knowledge and contacts. The important thing is that you should never be lulled into complacency when you are filling a managerial role. And you should have a realistic view of the value of your managerial services to the company in its pursuit of profit. All too often companies flush wih success reward employees by giving them fundamentally unnecessary management-level jobs, inserting level after level of supervision between the people making the decisions about what should be done and the people doing the work. When cost cutting becomes imperative these people's salaries are the logical place to begin cutting—and that is exactly what a growing number of firms are doing.

When times were hard for one Hartford area company upper management went so far as to send one group of managers an ultimatum: Go back to work as programmers (doing something the company really needed) or get fired. The affected managers were horrified and at least one quit. But nobody who had worked under these individuals was surprised, nor, may I add, did the departments run any the less smoothly without them.

### Using Your DP Apprenticeship to Position Yourself for Management

If you've decided you want to pursue a career that will lead you up the management ladder you will have to be very careful to craft the best possible apprenticeship for yourself during the first five years of your DP career.

You need to select jobs in those years that will do the following for you:

- Teach you the business fundamentals of the portion of your company's DP shop that is going to be the most active in the next decade.
- Give you visibility to management.
- Give you the grounding in technical matters that will let you make wise management decisions in the future.

If you want to get somewhere in management, you simply have to be where the action is. Determining where that might be is no simple task, and getting yourself a job there can be even harder. There is definitely a certain amount of luck involved, but if you are to succeed in business you need to be able to make your own luck. You must do a lot of research about the DP operations of a company before you take your first and subsequent jobs to find out whether you are joining an area that expects to see a lot of future development team formation and will therefore need more managers, or whether you are coming into an older, more established part of the

DP area where opportunities to make a real mark will be harder to come by.

This is particularly hard to gauge because often the areas of a DP shop where there are the most opportunities for major growth are those where the budget is axed first if belt tightening occurs. The new and innovative can be dispensed with, but the old, established systems must be maintained.

Once you have found your job you must do two things. You must do the best possible job with any work you are assigned, no matter how seemingly menial, and you must begin thinking like a business person.

No matter what your ultimate career goals are, you have been hired to be a programmer. You will have to establish your competence as a programmer before anyone is going to give you an opportunity to do more. But the way you will hasten your advancement into business is by showing that in all situations you are aware of the business implications of everything you do. This means simply that you must realize you are a business resource and start out by managing yourself effectively. If you have a choice between doing something that is technically challenging or doing something that will save the company money, you must choose the money-saving option. This may sound obvious, but too many programmers operate as if they were visiting scholars on loan from a university rather than people hired to make money for a company. You will stand out in the crowd if you show that you remember what the company thinks you are there for.

Besides working hard, you must do something equally important—you must let management *know* just how hard you have been working. This is called gaining visibility and is a very subtle thing to achieve. The basic truth is it is simply not enough to do a job, you must make sure that the people with the power to reward you know what a good job you did. The much-maligned business memo is often an invaluable tool to help you in this. Managers complain that the biggest obstacle faced by technical people who want to get into management is their poor communications skills. Get started early working on this. Write memos, write documentation, send out project summaries and monthly status reports whenever you can justify it. And try to get some feedback from your manager on the stuff you send. How would he suggest you improve it? It is not so

much what you say but the fact that you are saying something—
demonstrating your communications skills and your awareness of
the group nature of the situation you find yourself in that makes an
impression on your bosses and shows that you are a contender for
leadership positions.

Take advantage of opportunities to address groups too. Teach
classes if you are offered the opportunity. Never miss a chance to
give a presentation at a meeting, and when you do, take the time to
do a professional job with your slides and other illustrative material.

Remember though that visibility is a two-edged sword. If your
project hits a snag, your visibility is not going to go away. But your
ability to function in a strong and confident manner despite a negative situation may, in the long run, win you more respect than anything else you do.

You must take initiative, but remember this does not, repeat,
*does not*, mean doing other people's work, the sure mark of someone
who does not understand the rules of the business game. Taking initiative means finding things that are currently nobody's work and
doing them in your spare time. By identifying a problem and solving it without ever causing your manager to have to add it to a
schedule you will begin to stand out as a self-starter, and managers
will want to have you on their teams, especially if you tactfully and
modestly announce what you've done in a tasteful memo.

Don't think that because you want to be a manger you don't
need to become a good technician. You don't want to be thought of
by management as a head-in-the-clouds technical person but you
want to be sure you know your stuff. So many of the managers you
will be competing with are technically weak that you will be able to
accomplish things they can't and and avoid debacles simply by
having a good enough grasp of technology to make use of what your
subordinates tell you. The most effective managers in technical areas
are those who know how to use their people's technical knowledge
in combination with a strong business perspective. Rhetoric about
team spirit won't get the job done on schedule unless you have a
good grasp of the obstacles that you are likely to encounter on the
way.

Finally if you come into a new job situation with hopes of becoming a manager, be very careful how you treat your coworkers.
In the period when you are working to become a team leader you
will be very dependent on the help of the people you work with to

get things done. If people view you as a self-seeking opportunist you may find that help is hard to find when you need it. People don't rush to rescue people they loathe.

Many would-be leaders tend to copy the management styles of the successful managers they see around them. There is nothing wrong with this but don't forget you can learn just as much by watching those who don't make it, observing their failures, and taking them to heart so you can avoid their fatal mistakes.

### Benefits of a Corporate Apprenticeship for Those Planning Careers Outside of the Corporate World

We stated earlier that you were going to have to serve your corporate apprenticeship in a corporate environment if you wanted a mainframe-based career simply because that is where the mainframes are. In chapters five, six, and seven I will discuss what steps you can take to use the corporate apprenticeship period to prepare yourself for noncorporate and entrepreneurial alternatives. What I would like to do here is briefly summarize the broad contributions that the corporate experience can make to the person who wants ultimately to leave the corporation.

The major benefit, of course, is that you learn a lot about programming computers. But beyond that you should pick up the following:

- Knowledge of how business operates
- Contacts within the corporate community
- Knowledge of the needs of the business community, which can lead you to base a successful business on filling those needs

If you are like many technical people you have always felt convinced that you would end up with your own business because you have such great ideas, but you don't see yourself as a business type. A few years of working in a profitable, well-run company can teach you a lot about how to think like a successful business person. When you encounter marketing people, production staff, and financial professionals and see the responsibilities they must take on, you begin to get a feel for what you will deal with in any business of your own, even though yours will be on a much smaller scale. You should gain respect for the problems you can encounter in each of these areas. You should also begin to see people who have a knack for getting people to give their best and conversely, people who can create interpersonal havoc with their management style. All this is real-world experience, and it may prove far more valuable to you as a fledgling entrepreneur than any business school course work. Should you start a business of your own you will need to perform most of the functions that the larger companies do, the only difference being that you will have to be a lot better at it than they are since your margin for error will be a lot slimmer.

If you are planning to take off in an an entrepreneurial direction you will need more than experience. Chances are that you will need business contacts. If you are selling something to business you will need to know who has the authority to buy what you have on the market. If you have paid attention while working in a couple of companies you should know who these people are. Keep aware of who does what in the companies you work for. Make sure that middle management knows you by name if at all possible. When you leave a job, do it carefully, and don't use leaving as an opportunity to blow off steam and let management know what you think of their lousy way of doing business. If you want to sell services or software your current managers (and some coworkers) will be your future customers. Many of those who enter as trainees when you do will be entering management just around the time you will be beginning to get your business off the ground.

So no matter how confining you might find the corporate world as a potential entrepreneur, tell yourself you are prospecting for customers. Establish your reputation for competence, and your DP apprenticeship may build a very strong base for an entrepreneurial future.

Finally, if you are alert during your corporate apprenticeship you should start seeing all sorts of niches in the corporate world where services or products you could provide might fit in. Corporations are the best customers to have because they have lots of money to spend and they tend to think in big numbers. Keep your eyes open for the ways some of that money could be spent on things you could sell.

Not everyone is cut out for corporate life at the end of a four- or five-year corporate apprenticeship, though the intelligent programmer will have a wide range of choices open to him.

# 4
# *Job Hopping—*
# *A Programmer Tradition*

No discussion about a mainframe programming career in the corporate sector would be complete without some discussion of the role that job hopping plays in the development of a lot of programming careers.

In most fields it is assumed that you get your first job and then work in the same firm for a period ranging from three to seven years. In these fields to change jobs more frequently is a sign that something is wrong with a person, that he has trouble holding a job.

In the short history of DP as a career path this has not been the way that job hopping has been viewed at all. Because of the unique opportunities provided by the programmer shortage, some talented programmers have been able to change jobs once a year a part of a career strategy and have received hefty raises every time.

Job hopping has its place, and you need to understand what that place is to use it most effectively. You need to understand what benefits you get from switching employers and what you are loosing in the exchange. Finally, you ought to know a few key facts about headhunters, the main promoters of job hopping.

## What Job Hopping Can Do for You

Job hopping can, pure and simple, lead to dramatic leaps in your salary early in your career, especially if you started out at a salary toward the lower end of the range. This is due to the fact that while almost no one, except large corporations with sophisticated education organizations, wants to take on neophyte programmers, there are a herd of companies yearning to hire programmers with one or more years of experience. The companies that provide training to neophyte programmers are often those that pay relatively low starting salaries. Often they are banks or insurance companies that must employ hundreds or even thousands of programmers to sustain their operations. Because their corporate guidelines limit how large a raise any employee can be given these companies can only offer their best trainees raises in the 15 percent range. This sounds like a good percentage, but 15 percent of $17,000 is only $2,550 which brings the programmer's salary up to $19,550. In come the companies that don't pay for expensive trainee classes. It is easy for them to offer the trained programmer another three or four thousand dollars. After all it is a lot cheaper than paying trainees a salary while they sit in a costly class!

The best companies of course start their blue ribbon college hires at much higher figures so changing jobs will not give one of these a significant boost. But for the person whose credentials are marginal at the beginning, job hopping early in the career is about the only way to close the salary gap with his more credentialed confreres.

Job hopping usually leads to dramatic salary growth for the first four or five years of a career. However once your salary reaches a certain level which currently is somewhere in the middle $30,000 range, this is no longer true. The reason is that you have become too expensive for most of the jobs that are available. You will need to have picked up a technical skill that is in great demand to be able to continue improving yourself through job changes once you have reached this salary level.

The other benefit of changing companies early in your career is that you get a chance to broaden your experience. Many people who stay in the same job for five years don't have five years of experience, they have one year of experience repeated five times. When you change jobs you increase your chances of seeing new techniques and learning different kinds of software and applications. No two companies are the same, even though they might have similar applications running in what are supposed to be the same software environment. You won't realize the extent to which companies have distinct personalities until you have worked in more than one.

Job hoppers usually get a wider experience with different software environments too, which can be useful if you plan to be a consultant in the future. However I would caution you not to change jobs just to pick up some particular technology you have been yearning for. Headhunter ads often use "Learn Database" or "Learn CICS" as a come-on to get people to answer ads. Ask yourself why a company would train you in something valuable when they could train proven in-house staff first.

Sometimes changing jobs is the only way out of an impossible situation. When you find yourself stymied because of personality conflicts with your management which are not going to go away, or when you are convinced that you will never be allowed to move into any area in the company that you don't loathe then there is no reason to stay in a hated job. Because of the prevalence of job hopping among programmers no negative motive will be attributed to you if you change jobs every two years or so. Just be careful that you don't suggest to a potential employer that you are changing jobs because you can't get along with anyone at your old job!

## How Job Hopping Can Hurt You

If your only reason for changing jobs is that you are discontented in your present job you need to be aware of the sad truth that the majority of open jobs in most companies that are filled from outside the company are those that no one currently working in the company wants. The only exception to this is when a company is bringing in a new technology that no current employees are familiar with and wants to bring in a person experienced with that technology to get things going.

While it is true that many companies are looking for people with one or two years' experience to fill what are for them entry-level slots, a lot more companies are looking to fill the job slots vacated by people with the same experience level as you who fled them as intolerable. You will have to do a lot of research to find out why a company is offering you the great deal it is, and often paying an agency a fee of up to 30 percent of your annual salary on top of what you are getting.

You need to be skeptical about anything you are told by a hiring manager. It is not uncommon for desperate managers to lie to interviewees about jobs they are trying to fill. They have deadlines to meet, and need bodies to sit in front of their terminals. A common ploy of such managers is to tell you that his company is a CICS shop or that it is bringing in IBM's exciting new database product DB2. Hiring managers know that these are products a lot of programmers would like to get experience in. What such managers do not mention is that although the company does have the software installed you will be nowhere near it.

Many companies find themselves with a desperate need to maintain old boring batch systems which most ambitious programmers regard as the lowest kind of assignment, and it is these kinds of jobs that usually call forth the greatest use of imagination from hiring managers.

Other ploys include telling you that you will be a team leader which sounds great until you discover that your department of ten people has four team leaders—or promising to train you in systems programming, which translates into letting you move production modules into the hold libraries or other clerical level "systems" tasks.

Ideally you should have been developing a network of friends in different companies in the period before you consider job hopping so that you can talk to them and build up a realistic picture of the DP shop in a company you are considering. You can usually find out where the sweatshops, slums, and disaster areas are, and conversely, locate the departments with the reputation for turning out the people who go on to leadership roles or get the technical training that leads to real technical growth.

Best of all is to be offered a job by someone who has worked with you before and knows and respects your proven skills.

As a footnote here I urge you never to take a job with a company that makes you sign a contract that makes you liable for employment agency fees should you decide to quit. This sounds like an obvious statement, but I know of one major employer of programmers, a blue chip company no less, that recruits programmers with press gang tactics. Programmers come to work for this company assured of career opportunities that are pure fantasy on the part of hiring managers, only to find themselves facing law suits for thousands of dollars when they try to leave the company before the contract period is over. You will never be able to afford the legal talent that a large company can, no matter how much right you have on your side, so take heed. There are enough good jobs around that you don't have to put yourself in that kind of position. Likewise you should never sign anything that makes you liable for relocation expenses.

While the most obvious problem with job hopping is that it might land you in a position much worse than the one you left, there are other problems with it too. If you are a competent "star performer" in your current company you must be prepared for the fact that the minute you leave your old job behind you have left your old reputation behind as well. You will have to prove your competence all over again. Typically most of us have to live with the reputation we acquire during our first six weeks on the job. You will have to put out your very best effort in those starting weeks if you want to win again the respect that you already enjoyed at your previous job. And there is always the possibility that bad luck will intervene, making it much harder to prove yourself a second time.

There is an up side to this though. Having changed jobs several times and having reestablished my reputation most of those times, I've gained the confidence that my reputation was something real and not a fluke. But there are some jobs out there, and most people encounter at least one in their careers, where nobody can look good. If office politics are out of control, or you have an antiquated system that has no documentation, no one around who understands it, and one test job a day turnaround, you are going to have to walk on water just to keep from drowning. If your reputation as the local guru is important to you, keep this in mind before changing jobs.

Another fact to consider before changing jobs is that when you change jobs your new company owes you nothing. The good work you did somewhere else is irrelevant, and you must expect to wait at least a year before you can ask for any education or other special treatment. You won't be able to take off the three weeks you'd been planning for that trip to Venezuela either—your vacation credits are gone, unless you explicitly bargained for them before accepting the offer. So if you have grown accustomed to taking long lunches, the occasional day off, and still receiving great performance reviews you should think twice before giving it up. Similarly if you have children, you can count on their coming down with the chicken pox one week after you start your new job, just in time to give you a reputation for being undependable!

## How Headhunters Work

Every Sunday programmers who feel that their current situation is less than ideal turn to that ego booster, the EDP classifieds in the Sunday "Help Wanted" section of their newspaper. It is heartwarming to see a multitude of ads crying out for people with your own job skills and offering salaries better than what you are currently receiving. The ads are usually divided into two groups. Some are display ads in large boxes with fancy graphics, which don't mention salary, and often misspell the acronyms of the software experience required. These are placed by personnel departments. The second group consists of detailed descriptions of what sounds like actual jobs with actual dollar amounts following each description. These are placed by headhunter firms. ("Headhunter" as I use it, refers to employment agencies that specialize in DP personnel; however, don't confuse these with the far classier executive search firms that raid corporations for high echelon executives. The latter are the ones usually referred to in books and articles on "headhunting.")

If you venture to answer a personnel department ad the result will usually be a polite form letter claiming that your resume will be kept on file for future requirements. This means, sad to say, that it has been tossed in the trash. The chances are, however, that if you had gone to a headhunter you could have swung an interview for the same job, assuming that you were correct in thinking that you did have qualifications that would let you do the job.

Headhunters flourish in the DP world because they are able to circumvent and bypass corporate personnel offices, which usually are out of their depth when it comes to evaluating the resumes of technical personnel.

Here's why. When a position opens up personnel usually requests a form from the hiring manager, listing the specific experience that is required for the position. This works well with clerical personnel, after all it is easy to determine if someone can type 65 words-per-minute. Unfortunately it is much harder to quantify on a short form all the different kinds of experience that a technical candidate should possess. Personnel people when considering a resume, slavishly look for a one-to-one correspondence between the items listed on the resume and on the requisition form. They do not have the technical knowledge to understand that often an item on the applicant's resume is equivalent to what has been requested although it looks different. Thus a person who lists IMS on their resume might never make it to the interview for a job that requests DL/I experience, even though any technical person knows that to program in an IMS environment you must use the DL/I access language.

Managers have learned that they are unlikely to find the candidates they need through the personnel department. After allowing personnel to flail around for a polite period many DP managers accept the necessity of going to the better headhunter firms, staffed by people qualified to match requested skills with available applicants.

In some organizations personnel has tacitly admitted it is out of its depth and works closely with headhunters. One personnel recruiter at a small insurance company I contacted during a job hunt expressed real surprise to have a programmer call her. She referred me to the headhunter firm her company uses to find programmers.

Headhunters, then, can usually get your resume past the trash can, but to use them effectively you must realize that most headhunters are not what they attempt to present themselves to you as. The majority of headhunters try to appear to be "career counselors." They will interview you and ask many questions about your career goals and long-term plans in an attempt to build your confidence that they are helping you and looking out for your best interest. However, headhunters are not career counselors. They do not receive a single penny from you for their career advice. They are salesmen and saleswomen, and they make their money, tons of it, by placing you in a job—any job that is open where the hiring manager can be persuaded to accept you, and you can be persuaded to go.

When a headhunter places you he gets paid a percentage of your yearly salary by the hiring company. Most programmers know this. What they often don't know is how large a percentage the headhunter gets. Usually it is 1 percent per thousand of your new salary up to some cutoff, usually 30 percent. That means if you are placed in a $30,000-a-year job the headhunter is getting $9,000, which is then subdivided between the owners of the headhunting company and the salesman who made the placement. In the world of the head-hunter you are the merchandise he needs to push and he is working for his customer, the firm buying his services, not for you.

Many headhunters claim that they have a pipeline to the best jobs that are never advertised. This is not usually true. Usually they have exactly what was in the paper a few weeks back for the reasons sketched out in our discussion of personnel department recruiting. Not only that but if you carefully follow the ads you will notice that often all the headhunters in town are describing the same few jobs that are open that week and that were advertised in display ads a few weeks back.

Other headhunter ads run constantly and you will realize after a few weeks that they are just come-ons designed to get you to call the office since a major problem headhunters have is attracting people (product) that they can then sell to their customers.

Less-reputable firms engage in all sorts of creative maneuvers to get their hands on programming flesh. *Infosystems* magazine tells of headhunters calling up managers and pretending to be watch repairmen, claiming to have lost the last name of a programmer who dropped off a watch to be repaired, just to get the names of people in the department so that they can be called later and offered a job.[1]

Out of curiosity I once interviewed for a position as a head-hunter with a sleazoid local firm. The owner explained what my job would be. In return for about 75 percent of the fee the company would get when I made a placement he would give me a desk to use and a spiel which he claimed had almost magical powers to per-suade. I would memorize the spiel and then start calling everyone in the phone directory of local companies who might possibly be a programmer. If I found a programmer among the irritated typists, actuaries, and maintenance supervisors I'd called, I would launch into the spiel offering the programmer a shot at a much bigger salary, suggesting I had inside information on a position for someone with skills just like his. If he took the bait, then my work would really begin, since I would have to coax his resume out of him and then scurry around pestering managers until I found one desperate

[1]Infosystems, "Winning the Talent Contest; in a demand driven personnel market, providing professional challenge and career development are key factors in attracting and retaining capable employees," September 1985, p.78-81.

enough to interview him for a job. I could expect that this routine might bring in one or two prospects per one hundred calls, if that. I would also work any likely prospects for the names of their friends and coworkers.

People really do do this for a living, and it is not at all unusual to have one of these hopefuls call you at work.

That people can make a living doing this kind of thing is a sign of how hard it is for managers to locate qualified, experienced personnel. As irritating as managers might find these headhunters *Infosystems* reports that they must maintain an uneasy alliance with them because when they do need people the headhunters are often their only source[2].

How best can you deal with this situation? You may very well need the services of a headhunter when you do decide to change jobs, but you need to remain in control of the situation at all times. The place to start is by being very choosy about the headhunter you work with. There are reputable firms that are run by people with a lot of experience in the DP field and a solid base of contacts among local managers. Often these companies place only DP people. If you choose a reputable firm that has been in business in your community for a long time, the chances are that they can place you in a job you might not have known about or might not have been able to get an interview for on your own.

The important thing to remember here is that a headhunter can only place you in a job that calls for someone with the skills you already have. A company is not going to pay a headhunter to provide an unqualified person or a person, whatever his credentials, who requires expensive training. They can usually find lots of people who don't have the specialized skills they want. The premium paid to the headhunter is for finding a person ready-made for the position.

You should use the following guidelines when approaching headhunter firms and refuse to even give your phone number to anyone that you have any feeling of uneasiness about. You don't need to have an imbecile headhunter calling your manager and leaving messages for you to call him at Scumbo Placement Services! Ask the following questions:

[2]*Infosystems*, op. cit.

   **1.** Is this a firm that specializes in DP jobs and whose salesmen are knowledgeable about DP? This is extremely important. Agencies that really specialize in clerical personnel have jumped into DP placement because the money is so good. Often the recruiters in these places are as bad, if not worse, than the people you encounter in personnel. If you use one of these the result is likely to be that they send out a garbled resume that will hide from prospective managers any skills you might actually have.

   Ask what the background of the person interviewing you is. You want someone with a programming background who is capable of understanding, interpreting, and making the best of your resume to potential employers.

   Try and get a feel for how much the recruiter knows about your current job. Does he know the names of the managers? Does he know what your department does without your telling him? If he doesn't you have to wonder what use he will be in finding managers and jobs elsewhere. A good headhunter should show you that he has some familiarity with both your company's DP operations and other companies that you are interested in. He should be able to suggest several places that you haven't heard of where you might be interested in working. And, most important do not let him use the interview as an opportunity to grill you to find out the name of your manager and the details of your job so he can fill your job when you quit!

   If he wants you to sign anything, politely refuse to do so until you are very sure that you want to work with him. The more reputable firms will operate only by your word.

   **2.** How long has the firm been in business? Some companies pop up like mushrooms after a rain. If you deal with one of these you have no way of checking on their performance or ethics. In a worst-case situation you might fall into the hands of an opportunist who finds a position for you and then lets your manager know you want to quit your current job, putting you in an intolerable position. The fact that this shyster goes out of business a few weeks later will be no consolation if you get canned.

   Be aware, too, that in some headhunter firms each recruiter is working entirely on his own and that means when he leaves his company, your file leaves with him. If someone who you have been working with does leave, it is very unlikely that his replacement will tell you where he went, since he wants to make his commission selling you. In that case you are back to square zero. The more reputable firms don't operate this way.

**3.** Does the headhunter suggest inappropriate jobs to you at the interview? If he does it is a sign that he is just shooting in the dark and doesn't know much about the DP marketplace.

**4.** Do you know anyone who has used this firm and been happy with the results?

Treat a headhunter with the same circumspection you would use with a car salesman. Let him describe what he has to sell, but ask a lot of questions. Don't rush out to interview the moment he calls you with a "terrific position." Try to get as much information as possible on the phone. If he won't or can't give it to you it might be the tip-off that you would be wasting time going to the interview. If you do go to an interview and find that the headhunter has misrepresented the job to you, tell the interviewing manager that you don't want to waste his time and then leave. Have nothing more to do with this headhunter; your time is too valuable to waste, and you don't need to raise questions at your current job about your long lunches.

Finally, if you get through the job interview and are considering a position, avoid any lengthy conversation with the headhunter until you have made your mind up about whether you want the job or not. The headhunter is a salesman, remember, and will get paid only if you take the job. Naturally then it is in his interest to sell you any job where a manager has expressed interest in hiring you. The headhunters who have stayed in the business for any period of time have succeeded because they are good at what they do. You should make your decision after considering all the different factors discussed in these pages and after talking it over with concerned family members and a few friends. You may regret it if you put yourself in a position to be influenced by a headhunter's hard sell before you know what you really want to do.

If you take a realistic attitude toward the headhunter while continuing to do your own thinking and research, the result can sometimes be a better job that furthers your career goals.

## How Often Should You Change Jobs?

If you are starting in your first job, the chances are that you will have to spend at least a year there before you consider changing. If economic times are tight you might have to wait two years before you make a switch. In tight economies headhunters cannot place people who do not have at least three years of experience, so, in this situation, you will be able to change jobs only if you do the footwork yourself.

When you are looking for a job that is not your first the rules are a little different. By now you are an experienced person with the proven ability to get a new job. Common sense dictates that you should spend a solid amount of time in your new position and thoroughly exhaust all opportunities for advancement in your new company before leaving. But if you discover that your job hopping has landed you in a terrible job, if you have fallen prey to dishonest managers and imaginary promises, you should not, as many people do, feel compelled to wait out an entire year before leaving the position. Wait three months and see if your initial feelings of hating your new job or finding it a dead end persist. If they do, go out and get yourself a new job. It can be done. This time, though, ask penetrating questions at the interview and be honest with interviewing managers about why you want to leave your current position. If you were lied to, politely mention it to the interviewer. If nothing else it will keep him from following the same strategy with you. If you really have found yourself in a dead-end job that does not make use of your current skills a manager who needs those skills should not balk at hiring you before you serve out your year.

## Alternatives to Headhunters

### Job Posting

Many companies use a system is known as "Job Posting." This means that any open position within the company must be advertised to the company's own employees before outsiders can apply. Usually the jobs are listed on bulletin boards around the company, but some companies might list them on-line, or make you go to a personnel office and look at a notebook. Usually the posting will list the job title, the job class, the offering department, and possibly the offering manager, and finally the qualifications needed to get the job. Often these are broken into two groups: the qualifications that must be met for an applicant to be considered, and those which would be nice extras.

Watching the posting boards—starting from your very first day at work—is an excellent way to keep tabs on the kinds of jobs that are available within your current organization. Most companies have strict guidelines about how long you must be in a position before you are eligible to "post out." In most you must stay in a job for at least a year. Sometimes a longer period is required. Find out as soon as you enter a company what those guidelines are.

It is very unlikely that at the time you become eligible for a new job within the organization, the very job you would like will come open. But you can still use the posting boards to help you find the position you want. Here's how. Long before you are eligible to post out you should be getting a very good idea of what qualifications are required for the different open positions and the different job grades your company has. You should also note the names of the managers or departments who have listed jobs over the year that have interested you. When you are ready to switch jobs the smartest thing you can do is call those managers whose departments have had the interesting openings in the past and alert them that you will soon be eligible for a posting. Ask them if they have anything opening up or, alternatively if any related departments might have something appropriate for you.

By staying abreast of the job postings you will not only get a jump on job hunting within your own organization, which is almost always the best way to get a more interesting and challenging job, but you will also be able to notify friends working at other companies when a position that might interest them is available. Many companies will pay you a cash bonus for such referrals.

If you are determined you cannot progress by staying in your current company, the best alternative to getting a job through a headhunter is, of course, to get a job through your personal network of friends and acquaintances. However, research shows that this technique, much popularized in general-purpose job hunting books, is less successful for technical people[3]. This is because hiring managers usually have very specific skill sets in mind and can rarely consider anyone who is not a close match. Thus unless you have a lot of contacts in companies with needs very much like the one you currently work for networking may not do the trick.

This leaves you with the alternative of responding to advertisements in the newspaper and trade press.

If you take this approach you must pay close attention to the way you write your resume. The first thing you should remember when putting it together is that the person who will first read it and decide whether to pass it on or throw it away (generally referred to as "keeping it on file" in the rejection letter you receive), will in most cases not be a person with a technical background. Since this person rarely has a basis for understanding what he sees on a technical resume he usually resorts to reading it looking for an exact match with keywords specified on the requisition submitted by the hiring manager to personnel.

Make sure when you put your resume together that you include as many keywords as possible that appear on the ad you are answering, exactly as they appear in the ad. Do this even if at times you have to stretch. The time to go into detail about your experience and its limitations is when you are sitting face to face with an interviewer who has enough technical background to understand what you are talking about. If your resume is too detailed it might just go over the head of the personnel gatekeeper.

Obviously you should not lie about your experience. But if you have extensive database experience using a database that is very similar to one requested in an advertisement and light exposure to the actual one stipulated, you would be wise to highlight that light experience. This way it will be the hiring manager, not a personnel functionary, who makes the call on whether your skills are a close-enough match.

When answering ads it is almost always a complete waste of time to phone first. The number in the paper will always be that of a personnel administrator who will politely request that you send your resume to the address featured in the ad.

---

[3]Lee Bowes, *No One Need Apply: Getting and Keeping the Best Workers* (Boston: Harvard Business School Press, 1986).

Be aware too of another strange phenomenon. You will from time to time see advertisements that list extremely detailed job qualifications. These usually demand a high educational level and offer a low salary. The explanation behind these is found in immigration law. In many of these cases employers are planning to sponsor a foreign national for his green card, which allows him to apply for citizenship. The law requires that in some of these cases the employer must make a good faith effort to determine that the job the foreign national will fill could not be filled with an American citizen. The advertisement is designed to fulfill this requirement and that explains its peculiar form.

## Job Fairs

Beyond answering advertisements there is another alternative you might try. You will often see "Job Fairs" advertised in the newspaper. Companies exist whose entire business is running "Career Fairs" dedicated to bringing together employers and technical personnel. Before you waste your time going to these you should realize that most of these are not going to do anything for you that sending your resume to personnel did not. Unfortunately most career fairs feature booths set up by each hiring company and are staffed either by a few technical people (who speak with all applicants for all jobs, not for the jobs they personally have open and, in addition, often are woefully ignorant about any but their own departments) or again, by the folks from personnel. After standing in line and showing your resume to such a representative you are usually informed that you will hear from them or given an application to fill out. The resume is usually sent to the company personnel department staffer who handles resumes and in many cases that is that. The most frustrating feature of these career fairs is that you usually cannot get answers to the simplest questions about what positions are open in the company, what qualifications the company requires, and what the salient facts are about the company's DP shop.

A few companies run their own open houses where managers interview people for actual openings. In this case you can tour booths belonging to different departments, speak to the actual hiring managers, and learn a good deal about the positions that are currently open at the company. These open houses are a terrific opportunity to learn about a company, and you should make an attempt to attend even if you are only mildly interested in changing jobs, since they are usually only held once or twice a year.

---

Job hopping can be a useful strategy for the first five years of your career. Use it to improve your earning level, your skills, and your knowledge of local companies. But when you find a company that you enjoy working for, where you see real possibilities for your future, stick with it and build up your reputation there. Don't let yourself always be led on by dreams of greener pastures. By the time you have reached your fifth year as a mainframe programmer you should have positioned yourself where you want to remain and grow in the corporate world, or you should be ready to bid the corporate world good-bye and venture out to begin your entrepreneurial phase.

# 5
# *Consulting— The Quasi-Corporate Alternative*

Some people are cut out for the corporate life. They enjoy the security of knowing that their paychecks will arrive regularly. They are proud of the products that the XYZ Corp. produces and proud to have something to do with producing them. They are joiners and feel good about being part of a large powerful company. They enjoy the people they work with, too, and feel confident that their efforts will be rewarded fairly.

Other people are different. After four or five years of working in a corporate environment they know that they are cut out for something else. The predictability of their paycheck is irksome because while it is always there, it is always the same amount and they know that they are never going to get rich at their current rate. Maybe the rigidity and the bureaucracy of large companies gets to them. They find their creativity stifled and are frustrated by a system in which it seems mediocrity, not originality, is rewarded. Maybe it's just the fact that no one ever laughs at their best jokes. Whatever the reason, there comes a time for many people when they decide that it's time to work for the only boss who is ever likely to put their own interests first—themselves.

Once you have served your DP apprenticeship and garnered your five or more years of corporate experience you have a range of alternate career possibilities open to you. Some demand entrepreneurial skills and the willingness and ability to take on high levels of risk. Others let you trade off the money you would get in the corporate world for more control and greater freedom both in terms of time and personal expression.

I will try to describe the most popular alternative career paths that programmers take and suggest to you the best way to prepare for them during your preliminary apprenticeship phase.

I will cover the consulting option first, since it is the one that the largest number of people take. Then I will talk about developing software on your own, teaching in colleges and outside of them, and, finally, entering one of the sales fields open to experienced programmers.

## Consulting as a Career

The term "consultant" is a frequently abused one in our society. A computer consultant may be anything from a corporate programmer who just got fired and needs a polite way to describe himself, to a person who is paid $100 an hour or more to advise bigwigs how to design technically sophisticated systems.

Some so-called consultants are merely employees of large consulting corporations like Arthur Andersen & Company, which employs over 9,000 consultants worldwide. Some of these may just have graduated from college and "consulting" is their first real-world job. Other consultants are true entrepreneurs who have built up a customer base in their region and work on several projects simultaneously, billing their clients themselves and qualifying as a small business under the tax code. Still others fall into an intermediate group, finding consulting jobs through brokers who take a hefty cut of their earnings, but are earning much higher rates than regular employees.

Most regularly employed programmers encounter consultants on the job. They are usually brought in to complete high-visibility projects that are falling behind schedule and the consultants work side by side with regular employees. Usually the word quickly gets around the department that the consultants are billing at $40 an hour and more. It is when salaried people see consultants doing work exactly like their own at much higher rates, that a lot of programmers become interested in consulting themselves.

Let's look at what consultants do. First we will look at the consultant who works for a firm as an employee. Then we will look at what are usually called "independents" and discuss what it is like to work through brokers and on your own.

## Consulting Firms

Although the term "consultant" conjures up the image of a wise adviser sharing his wisdom with admiring recipients, most so-called consultants in no way consult. The term "consultant" in the DP world has come, more and more, to be an upscale synonym for temporary help. Almost all consultant positions that are advertised, both internally within companies and externally in the newspaper or by employment agencies, are positions that call for people to do exactly what they would do as full-time corporate employees but to do it for a limited time.

Using this kind of consultant makes a lot of sense for corporations. Although when interviewed, executives generally claim that they are cutting back on their usage of consultants, replacing them with permanent help, the actual findings of those who study the situation are quite different. *Datamation* reported that management claimed they were aiming to have less than 10 percent of their staff be on a temporary basis at any given time, but the results of *Datamation's* salary survey in October 1986 showed that 17.2 percent of all surveyed employees were consultants.[1] Between March of 1985 and 1986, the outside DP service sector grew 13.3 percent, reflecting an increase in the use of programming (consulting) services.

Hiring consultants keeps a company with fluctuating manpower needs from having to lay people off and having to deal with the ill will that that can generate. It allows them to dispense with having to train employees and it lets them bypass all the restrictions

[1] David Stamps "Is Anybody Really Using Consultants," *Datamation*, October 15, 1986, pp. 99-102. The next year however, *Datamation's* Salary Survey reported a large drop in the use of consultants, possibly due to tax reform or the softening economy.

that the personnel department might impose on them as far as treating employees fairly. Consultants can be hired and fired at will and with no lengthy personnel justification, they receive no performance reviews and do not need company picnics to motivate them.

Consultants will often take jobs in areas that regular employees would shun as dead end or low status. A surprising number of highly paid consultants can be found doing the most boring kinds of scut work on aging batch systems so that the company can offer its regular employees more challenging assignments.

Since providing DP consultants has become big business many corporations that used to provide management consulting or accounting services have gone into the field. The arrangement that these companies prefer to use is to hire experienced programmers from local companies as their own employees and then send them out to work as consultants. The pitch that these companies use to recruit employees usually appeals to people who are bored with their career but not willing to give up the security of a permanent job. Typically these companies emphasize that their employee consultants will get intensive education in new software and will work on exciting state of the art projects. The salaries that these firms pay are usually a little higher than the salary the employee received as a regular corporate employee but not by much. The recruiters stress that they offer benefit packages and also promise the potential consultant that if they are unable to find him a consulting position he will have paid time off while he is "on the bench."

Needless to say, these companies are not in business for their health. Most employee consultants that I have encountered work at least full time and often a lot of overtime. If the company cannot find them work that they can bill out at $40 an hour they will usually drop their rates and bid less, since anything over about $20 an hour represents profit to the company. Some of these consulting companies represent valid corporate career paths and do provide their employees with excellent training and exposure. The very best companies offer the potential to become a partner in the company at some future time with the possibility of an income in excess of $100,000 a year.[2]

If you can get explicit statements to the effect that partnership is a real possibility, and are shown people now in the company who

[2] Parker Hodges "Do the Big Eight Add Up," *Datamation*, February 15, 1987, pp.62-68.

have achieved partnership through this pathway, then you should definitely consider the employee option as a consultant.

However, there are several large, powerful, unscrupulous consultant companies around who are called in the trade "body shops" because their forte is supplying warm bodies at cut rate prices to desperate employers. If you are thinking of working for a consulting firm I urge you to talk to several people who have worked for that firm for a few years and find out what kind of assignments and working conditions they have experienced.

If you are swayed by the promises of benefits, education, and interesting work find out how long people work for this company. Do they lay people off quickly when the business cycle enters one of its contractions? Do they send people out on projects that sound interesting to you? What education have they provided their employees in the previous year and what did the employees have to do to get it? Finally, check out the average number of years of experience of their so-called consultants, and beware of those firms who are peddling people with little or no work history. These are often the firms that are the most unscrupulous to deal with.

Common sense should tell you that no one is going to pay your salary while you loll on the beach, so if you are recruited with promises of lots of time off take it with a grain of salt.

Some consulting firms specialize in creating project teams. They work like this: The company is brought in to bid on a specific project, competing against similar firms. The company asking for bids will provide the consulting firms with some kind of specification package describing the job they want done. The consulting firm then gives its experienced systems analysts the job of estimating the project in terms of how it should be done and how much time and effort will be required to complete it. Based on these estimates the company submits a bid offering either to do the job for a fixed amount or else offering to do it in a specific way but billing for time and materials. If they are awarded the contract the consulting firm then assembles a team made up of experienced systems analysts with project management experience and other programmers with the specific skills needed for the project and sets them to work on the job. If the customer changes his specifications or requests more function the price of the project must be renegotiated.

Small companies and mom-and-pop consultant groups rarely get to bid on these projects, since the larger companies can devote full-time sales forces to lining them up. Programmers working on a project team like this might get good experience in learning how to effectively estimate and manage projects, since a company working under such arrangements has the strongest possible incentive to estimate correctly: if they are wrong they may have to eat the difference. Sometimes, however, this kind of contract leads the consulting firm to subject its employees to sweatshop conditions; unending overtime and intimidation tactics have been known to occur in this kind of situation, particularly when the company is employing salaried personnel.

You will have to judge any consulting opportunity with a consulting firm on its individual merits. You must, as usual be highly skeptical of any claims made by those who hire you. You should also try to track down people who have worked for the firms, even more so than when looking at other kinds of work since the potential for abuse is greater. Nevertheless, positions with dynamic consulting firms run by ethical, intelligent data processing professionals can offer a welcome change from working at a single corporate employer.

### Independent "Contractor" Consultants

But wait a moment, weren't we supposed to be talking about alternatives to being a company employee?

Well sit tight, and I will explain. The consulting companies that employ the consultants we've just discussed face the same problems recruiting experienced personnel as other businesses do. While some companies get around this by hiring people with minimal skills and giving them intensive in-house training, others recognize that their appeal to their client base is in the high skill levels of their consultants and so these consulting companies turn reluctantly to a second kind of person, who is called in the industry an independent subcontractor, or "contractor" for short.

Up until December 31, 1986, a contract programmer was a small business person who contracted with consulting firms to do work at sites where the consulting firm had negotiated a contract. Under this arrangement the consulting firm contracted with the client to provide the specific programmer's services for a specified period of time. The consulting firm would bill the programmer out at a rate anywhere from $30 to $60 an hour and then pay the contract programmer a percentage of this rate, usually 70 percent to 80 percent.

This arrangement was set out in a legal contract that bound the contractor to work for the term of the contract and specified penalties if he were to break it. The contractor was usually enjoined from going to work directly for the client for a period of anywhere from six months to three years. Other obligations and penalties were spelled out as well, such as when he should receive payment for his services. The contractor received a check for the full amount of his services with no withholding or social security tax removed and at the end of the year he was sent a 1099 form rather than a W-2. As an independent business person the programmer had the full responsibility of making estimated income tax payments quarterly and paying his self-employment tax to social security.

As a small business person the contractor could write off business expenses including his car and sometimes a home office. He could also deduct travel, entertainment, equipment, magazine subscriptions, and other such costs from his income. He could also contribute to a Keogh plan pension fund, which was very important since he had no other source of retirement funds as a self-employed consultant.

This represented a good deal to many people, and they used it. Unfortunately, it was such a good deal that the Congress slipped some wording into the Tax Reform Act of 1986 that made it far more difficult for mainframe programmers to qualify for contractor status. Briefly, what Congress did was toughen the standards by which a programmer or engineer was judged to be a contractor as opposed to an employee and threaten major tax penalties to employers who did not withhold taxes and social security from the pay of what the IRS considered to be employees.

The portion of the Tax Reform Act of 1986 that did this was called Paragraph 1706. Up until the passage of Paragraph 1706 programmers were exempted from having to fulfill all the conditions of the common law definition of independent contractor because of an earlier law, called Section 530 of the Revenue Act of 1978, which provided a so-called "safe harbor" relieving technical contractors from having to fulfill these conditions.

To modify this, Paragraph 1706 of the Tax Reform Act of 1986 stated merely that Section 530 "shall not apply in the case of an individual who, pursuant to an arrangement between the taxpayer and another person, provides services for such other person as an engineer, designer, drafter, computer programmer, systems analyst or other similarly skilled worker engaged in a similar line of work." Needless to say given the clarity of this language, no one, including the legal department of every large company I have dealt with as a consultant agreed on what the law really meant, or even to whom it applied. Particularly questionable was whether the paragraph applied to all contractors or only to those who worked through brokers.

However, the common law definition of an employee as interpreted by the IRS says that an employee is a person who works at the premises of his employer, for an hourly rather than a job rate, can be fired by the employer at will, has his work directed by the employer, has his tools furnished by the employer, and runs no personal risk of losing money on an assignment, among other factors.[3] This definition clearly embraces almost all erstwhile computer consultants.

While this change to the tax law might have raised a small amount of revenue for the government, opponents suggest that more sinister motivations led to its passage. The paragraph, which was written into the tax law without having been read aloud on the floor of Congress, appears to have been the direct result of lobbying by a trade group, the National Technical Services Association, which represents only eighty-five member consulting companies, the largest ones. The Computer Consultant Association claims that the effort was spearheaded by CDI Corporation, which is listed in *Standard and Poor's Register* as the "largest U.S. engineering, technical and scientific contract services organization."[4] The supposition is that these large consulting firms wanted to drive the independents out of the marketplace either to force them to work as consultant company employees or to drive up the need for their own current employees by reducing the overall pool of available consultants. Not surprisingly, Paragraph 1706 caused consternation among contrac-

---

[3] These are spelled out in a xeroxed copy of a typed manual passed around by consultants in December of 1987, and in my possesion, which unfortunately has no attribution, but may come from the Independent Computer Consultants Association. *The Wall Street Journal* published a similar list in an article, "Technical Specialists Lose Tax Breaks Under the New Law" by Sanford L. Jacobs in the December 9, 1986, edition.

[4] *Computerworld*, October 5, 1987. Letter from Richard Kuper and Harry A. Cozzi, p.20.

tors and their clients and immediately changed the face of computer consulting. Many client companies will not deal with independent contractors for fear of encountering tax penalties. Erstwhile independents who had been able to set up and bill contracts wholly without the intervention of broker firms have been forced to work for consultant firms, who are now getting a big chunk of the consultant's billing, and many former consultants have gone back to work as regular employees of hiring companies, rather than become employees of consulting firms.

For those who remain in consulting, what the consulting firms have done in general is to establish a special class of employee for the former independents. These employees are still bound by legal contracts almost identical to their old ones. They receive no benefits, as before, and are paid an hourly rate which is computed as a percentage of the rate billed to the client, as before. However the consulting firms now take an additional 7.5 to 10 percent from the consultant's billing rate to cover the employer's share of the social security tax and unemployment insurance. This is besides the additional amount the consultant must pay for his own share of social security taxes. They also withhold for federal and state taxes. The contractor has lost the ability to deduct business expenses and to contribute to a Keogh pension plan, nor can he deduct the cost of his self-paid health insurance as he could were he still considered an independent businessman. The only bright side to this is that the contractor still gets a much better hourly rate than the regular employee. Rates vary geographically and according to skill levels, but net rates from $20 to $35 an hour are common, while in New York's Wall Street area many contractors have been billing double that amount.

If you intend to become one of these special-class hourly employees, make sure to check up on the latest IRS rulings on this status. A November 1987 IRS "private letter ruling" suggests that the IRS wants to consider hourly contract employees to be the employees of the client rather than the broker firm, but other IRS private rulings have suggested the opposite.[5] Whatever the gyrations of the IRS, it is likely that programmers who prefer high hourly rates to lower salary rates will still be able to get them, one way or another, as long as there continues to be a programmer shortage.

[5] Davidf Ludlum, "IRS ruling raises cloud over contract work status," *Computerworld*, March 14, 1988, p. 105

## Drawbacks of Consulting

The major problem with consulting is that it is a very unpredictable way to make a living. In return for immediate cash you are giving away any claim to long-term job security. Furthermore, you are utterly at the mercy of your client and the consulting firm, and you do not have the protection of the usual personnel guidelines you have taken for granted as an employee to protect you when things go wrong.

Although your contract specifies an appealingly high hourly rate, all kinds of factors can limit the number of hours you actually work. For starters, you don't get paid on company holidays. Getting sick becomes painfully expensive when you are loosing upwards of $200 a day for each day of the flu. The hour or two that you are accustomed to taking as an employee to drop in at your kid's school play or to see the doctor suddenly costs you a bundle. So when you try to estimate your earnings from a contract you must plan for these inevitable unpaid hours. I find that the best thing to do is to allow for three unpaid days per month. If your financial situation is that you must have a certain amount coming in each month and you have no cushion of savings to tide you over, consulting should probably be your last resort. To be on the safe side, you should probably consider consulting only if you have six months worth of living expenses stashed away. And don't fool yourself that you are covered because you have been offered a six-month-long contract. As we will discuss later, these contracts can disappear in a moment leaving you with no recourse and no visible means of support.

Some companies will let you keep more of your billing dollar if you wait for your pay until the client company pays the consulting firm. This can be an excellent way to add another $2 or $3 an hour to your check. However if you go this route be aware that it may be two months after you submit your invoice for the time worked until you receive a paycheck. Companies are often agonizingly slow in paying and the consulting firm is not going to antagonize a customer by hounding them if they are assured that the company eventually will pay (as most do). Again, don't take this route if you could find yourself in economic distress from missing a pay period.

If you have a spouse who has a job that provides good health benefits you don't have to worry about providing your own health insurance. But if you are supporting yourself or are the family's main breadwinner, insurance becomes a major issue if you are a contractor. The extra pay you earn as a contractor can comfortably cover paying your own health benefits, but this will represent a major line item on your personal budget. Now that tax reform has taken away your small business status, you don't qualify for small business insurance plans either so you may have to pay horrendous individual rates to get coverage. Your best bet, if the option is available to you, is to join an HMO that lets individuals have membership. You should expect to pay anywhere from $200 to $300 a month for this kind of insurance.

There is a real potential land mine here however, which you should be aware of. If you go out to join an HMO or otherwise apply for health insurance you might be horrified to discover that you can be rejected if anyone in your family has anything in their medical history which suggests anything less than perfect health. In this case you may be forced to pay large sums for examinations by doctors to determine the extent of your family member's problems and then be rejected when the doctor makes his report. The only insurance open to you then can be ruinously expensive.

A federal law, the Consolidated Omnibus Budget Reconciliation Act (COBRA) of 1986, requires employers of more than twenty employees to offer former employees continued coverage under their insurance plan when they leave the company, assuming of course that the employee pays the premium. In addition, some state laws force your previous employer to allow you to remain as a self-paying member of a company health plan for a longer period than the federal law. In Connecticut, for example you may stay in a plan for up to twenty months. Since the group insurance rates charged by these plans are considerably lower than what you can get on your own it is in your interest to stay with group insurance as long as possible. Besides, the group insurance often covers things that the individual plans offered by the same organizations do not, like prescription drug reimbursement. Before you leave a job that includes health coverage, be sure to find out how you can take advantage of this and ensure that you have affordable health insurance. The company you are leaving may make it as difficult as possible for you to continue on their employee plan, too. For example while you must make your monthly payment on time, the company may refuse to bill you or send a reminder, and will terminate your coverage if you are late with a single payment. Make sure you make the payments! A single uncovered health emergency could drive you into bankruptcy. Remember that no federal assistance programs help people who have modest assets. You could lose your home if someone in the family came down with a sudden serious illness or had an uncovered accident. This is not an area in which you can afford to be sloppy.

When you no longer qualify for group insurance you might be able to join a group sponsored by a small business organization. The Small Business Service Bureau, Inc., for example, is an organization that offers various group plans, including HMO's in many states. Unfortunately, since the Tax Reform Act of 1986 took away independent contractor status from a large number of consultants you might not be able to qualify for small business plans unless you have some other source of small business income besides consulting.

Finally, some small consulting firms will let hourly employees (erstwhile contractors) join their health plans by subtracting a fixed amount from each dollar you earn for the premiums. This is a good deal for you if you have no other alternatives. This might be a good point to add to your negotiations when you are establishing your rate too, since the money that is taken out to pay your premium reduces your paycheck rather than appearing as taxable dollars. A slightly lower rate with company benefits paid for by the missing dollars is probably a good deal for you.

If you are contributing an important part of your family's income you should also consider paying for disability insurance since the day that you stop being able to work because of an illness or other serious problem you stop getting paid. Consult with a capable insurance salesperson and find a plan that has the least restrictive payout conditions. If you are making $50,000 a year as a consultant you can afford it, and it would be foolish to leave yourself open to disaster.

A major problem with contracting is your fundamental helplessness when dealing with both the consulting firm and the client firm where you do your work. Although you sign an ornate contract that specifies a term during which you are supposed to work, this contract as far as you, the contractor, are concerned is a piece of junk. If you break it you are in real trouble and can expect to have wages denied and even face a lawsuit. However the client company you are contracted to work for can dump you at any time it finds convenient, and there is not much you can do about it. Many a shocked programmer has thought that if the client terminated the contract before the specified term ended he was owed some compensation, possibly the full amount of the contract. Absolutely not. Business needs change and projects are canceled. No client company would sign up for a contract that bound them to pay you no matter what their needs. If the project you are hired for gets the ax you can be on the street with five minutes' notice. Worse, if you encounter a personality conflict you can be canned instantly, with no recourse to the usual procedures that companies have in place to prevent vindictive firings.

True, your contract might technically enable you to go to court when you are the victim of real abuse, but the company can always claim that you were not doing a satisfactory job. Obviously if you had been satisfactory, they can say, would they have fired you? Most consultant contracts are written in a way that this "unsatisfactory performance" is grounds for immediate termination. No matter what your legal rights, are you really ready to pay a lawyer to take on a multimillion dollar corporation? Who needs that kind of hassle?

And don't expect the consulting firm to act in your interest either. If a company employee lodges a malicious complaint against you and the client firm throws you out without even considering your side of the story (it does happen), the consulting firm is not going to jeopardize the future business it could do with that company to stick up for you, even if they know that the charge is not true.

This is not a trivial problem; a large number of the projects that are forced to hire consultants are projects that are in trouble. As a consultant you have no clue as to what political forces are operating, but you may find yourself at the very center of them. In a project that is failing to meet its dates or has insurmountable technical problems it is not unusual to have management desperately seeking scapegoats to blame for the disaster. Blaming the consultant can be the perfect short-term solution in this case, and you might find yourself fired for no better reason than that a manager needed to show his boss that he was taking aggressive steps to "solve" the project's problems.

Even in a project that is not a complete disaster the consultant can find himself the target of unreasonable abuse. Disgruntled employees often focus on the consultant's high pay rate and try to shoot the consultant down, loudly pointing out to their management and coworkers any errors the consultant has made. If you are unfortunate enough to make the kind of mistake that results in a dolly-load of paper being delivered to your output drop (it's happened to us all), or if you move something into production that bombs on its first run (this too has happened to us all), this kind of employee can make a federal issue of it. If, for some reason, management considers the complainer important enough to pacify, out the door you may go, no matter what the quality of the rest of your work.

What this means is that as a consultant you must exercise incredible care in your relationships with everyone you work with. You cannot survive more than one or two complaints about your work since there is no review procedure as there is for a full-time employee. It is safest to never assume that your contract will run the length of the time that it is written for, and you should at all times maintain your contacts so that you can get a new job if one is needed.

Beyond these drawbacks there are further issues you need to take a hard look at before jumping into contracting. The first is the nature of the work that contractors are given to do, and the second is the existence of unethical consulting firms.

As I said earlier, many people have a somewhat glamorous picture of consulting. The reality is that probably 80 percent of consulting jobs that you turn up will involve doing work which would cause you to quit had you been given it as part of a regular, full-time job.

Consultants get to do the most boring parts of any project. There is a simple reason for this: The company gives the interesting stuff to its good employees so that they will keep working for the company. As a contractor you can expect to do a lot of brute coding off of other people's detailed specifications, a lot of setting up of print lines for reports, of writing reporting programs, fixing up JCL, and creating test data. This frees up the regular employees to do the fun stuff.

The fact that you have terrific experience, much better experience than the people running the project, means nothing. Clients hire overqualified contractors to do simple tasks because they thus guarantee themselves that the work will be done perfectly. This can result in situations like one I've seen where a consultant who was a real CICS maven and had contributed articles on the subject to the trade press, spent several months doing nothing more than typing in the text for help screens.

This can be very frustrating if you are used to being a team leader or having your opinions taken seriously when design issues come up. You will always see the employees getting any interesting work while you deal with boring junk. You rarely will be asked to do any true knowledge work unless you work as a contractor in the same department for several years.

Closely related to this problem is that if you consult for a long time your skills may atrophy. You will almost always be hired to do things you know how to do already. I have managed to pick up a little additional software experience as a contractor, but only by reading manuals on my own after work. You will rarely get any formal training. After a few years of contracting you may find that you are not getting exposure to the newer things appearing in the software world, and it is the new software that is going to be most in demand for contractors.

Finally I must remind you that there are sharks cruising the business seas. If you are used to dealing with large corporate employers bound as they are by complex federally enforced labor laws you might find it a shock to discover that a small consulting firm can get away with not paying you for work you have done. It doesn't happen a lot, but it does happen, and most working contractors can tell you war stories. In many cases your money is held back because of a dispute with the consulting firm. If your consulting firm interprets your contract to mean one thing and you disagree, or if you terminate the contract before they want you to, you may have real difficulty collecting your last few weeks earnings. In cases like this you might have unequivocal legal right on your side, but it will cost you as much as you could recover to get the money due you.

If the amount is not large you may be able to recover it in small claims court. Look into what the dollar limits are in your state. But if it is more than a few thousand dollars you are looking at serious litigation to recover it. Some of the situations that have caused this to occur are: terminating your contract before the specified end date, going to work at the same company for a different consulting firm, and most blamelessly, business failure of the consulting firm.

Your best protection against this kind of thing is to know whom you are dealing with when you enter into a relationship with a consulting firm. Check with the Better Business Bureau, although their listings are by no means all-inclusive. Talk to contractors who have been in the business for awhile. Ask explicit questions about firms you are considering too. After a harrowing brush with one outfit, I found that all my buddies had anecdotes to tell about the company's unethical practices, but they felt somehow constrained against telling them to me until I had had my own experience.

Scrupulously examine any contract before you sign it and make sure that you are prepared to observe every clause in it to the letter. We all know that we should go to a lawyer before signing any contract but of course most of us never do. I'm not going to insist that you talk to a lawyer, although it is a good idea if at all possible. However you must make sure that you understand everything you are signing. Don't rely on any verbal assurances you are given that contradict what is written on the paper. If there is a difference, insist that the assurance be written into the text of the contract. There is nothing that says that you can't add terms or cross them out. In particular, be very careful to limit the scope of the consulting company's exclusivity clause.

Exclusivity clauses are little bombshells buried in most broker firm contracts that bind you to working for the same consulting broker in subsequent contracts at the company where the broker is placing you. Try to limit the scope of the clause to the department or the division that you are going into. Otherwise, if you have a falling-out with the broker company you might find yourself unable to work at a customer site where you are very much in demand. You might also have to turn down contracts offered by other brokers at that company which would have given you a better rate. Since your goal is to work for yourself, the shorter the time period of the exclusivity clause, the sooner you work directly without a broker. You should also exclude from the exclusivity clause, in writing, the names of any managers or departments you have previously established links with that might yield future contracts.

Technically, these exclusivity clauses are probably illegal in many states since they contradict right-to-work laws; however, the amount of legal hassle you would have to go through to defend yourself in court is not worth it, and I do know of companies prosecuting cases involving this issue—even though they lost.

In negotiating the contract make sure that there is some way you can get out of the specified term. Most places will accept your leaving if you give a few weeks' notice. Make sure that this is in writing, though, so there is no conflict if you do have to leave. Otherwise the company may withhold your last paychecks.

Finally, be very careful when the question of signing again comes up. Make sure that the original contract does not somehow specify that you must extend the contract at the original rate. You should be able to negotiate for more money when a six-month or year-long contract ends.

## Benefits of Consulting

Having just painted a rather bleak picture of consulting I would like to remark that it is the way I've made my living the last few years. With all the possible pitfalls, it offers some unbeatable advantages.

Primary, of course, is a sense of freedom. Many of the contractors I know who have been in the business for as many as ten years admit they couldn't work any other way. While you must behave circumspectly and do excellent work, you do not have to take seriously a whole set of things "real" employees do. You do not have to pretend to be loyal to the company. You don't have to get involved in the struggle to get ahead in the company. You don't have to feel bad when dumber people get promoted since you are not playing the game, and finally, you have the tremendous consolation in every situation of knowing that you are getting paid as much as just about anyone you meet—often more than the managers giving you your assignments.

Being a contractor lets you distance yourself from the business mentality if you should choose to do so.

You also don't have to pretend that you are never going to leave the company. If the headhunter calls with a great job offer and leaves his phone number it's okay. Everyone knows you are only there temporarily. If you trying to get a business of your own off the ground you can realistically contract half the year and work on your own business the rest of the time and yet make enough money to pay your bills.

Contracting offers people who would like to spend time with their small children a realistic alternative to year-round day care. While you will probably have to work full forty-hour weeks while you are contracting, you can get by working a lot fewer of those weeks. It is easier to leave an infant or small child with someone else knowing that it will last for only ten or twelve weeks and knowing that at a specific time you will be done and can spend undivided time at home with your child, having put a nice chunk of money in the bank.

*Consulting Versus Working Part Time*

Having worked both as a year-round, part-time employee and as a short-term consultant while my children were little I would say that being a consultant has several advantages, although unlike me, the majority of people I've met who have a choice prefer to choose the part-time option.

First of all, it is a lot easier to find short consulting jobs than it is to find part-time positions. In fact, it is almost impossible to get a part-time position unless it is with a company where you have worked full-time for a long time and rendered yourself indispensable. Even then some companies, like IBM, simply refuse to let people convert to permanent part-time employment no matter how good their work. In contrast, short-term contracts of three months and under are usually available, particularly when businesses are trying to cut back on other consultants. You may find it easier to get these contracts since most programming contractors don't like them, preferring the relative security of longer contracts.

Second of all, you are given far more respect as a full-time, short-term consultant than as a part-timer. Business people do not generally like to deal with part-time workers. They fear, rightly, that you won't be there when something important comes up, and wrongly, that you won't work as hard as full-time employees. In truth, part-timers often work harder than full-time employees, not taking the leisurely lunches and long telephone breaks that full-time workers feel entitled to. The real reason that businesses don't like to use part-timers is probably that they think it demoralizes full-time staff to see others going home early. Whatever the reason, as a part-time worker you will find you have to deal with a lot of unspoken resentment that is not an issue when you work as a short-term consultant.

Finally, there is one overriding advantage to being a short-term consultant. Money. When I worked as a part-timer my bosses let it be known that they were doing me a tremendous favor by letting me work at all, and I, out of gratitude, was expected to sacrifice some of the benefits and pay I would have received had I been full-time in the same job. The standard arrangement was to pay me an hourly salary that was exactly what my old job paid on an hourly basis *without benefits*. I got paid for holidays that fell on my working days and on one job, for some earned vacation pay, but I did not get sick days or any health or other insurance benefits even though I worked over twenty hours a week. This is a typical part-time arrangement.

I felt very lucky to be able to work under this arrangement until I had my second child and discovered that I would net about $75 a week for three full days' work after paying taxes and day care charges for two children. That was when I discovered that I could get *twice* my old hourly rate if I worked instead as a short-term consultant. I didn't get the paid holidays, but I found that I made more money working eleven weeks under this arrangement than I had working six and one-half months under the other one. Another advantage of this, too, was that I only had to pay for eleven weeks of full-time day care as opposed to the twenty-eight weeks of full time care I paid for when I worked part-time. (Most infant day-care providers charge full-time rates if you use their services more than twenty hours a week.) With infant/toddler day care running from $100 to $200 a week per child, you can see that short-term consulting makes terrific sense economically as well as emotionally for the mothers of young children.

Incidentally, after working short-term contracts and establishing inghinga reputation you may find employers willing to let you work as a part-time consultant, which may be the best possible arrangement since you will have time off during the week for your outside interests and still make high consultant rates.

Another part-time possibility to consider if you want to be at home more is PC-based, small-business consulting. If you are familiar with off-the-shelf PC software you might find a niche doing this kind of work. In general, experienced DP consultants with mainframe backgrounds avoid this kind of work since it is hard to pursue full time and still make a living that compares to what they can earn working for large corporations. Many of the people who bill themselves as "computer experts" for small business PC owners are self-taught or have dubious credentials. However, if you know your stuff and are looking for an income sideline, PC consulting might be a good solution. You may be able to do new system setups for small businesses, counseling them on what software to buy and setting up their databases and spreadsheets for them, while you are at home with your children. Another possible PC sideline is trouble shooting: for a charge you will ride in, trailing clouds of glory, to save the day when small business users get those wonderful user-friendly messages like "FATAL DISKETTE ERROR" which convince them they have destroyed their entire system.

## Further Benefits of Consulting

I know numerous contractors who have traveled around the world taking contracting assignments in foreign countries. For example, you could work in Israel or, alternatively, in Saudi Arabia (if you are male and not Jewish), or in the Far East. Many non-U.S. citizens have been able to get work visas to work in the United States by coming in as contractors too. Currently many programmers from England, Ireland, New Zealand, and Australia are working in the United States as contractors. Much of the software used in the United States is used internationally, so your skills transfer. In fact you might even be able to work in foreign countries with limited language skills since English is used by many international companies as the company language. If travel is important to you, consulting opens some real possibilities. Then too, you can schedule lengthy trips abroad during the two or three months each year you are "on the bench."

Finally, contracting offers you the opportunity to see local companies as a "tourist." What I mean by this is that you can work short stints in area companies and get a better idea of what they feel like and the opportunities that exist in them. If you would like to be a corporate employee but don't have a feeling for what you would be happiest doing or what local company would be best for you, working short stints as a consultant will not only help you make up your mind but will give you a reputation within the company, making it much easier to get a full-time job there that suits you. It is not unheard of for contractors who have worked extensively at client companies to eventually be hired directly into management, at very nice salaries too.

Contracting also exposes you to a lot of situations that sharpen up your systems analysis and development skills, not because you do a lot of systems analysis, mind you, but because you see a lot of poorly managed projects that have gotten in trouble, resulting in the need for you, the contractor, to be brought in! Since you see a lot of crisis situations you should learn a tremendous amount about how *not to* manage a project, which, should you incline toward management later in your career, can be of tremendous value to you.

The final benefit of consulting is that if you are persistent and handle yourself well you can, after a few years build up a client base of your own. This will enable you to dispense with the services of the consulting firms and start making some serious money. Although tax reform has confused the issue tremendously, some companies are interpreting the law so that the employee restrictions apply only to programmers working through brokers (the consulting firms). If you get the contract completely through your own efforts you may still qualify as an independent contractor. You may also eventually be able to contract for fixed-bid contracts where you do a specific project for a specific amount. You can come out way ahead in these situations if you are a fast worker, and in these situations there is no question about your independent status. If you can build up this kind of consulting practice you can make an enormous income, be treated as an independent business person, and build a very satisfying career for yourself.

## DP Audit and Computer Security Consulting

One last area to consider if you are thinking about consulting is the expanding DP audit and computer security business. As companies invest more and more of their resources in expensive and vital computer systems which contain business information that, should it be revealed, would give their competitors a real advantage over them, they are becoming highly sensitive to the issue of computer crime and data security.

Companies often bring in outside computer security specialists to examine their systems and ensure that their data is secure and that their procedures for protecting that data are effective.

Other functions such outside auditors might perform include analysis of the company's computer systems looking for waste and fraud.

One way consultants get into this business is to write articles in the trade press about data security issues. There is no hard and fast credential. If you are technically sophisticated about operating system-level software and interested in sleuthing, this might be an interesting path to explore.

## What Experience do You Need to Begin Contract Consulting?

If you are a working corporate programmer who has been considering going the contractor route you have probably wondered what qualifications you need to break in. You probably also wonder how to get started. Let's address these questions.

The amount of experience you need to break in is a direct function of the demand for programmers that exists in your geographical region. When business is painfully short-handed you may be able to work a solid contractor year (about eight months) after three years of solid experience. In areas where there is less demand, whether it is because there are fewer mainframes around or because of a business slump, you might need seven or eight years' experience to break in, and that experience might have to be with certain in-demand software only.

One indicator is the number of advertisements for contractors in the paper. These are usually very specific as to what skill levels and software experience are in demand. Be aware however that five contractor ads requesting IDMS/ADSO doesn't mean that there are five IDMS/ADSO positions open, just that the five consulting firms are all trying to fill the one opening that a client has for that skill set. Watch the papers for a couple of months to get some idea of how steady the demand for contractors seems to be.

If you are looking at out-of-town ads that promise huge salaries be aware that these often reflect skyrocketing costs of living, particularly in New York and Boston. You might get the rate and still not be able to find a place to live.

Most of the demand for contractors is for applications programmers with backgrounds in COBOL, popular databases, and CICS online. Clients need programmers who can crank out the code on development projects that are in danger of missing their dates, and they need programmers to take over maintenance on systems whose regular employees keep quitting.

This means that if you have highly specialized systems internals skills you will be overqualified for the majority of the positions that come up. Your rate will be higher for the specialized work but you might have to wait a long time to get it, or you might have to take work that is less technical.

If you are interested in trying consulting there is nothing wrong in interviewing with a few consulting firms and then waiting to see if they call with anything you would be interested in. No matter how interested they seem in your resume it is only if they call you with possibilities that lead to interviews that you know you have a future in consulting.

If you do begin dealing with consulting firms, make it very clear that they are never to send out your resume to a client before checking with you first. This avoids having two firms send your resume to the same place, a situation which irritates everyone involved. You should give your permission each time your resume is sent out and you should insist on seeing the resume that is sent out too, since many broker firms insist on rewriting your resume in their format. Second-rate consulting firms will often hopelessly garble your qualifications on the resume and thus ensure that you will never get the contract. You must use all the criteria in evaluating a consulting firm that you would use in evaluating a headhunter, because ultimately the consulting firm salesperson is doing for you exactly what the headhunter would. Make sure that the consulting firm's sales reps are intelligent people with solid programming backgrounds who are capable of interpreting and representing your skills to a potential employer. You deserve the best, because with the consulting firm taking 30 to 40 percent of your billing rate you are certainly going to be paying for it!

You may encounter a Catch-22 situation when you first decide to consult. Many consulting firms have clauses in their contracts with clients that forbid them to recruit the client firm's employees. If you work with a company that uses consultants you may find that none of the better companies can hire you! Your only hope then is to sign on with a company that does not do business with your current employer. But be careful, sometimes the reason they don't do business with your employer is because of a previous history of unethical conduct. Take care!

Perhaps the best time to try consulting is when you are at a major turning point and find yourself between jobs. Perhaps you have come back to the work force after having taken some time off to care for children. Perhaps you have just moved to a new city. Or you may have just, for whatever reason, been fired from your last job. In this situation you might consider giving consulting a try before you turn to looking for a full-time job.

In making the decision to become a contractor you should always weigh your ability to take on additional risk with the benefits of your current situation. The time to quit a decent full-time employee situation is only when your consulting contract has been signed and you are sure that you could survive financially if it should fall through the next week. Having prepared for the worst possible case the chances are that you won't encounter it. Many contractors work at delightful contractor rates for four or five years in the same company. I've even seen projects where all the old-timers were contractors! Consulting can be a wonderful way to make a living as long as you keep your eyes open.

## Foreign Consultants Working in the United States

There has been such a strong demand for contract consultants in the United States over the past several years that many of the larger United States consulting firms have taken to importing foreigners, particularly programmers from the U.K. and the British Commonwealth. These prog    nmers are familiar with the software environments used in the United States and, of course, speak English. Foreign consulting firms, too, have been opening United States offices, trying to break into this market. Foreign consultants can have a wonderful experience working in the United States, if they know what they are getting into. Unfortunately, many of them do not. So many consultants brought from abroad by these companies tell stories of having been bamboozled or told tall tales about conditions in the United States that I would caution anyone considering coming to the United States from abroad to exercise real caution.

Several foreign consultants I've encountered have run into real problems with their immigration status. Some consulting firms have promised the consultants that they will sponsor them for their "green card," the permanent visa that allows an immigrant to apply for United States citizenship, when the firm actually had no intention of doing so. You should be aware that getting a green card is quite difficult. Consultants are usually brought in on temporary work visas that typically allow the consultant to work in this country for a period of eighteen months. When that work visa expires a foreign contractor may find himself forced to leave the country. If you are a foreign contractor working under such a visa you should assume that you are going to leave at its termination and plan accordingly, no matter what you are told by agencies or potential employers. Consultants who have counted on getting permanent status have sometimes been shocked when it fell through, and they were forced to hurriedly sell cars and furniture, acquired in the expectation of a long-term stay, at a great financial loss. Don't make plans based on having permanent status until your permits are in your hand.

The other major problem foreign consultants encounter is that they are totally unprepared for the cost of living in the United States Several foreign consultants I've met in Connecticut told me that they were assured by agencies that it was quite cheap to live here. The rates that these consultants receive were generous compared to those they received in England; however they were about half what United States consultants receive for the same work and barely allowed them to pay the outrageous rents common in this part of the country. Some foreign consultants were also shocked at how high travel expenses are here, since there really is not a well-developed network of cheap, family-run hotels available to visitors comparable to those found in Britain.

By far the greatest number of abuses, not surprisingly, center on the rates that these companies pay their subcontractor consultants. If you are a foreign consultant, try to talk with people who have worked in the area you intend to visit before you sign up and do some serious research to determine how much money you will really need. Most of all, find out what the prevailing rate structure is in your prospective area by talking to people who have worked there if it is at all possible.

As an example of how badly you could be exploited, a tale is circulating in Hartford about a British contractor who was quite happy with his hourly rate until he accidentally saw the invoice for his services that his company had sent his client, which revealed that he was only getting 40 percent of the rate his labor was being billed out at. Even the worst companies here usually leave the programmer 65 percent or more of his billing!

Finally, if you are coming to the United States as a contract programmer don't let anyone tell you you won't need a car—unless you plan to work in New York or Boston. In the vast majority of American cities public transportation is either nonexistent or limited to the inner-city area. You may not even be able to get to work without a car, let alone go out at night or visit local attractions. Make sure the rate you are getting allows you to afford a good, used car and that you can qualify for a license!

## Using Your DP Apprenticeship to Position Yourself for Contracting

If you would like to be a consultant, you should make sure that the jobs you take in your first five years expose you to as many as possible of the popular software products used for database management systems and on-line development. Particularly useful is any IBM product that is being marketed heavily by IBM. You need to have about three years of solid experience in what you claim as your specialty; however, any additional software you are familiar with should definitely be featured in your resume since often a week's exposure to an obscure software product that a client has a requirement for can get you the job.

Get the mainstream stuff and pick up any software experience that you possibly can. Avoid homemade system software like the plague. It will do nothing for you when you want to consult. In fact if you don't have easily recognized software skills you may not be able to get a contract at all. Clients are emphatic when it comes to paying for contractor skills. You must have exactly what they want, and usually what they want is the mainstream stuff. The only exception to this is when a client himself has nonstandard software or homemade code in which case he must train the candidate with the most congruent experience.

Be realistic about your talent too. As a contractor you are going to be thrown into some challenging situations and expected to find your feet very quickly. You need to be able to be productive in two or three weeks, maximum. If you can't honestly say that you are a better programmer than 75 percent of the people you have worked with you probably ought to avoid contracting situations. If you find during the apprenticeship period that you are better at dealing with the administrative parts of your job than the technical side you might make a fool of yourself as a contractor.

Analyze how long it takes you to catch on in a new assignment during the apprenticeship period. If you hate having to learn a whole new system you will hate contracting, since you need to learn a new system every time you start a new contract. If, however, you find the first six weeks of the job when everything is new the most exciting part and feel bored in the same position after a year, contracting might be just what you need to keep the juices flowing.

Use your apprenticeship period to pick up transferable software skills and test yourself to see if you could handle the requirements of contracting. And don't underestimate the contacts you can make in the apprenticeship period. The best kind of consulting is the kind you do without an intermediary. Most consultants are forced to use brokers because it is simply too hard to locate the manager who has a need for a consultant the very week that you are looking for a new job. If, however, you build up a truly sterling reputation in a large company you can build a good relationship with managers and keep current on the development projects that are being planned so that you can schedule yourself in on potential projects. Managers would much prefer to use a known performer rather than a stranger, so any effort you spend building up relationships with managers during your apprenticeship can be worth a tremendous amount to you as a consultant.

———————————

Consulting is not for everyone but for people who are temperamentally and intellectually suited to it, it offers advantages and long-term possibilities equal to any other DP career path.

# 6
## *Software Development—Becoming an Entrepreneur*

Just about the time a lot of baby boomers decided they were finally too old to make several million dollars as rock and roll stars, along came a new American dream to fill the void: millionaire software developer. While software development has been an industry since the 1950s, the introduction of the IBM PC and the fortunes made by developers like Ashton-Tate, Lotus Development Corp., and the Beatles of software, Microsoft, brought software development into the limelight. If you are a programmer you are probably accustomed by now to having well-meaning relatives inquire why you don't write some software and make some real money.

You may have been wondering this yourself. After all, the chances are that in your job as a programmer you do write software. But your net worth does not approach the $1.25 billion that *Forbes* magazine reported in 1987 as the minimum worth of then 31-year-old William H. Gates, the founder of Microsoft.[1]

---

[1] *Forbes*, "The Forbes Four Hundred Billionaires" October 26, 1987. Profile of Gates is on page 130.

The days are gone when you could write some code on the home computer in your basement, dupe it onto some floppies, sell it by mail through an ad in the back of computer magazines, and make "real money." You never could sell mainframe software that way, and the market for PC software has matured considerably since its first heady years. In particular, it has developed rigid distribution channels with which you must deal if you want to sell to the business community, which has turned out to be the only really viable market for PC applications. PC software publishing now resembles print publishing and the music business much more than it used to. The successful software developer will need more than an good idea to get ahead. He will have to master the intricacies of how the industry works.

Nevertheless, I've met several programmers with backgrounds in mainframe programming who have managed to build successful software companies drawing from their experience doing mainframe programming.

The products with which they made their mark include both mainframe software packages and PC packages that target specific needs of mainframe-using DP shops.

If you are thinking about going into PC software development on your own, it would probably be a good idea to realize that the large obvious applications like word processing and spreadsheets have attracted a horde of competitors and gone through a shakeout. The same goes for database packages. The strongest have survived and achieved the semipermanent status that comes from having a wide-flung distribution network in place committed to selling, and, more important, supporting that software. In addition, there now exists a large group of users who are trained in and accustomed to using the dominant PC software packages. If you have ever tried to get a nontechnical user to change the way he uses an on-line application once he has learned to do it one way, you know that this is no easy trick. So even if you were to come up with a terrific substitute product you would not only have to compete with rich, savvy, competitors, but you would have to struggle with the inertia of the installed customer base.

The companies that created the successful packages are no longer a couple of guys in the garage either. They have large staffs of employees and are constantly modifying and improving their programs to cope with the increasingly powerful upgrades that the computer manufacturers introduce. The competition is heightened further by the entry into the fray of many software companies who used to develop software for mainframes but now see the PC market as the fastest growth sector of the software economy.

Does this mean you should give up? Certainly not. Should you quit your job and start writing code right away for your brilliant idea? Certainly not either. It is probably going to take you a couple of years between the initiation of your product and the day you start cashing the checks. Unless you have an independent income, you should hold on to any job you have until you have a complete spec for your product and a business plan that has excited either a bank or a backer to give you enough money to get through a very long year.

### What Kind of Software Should You Develop?

Obviously you can develop and possibly make a hit with just about anything you can think of. An idea that sounds dumb to me might turn out to fill some need I have never even thought about. So I will preface this by saying that my discussion below is confined to sketching a picture of the kinds of software that have a higher probability of success, and to some extent reflects the histories of software developers I have encountered who have done well selling their own products.

*Applications Packages*

Many small but steady software successes for both PC and mainframe developers have been racked up by companies that provide packages targeted to a specific kind of business or to a portion of a specific industry. For example there is an entire software community that provides insurance packages designed to be sold to smaller insurance companies that do not have the resources to hire huge DP development staffs. Rating software for insurance companies, such as Gen-A-Rate developed by Programming Resources of Wethersfield, Connecticut, can be sold to agencies or even large companies that are glad not to have to develop it themselves.[2]

[2] Lawrence B. Rasie, "Software Industry Develops Bit by Byte," *Hartford Courant Business Weekly,* June 1, 1987 p 1.

There are many packages developed for the health care industry that enhance patient care or facilitate complying with governmental regulations. In any field where governmental regulation is particularly stringent, a small firm with up-to-the-minute expertise in the legal requirements of a certain industry can keep a software package abreast of rapid changes faster than companies with tight resources can.

If you have worked intensively in an industry and have a good background in the business aspects of that industry, you may be uniquely suited to developing generic application software for it.

There are also a lot of opportunities in the area of developing systems that address the needs of professionals who run their own businesses such as dentists, investors, and accountants. None of these is exactly virgin territory but to date there is no single package that has established dominance for these user groups, so if you come up with something truly useful you could be set for life. The key here is that before you plunge in to develop anything for a profession or industry, you must do a lot of research to find out what exists to support it already, and what that software's strengths and weaknesses are.

## Tool Development

An area that has been a fertile one for small developers is the area of systems tools and productivity aids, for both mainframes and PC's.

These are products that are useful to programmers themselves. One set of tools is designed for use by systems programming departments. Another subset is used by applications programmers. In both cases these kinds of software are very useful to companies when installed, but few companies can justify the costs of developing them within their own organization.

A good example of a systems tool designed for systems programmers is VSUM, developed by Software Technologies and Research, Inc. of Cromwell, Connecticut, which was acquired in 1987 by On-Line Software International, Inc. of Fort Lee, New Jersey. This product facilitates efficient definition of VSAM files. VSAM is an IBM product that is used almost universally; however, VSAM files can cause tremendous performance problems when they have not been designed correctly, and few people are quite sure how to design them. The VSUM product displays screens on which you enter requested information about your new or existing VSAM file. The system then analyzes your input and recommends ways to improve the file definitions.

Productivity tools directed at applications programmers include programs like On Line File Utility developed by MacKinney Systems of Springfield, Missouri, which allows programmers to browse and update CICS files easily. Other programs make up the currently ballyhooed family of CASE tools, (computer-aided software engineering). These products do things like draw flow charts, or restructure spaghetti code. An example of this is Language Technology of Salem, Massachusetts' Recoder product.

To give you some idea of the what you are looking at here the last product mentioned above, in 1987 cost $75,000 for an annual license and reportedly had 23 licensees.[3] That kind of money could buy you a lot of lunch!

Industry watchers report that there is as yet little market penetration of COBOL programmer productivity tools, but that may change as managers hunt high and low for ways to improve programmer productivity (and decrease the need to pay programmer salaries).

If you have an unusually clear understanding of the nature of programming itself, you might be able to see as yet unaddressed problems that could provide you with a huge corporate DP market.

Conversion aids are a third kind of tool that have been successful products for some developers. Companies that have committed themselves to a vendor or an operating system which shows signs of going bye-bye in the near future are faced with the unpleasant job of converting their systems from old languages or operating systems to new and hopefully more stable ones. Sometimes it is possible to write programs that mechanize this process. To be successful with such a product you need to have a very good idea of what the more popular conversions are going to be in the next four or five years and you must have technical expertise in both old the software that is being converted and the new software. Usually the people who develop software like this do it as an outgrowth of their work which involves doing this kind of conversion for a client on a contract basis. If you are planning to market a product you developed as part of a contract you performed for a client you must be careful to negotiate

---

[3] Karen Gullo "Steady as She Goes," *Datamation*, January 15, 1987, p. 37.

your rights to the conversion aid that results, otherwise you might face a legal challenge from an irate customer who feels he has a right to the code you developed on his equipment on his time.

## PC Software with Mainframe Features

Another area that has proven kind to some developers is developing PC software that mimics familiar mainframe software in function. This was the tack taken by Applied Systems Technologies, Inc. of West Hartford Connecticut, when it designed PC/DACS, a security package for PC's that resembles the mainframe security packages that systems departments are familiar with.[4] As PC's become more technically sophisticated there should be increasing opportunities for more mainframe-like software. Already a number of companies have done quite well developing networking programs as well as programs that allow PC's to communicate with mainframe databases. However, here we are getting into massive development projects probably beyond the resources of small entrepreneurs.

As PC operating systems start to incorporate multitasking it will take much more technical sophistication to write code for them. Systems programmers who have had experience writing reentrant operating system code for mainframes will have a unique advantage over PC developers who have previously not had to worry about storage violations and other problems posed by having programs running simultaneously in one machine.

## Important Steps in Developing Software

### Market research

Before you begin the actual design of a software product you have a lot of work to do first to determine if there really is a market for what you intend to produce.

Market research is of fundamental importance. If you are going to sell a taxidermy package you better find out how many taxidermists there are who make incomes high enough to justify buying

---

[4] Steve Kemper "Protection Offered for Data in Personal Computers," *Hartford Courant Business Magazine,* September 20, 1987. Also some of the suggestions about new product development in this chapter came from my personal discussion with Al Dube, Vice President of Research and Development of Applied System Technologies, in December of 1986.

what you hope is an expensive program. Obviously if only 3,000 full-time taxidermists are working in the United States and their average income is $9,000 a year you would not expect to make a fortune with a product retailing at $1,000 a copy. If on top of this there was already a product out that performed most of the functions you had planned to write, and it was available for free through hobbyist bulletin boards your future would be grim indeed.

You need to thoroughly research the hardware that you will be developing a product for. You will have to somehow come up with figures that tell you what kind of machines your potential customer base has installed.

A good example of what can happen if you don't pay attention to this is the story of a large, well-known company that attempted to break into the software development business after developing a programmer productivity tool for its own programmers. The product was useful for the programmers it was designed for and the company had high hopes of making a profit selling it to other companies. Unfortunately it had been designed to run on networked Wang PC's hanging off of a Wang minicomputer which communicated with an IBM mainframe. Since the product made use of some unique capabilities of the Wang machines it was not portable to other kinds of PC's nor to the more common programmer workstation configuration for a programming shop of this size which is 3270, style terminals going directly to the mainframe.

What this company soon discovered was that they weren't selling software, they were selling a whole hardware configuration, and an expensive one at that, since the only way a company could use their product was to duplicate their entire hardware configuration.[5] You could find yourself in a similar situation if you develop a mainframe product for companies who turn out to do the bulk of their work on IBM System/38 minicomputers, or if you require that your user have an expensive PC configuration before he can use your code.

The moral of this is that before you begin you will need to produce a coherent business plan that is chock full of numbers you

[5] This refers to the ITT Corporations' subsidiary HiTech which tried to market a Programmer Workstation product that had been developed for internal use by programmers at The Hartford Insurance Company. I inteviewed for a position on the development team for this product in February 1986 which is where I learned about it.

can substantiate. You must identify your potential market and document your assumptions. You must keep up with what other software developers are designing and keep track of which products similar to yours succeed and which fail.

If software development is where you want to make your mark you should be reading every DP magazine available every month starting your first day on your first job, in the hopes that four or five years down the line when you have accumulated the application and technical experience you need for your own project you will have mastered the knowledge about the software business you need to get started on a path that has some chance of success.

## Developing Your Code

When you develop software to sell you have to make sure that it is nearly perfect. If you used the methodology used by 98 percent of functioning DP applications shops, including the big vendors, you would be out of business in weeks, even if you could sell your product.

Basically you cannot afford to have a customer encounter a single programming error when using your product for the first several months (excluding, of course, those caused by his own ignorance.) No abends, no nasty bugs. Being human you will of course have buried somewhere in the code something that will emerge as a problem eventually. But you must do your absolute best to take care of 99 percent at least of the problems that could occur when your program runs.

This means you develop a test plan that is just as rigorously worked out as your code. You must develop a test case for every single error situation you can imagine. A single anecdote about your product's failure passed around the managerial lunch table could result in a shutdown of sales.

Even if you develop the greatest code on earth you are not done yet. No matter how debugged your software is the user will use it wrong. You must constantly provide for his most idiotic actions in your product design if you want to succeed. You must provide help screens and intelligible error messages. Just because none of the software you have had to work with in your career as a programmer provided either is no excuse. You are not IBM and cannot get away with what they do. For that matter, neither can they. Even IBM has had to clean up its act and is spending a lot of money on comprehensible manuals for its new products.

Therefore you must plan to spend a lot of money on professionally produced manuals written by competent technical writers and full of useful graphics.

And should you be lucky enough to build up a customer base you will have to spend a lot of money supporting your product once it is installed if you want to keep it installed. This means that you will have to have a help desk and keep it staffed with intelligent people who can answer the questions of users unable to read and understand your beautiful books.

You will also have to make sure that your programs continue to run every time that a new upgrade of the operating system it runs under is introduced. This means you must stay on top of all vendor product announcements so you can get to work on fixes before the new vendor releases hit the street.

Obviously, software development is not for the faint of heart. Nor is it a comfortable escape for the programmer who hates to deal with the business aspects of programming. Only the programmer with the sharpest business skills (or wisdom to locate a business-whiz partner) can have any hope of succeeding in the software development field. There is more to be done here than any one individual can accomplish so you will eventually have to face hiring people to work for your business. Clearly you will have to have tremendous managerial skills and business acumen as well as incredible programming talent.

## Marketing Your Product

We now come to the crux of the matter. How do you get customers to buy your product?

This is a question you must address from the moment you begin to think of a product to develop. You can't wait until the code is written to address marketing. It must be your first priority at all times.

Again your first need is to research the software business in depth. How are existing products marketed? If you are developing PC software and are hoping to appear on the shelf in Computerland stores you must find out who stocks those shelves. If your attempts to communicate with these people result in nothing but a form letter, that in itself should tell you something.

Instead of trying to market your software yourself, you might find an organization that is willing to add you to their list of products and give you distribution. Much of the software that goes out with the IBM logo on it was actually developed by independent developers who have signed distribution contracts with IBM. However you must carefully consider any contract you sign with such a distributor. You may discover, for example, that the contract contains clauses in which you sign away all rights to sue the distributor for any reason. What would happen if the distributor misrepresented your product, or distributed defective copies? Worse, once you sign your product over to a distributor he can pull your software off the shelf in favor of another developer's product even though yours was selling moderately well, and you will not be able to take advantage of other distribution channels because he has exclusive rights. Be aware too that if a big company distributes your software they will get a big chunk of any profits. Your cut may end up being only 5 percent of the sales price.

In response to the difficulty of launching new PC products in the marketplace, increasing numbers of software developers have turned to an ingenious method of selling their wares: giving them away for free. Their products are called "Shareware." Shareware developers distribute their wares through user groups and distribution services where diskette copies are typically distributed for a $3 to $10 handling fee (the developers get no part of this), and through bulletin boards where they can be downloaded for free. The shareware programs are copyrighted, and it is forbidden for others to sell them at a profit, but users may freely copy and use them. The developers see this as a way to get users hooked on their products. They request only that if you like their program you will send them a modest registration fee, usually under $100. As a further incentive, since, after all, the users already have the software, developers offer registered owners comprehensive hard-copy manuals, free updates, or even commissions on the registrations of their buddies.

While there is no question that this is a great way to gain visibility for your product, except for a handful of shareware "superstars," few shareware authors get rich. The reason for this is easy to figure out: Developers quoted by Tom Stanton in *PC Magazine* said that only 1 to 5 percent of their users pay the fee. For example, Bob Wallace, the developer of the very popular PC-Write word processor, claims he has only 7,000 registered users for his product, although he has sent out 40,000 copies through the mail and there are who knows how many other copies being used.[6]

An excellent source of information about shareware is Nelson Ford's organization, The Public (software) Library, which puts out a monthly newsletter and distributes what it considers to be the better shareware offerings. There is also an Association of Shareware Professionals that might be worth investigating.[7]

The success of a shareware product might make it easier to market your next product at a healthy price, especially if it is targeted to a business audience, since your previous product's success will give you name recognition and a reputation for quality, but you should limit your expectations for a shareware product to getting visibility, rather than big bucks.

If you plan to develop a product whose potential customer base is corporate managers your marketing strategy might be quite different. In this case you don't need to go retail. If you have built up strong personal contacts over the years you might be able to get a commitment from managers at a few local companies to install your stuff, probably by offering them a tremendous discount. This gives you the inestimable advantage of being able to tell other potential corporate customers that the XYZ Corporation has your code installed and that they love it. If your product is one that you can sell many copies of to a single customer you might be able to market it via a direct mail campaign, targeting managers, or through personal meetings with executives. Your personal reputation and business intelligence are the operant factors here.

The good thing about selling PC software to corporate customers is that they are much more likely to pay for each copy of a program that they use rather than just making copies.

An approach that has worked for some developers is forming a partnership with a large company. There are several advantages to this approach. What you are doing here is selling a percentage of your product to a large, well-known company. You still do all the

---

[6] Tom Stanton, "Shareware, Nominal Fees Can Yield Big Values," *PC Magazine*, May 13, 1986, p 195.

[7] The Public (software) Library can be reached at P.O. Box 35705, Houston, Texas 777235-5705

development work on the product, but they provide the following very important resources:

MAINFRAME TIME. The chances are that you do not have an IBM 3090 computer sitting in your family room (if you do, you probably don't need this book)! Even the smallest mainframe is way beyond the average person's means. Yet if your product is to run on mainframes you need one to do your testing on. Most companies take a dim view of your using their computers to test your own code while you are on their premises supposedly doing work they are paying for. You can purchase timesharing time on mainframes, but this is expensive. If you can make an arrangement with a large company to let you use its mainframe for your development work this will be of great use to you. If your product goes nowhere, at least you are not out the cost of all that computer time!

A TEST SITE. If you work in partnership with a large company that commits to installing your product in its final testing phase you get that most invaluable of experiences, the beta test. A beta test is the final test phase of a new product where the product is installed at a customer site with the understanding that it needs to run in production mode for a while to shake out otherwise undetectable errors. While you should have tried to debug every possible facet of your code, a beta test is going to turn up things you could never have dreamed of. The more people who pound away at terminals using your code, the better the prospects are for your product's long-term health.

MONEY. I don't know about you, but I develop code a lot better when I've had something to eat in the last week or so. If your arrangement with a partner company includes having them advance some cash for you, you can devote full time to the task at hand.

However the trade-off for getting all these benefits is that the company is going to get all their money back and then some if your product is at all successful. Any company entering a partnership with an unknown quantity—you—is going to give you most of the risk and themselves a tremendous cut of any profit.

You need to have excellent legal advice before entering into such a partnership. But even with the best advice you should be prepared to lose a substantial piece of the action if your product takes off. The realization of a decent profit is the only reason a corporation would be interested in sponsoring your efforts. And no company will show the slightest interest in your product unless it shows every sign of being a big moneymaker relatively quickly.

Whatever you give up, the benefits of corporate backing may outweigh the negatives. This is especially true if you intend to develop a series of products. Try to structure your partnership so that you retain total control of future products. If your software becomes successful and your company name starts to mean something you can eventually wean yourself from your original corporate backer.

The much-discussed "venture capitalist" is another alternative. Unlike the corporate sponsor the venture capitalist can only give you cash. In return for this you may find you have to sign away your first-born child. Think twice before putting yourself at the mercy of nontechnical backers whose only interest in your company is a 200 percent short-term return on their investment. You will be giving away a large part of your business for keeps. Again remember that venture capitalists will have no interest in you at all unless you are close to becoming profitable with a can't-fail product.

If money is all a venture capitalist could give you, look into alternative methods of raising funds. Some successful developers have been able to get bank loans on the equity in their homes. While this is chancy, at least when you do sell your product a good deal of the profit will remain yours, and you will not have to worry about investors selling out their shares to hostile interests.

## Using Your DP Apprenticeship to Prepare for Software Development

If you think you have what it takes to be a successful software developer, what is the best training you could provide for yourself in your first, apprenticeship, years?

The most obvious route would be to go to work for a software house and work for people who have been successful in the business that you want to enter. The best kind of software company to work for would be a relatively newly successful one because as companies get larger they lose their edge and become less efficient. I can guarantee that if you tried to develop software the way that the large vendors do you would be out of business in a year. Large companies have a momentum that overcomes the inefficiencies introduced by bureaucracy. They also tend to have large customer bases that have a significant enough investment in their products that they will tolerate problems that would put you out of business. Established companies can survive failures that newer ones cannot.

Unfortunately some of the failure that large companies can survive is introduced by hiring inexperienced programmers and training them, which large companies can afford to do but small ones cannot. What this means for you is that it is extremely unlikely that you can get recruited to work for a small, tough, software competitor straight out of school. You will have to have compiled an impressive resume and have very specific skills which such a company needs at the moment you appear to get such a job.

Small companies tend to be unstable too. So if you do get hired by a small company you might find your job evaporating at some hiccough of the business cycle. Successful small companies are often taken over by larger ones that fire half their staff or move them across the country to their own headquarters.

Thus, you might find it more advisable to work for a larger, stable company in the first years of your career. The successful software developers I've encountered received their training in large DP shops rather than in other software houses.

There are other benefits to a would-be developer in the large corporate DP shop. If you are careful about the jobs you select you should be able to build a solid base of technical expertise. You can also learn an applications area in depth, which is important if you want to develop applications software such as packages for insurance or financial users. Finally and most important, you will get to see what the business world is all about, an especially important consideration if you have been a sheltered techie throughout school as many good programmers have.

Corporations will provide the best customer base to you, the developer. They buy most of the software that gets sold, and they are accustomed to paying high prices for everything. Perhaps the best thing to do early in your career is to familiarize yourself with the nature of your potential customer so that when the time comes to create your product you can develop one with a good chance of success. The next best thing is get friendly with anyone who might ever rise to a position where they could buy your software for a corporation, or could place the resources of a corporate backer at your disposal.

Should you insist on a job with a "development" group? By now you might have noticed that I am less than enthusiastic about the way that most large companies develop code. You can learn a lot from corporate mistakes, and you will see a lot of these in a corporate development environment. But the only way you will succeed as a developer, I am convinced, is by religiously following the tenets of a structured design methodology. This is a practice to which most corporate development groups pay lip service but which very few practice. You may actually do your development career greater good by moving into a tech support area where almost no coding goes on but where you will learn the software internals of successful products. In the tech support world you will also get to see the technical problems that are costing companies big money—the very problems that you will profit from solving.

---

Of all the possible career paths open to you as a programmer software development is probably the hardest and yet it is the one that offers the greatest opportunity to take complete control of your destiny. If you are astute enough to develop and sell a successful product you may end up having a great number of programmers working for you in a few years. And you will be buying yourself the freedom to do things your way when you have proven in the marketplace that your way works.

# 7
# *Other Noncorporate Careers—Teaching and Sales*

You do not have to get a Ph.D. in computer science to have a satisfying career teaching programming. With the tremendous need for programmers in business a wide range of teaching careers has opened up for people who have experience as working programmers. These teaching careers range from those that might be poorly paid but are relaxed and enjoyable to those that are decidedly entrepreneurial and offer the opportunity to build a profitable training business.

You may be surprised at how few academic credentials are required to get the opportunity to teach college-level DP courses. Many technical colleges and two-year junior colleges will accept a long successful career as a programmer in a well-known local company in lieu of a college degree. If you are interested in teaching in such an environment you will probably start out teaching a single night course, usually for low pay. You can expect to be paid, at most, $1,000 a course. Considering all the time spent preparing assignments and correcting papers, and the time spent conducting lab sessions, your hourly rate is pretty low. However if you are interested in developing a teaching career you should look at teaching a course like this, not as a money-maker, but as an opportunity to discover whether you have a flair for teaching and whether it would be worthwhile for you to pursue teaching opportunities further.

The quality of the DP courses taught at two year colleges varies widely. My experience has been that Sun Belt states seem to have a greater commitment to providing high quality, inexpensive job-oriented classes to their populations. The programs I've seen in community colleges in Tennessee and Texas have been as good or better than the corresponding classes taught at the local four-year colleges. If you are lucky enough to teach in a well-run two-year school you will be expected to assign your students programs that closely mimic the kind of work they would produce in a business DP department. Your students would also be expected to code up five or six programs per course and run them until they get them to work. This is in contrast to the way mediocre four-year college often teach programming. In these schools students are assigned programs to code, but they submit them not to the machine, but to a teacher who grades them! Students in this kind of class are wasting their time since most of your real learning occurs debugging and resubmitting your code.

In a good school you will probably have to use the textbook that the department has selected, but you usually have a lot of freedom in how you structure your lectures. You will also have experienced teachers available to consult with when you have questions about teaching or when you encounter a problem.

In a well-run school you will be expected to flunk out a good number of students. It is only by maintaining the quality of those who graduate from their programs that the better schools earn a reputation for producing graduates who are worth hiring.

Sadly it seems that in the northeastern part of the United States there is still a more elitist attitude toward education. While technical colleges exist they often seem to be vocational schools designed for the academically feeble. The computer science courses taught in many of these are pretty dismal and do not prepare people for careers in the field. Some of the state community colleges teach mostly PC-oriented courses, of interest to the general population or to the small business person who wants to use off-the-shelf software in his business, but again these are not part of job training for people interested in programming careers. You will have to investigate which schools in your area offer good career-directed programming classes since this type of institution is the best place for a person with mainframe programming experience to teach.

In some areas of the country you might be able to teach in the local second-string four-year college. However four-year colleges tend to have more stringent qualifications for staff credentials than community colleges, and you might have to have at least an M.A. degree to teach credit courses at one of these. Look into the extension course offerings at one of these schools if you do not have the qualifications to teach credit courses. Some institutions, public and private, offer noncredit extension courses in subjects like CICS Internals, IDMS, and PASCAL. Such courses are usually taught by working programmers from the local community and are respected by local employers.

Teaching in a good local school can give you a little extra income and a lot of personal satisfaction if you are a person who enjoys the challenge of teaching. You will have the experience of being in charge of your class and winning their respect, and after doing it for a while you might decide to try teaching full time.

Landing a full-time teaching job is a lot harder than getting hired to teach a single course. If you have a master's degree in mathematics or computer science you may be able to teach full-time at a local college after you have proven yourself teaching a lot of single courses. However the competition for full-time academic positions is intense. These positions pay considerably more than teaching the same amount of part-time courses would, sometimes more than double for the same course, and they carry benefits that part-time positions do not. If you want to get one of these positions your chances are probably better if you cultivate your relationships with the administrators at the school and if your area is not full of unemployed programmers. If you have proven your worth by teaching evening courses you might succeed in promoting yourself into a full-time position if you are persistent and, I suspect, lucky.

There are also opportunities to teach at for-profit trade schools, but be wary. Often you will find such schools are more interested in hiring salespeople to promote their expensive programs than in getting excellent staff to teach them. Be careful not to associate yourself and your skills with a sleazy operation.

If you have a flair for teaching you might be attracted to the field of DP training. Companies that provide DP training contract with client companies to develop courses for their specific needs, or else they develop generic courses on timely topics which they sell to a number of different clients. These courses might cover technical topics, for example, the specifics of a software product like a database, or they might be more business oriented.

Many people who specialize in selling education to corporate customers focus on management training, since, not surprisingly, managers seem to like spending money on educating management rather than staff; they seem to have an endless hunger for courses on motivating employees, communicating, and dealing with stress.

Existing DP training firms sometimes recruit programmers to teach courses. Established seminar outfits like YOURDON, Inc., DBMI, or Digital Consulting work with freelance instructors who are paid on a daily basis. You might also be approached to teach such a course by a consulting firm, particularly if your resume shows expertise in an area that is currently a hot one in your region. If you have worked extensively with a database package that the largest local DP shop is about to install, you might be able to contract to teach the company's programmers how to use it. If you are a real entrepreneur you might be able to create and market such a course yourself.

A fellow consultant who has been trying for several years to establish his own indepenent training company tells me that the biggest problem is unreliable clients. This man quit his full-time job on the strength of a calendar full of scheduled corporate classes only to have his clients, one after the other, cancel the classes. Something as simple as snowstorm can cause your class to be canceled too. If you are teaching software courses you will be competing with software vendors who make money from their own courses. Nevertheless, it is possible to build up a business that does DP training if you are both a good businessman and the kind of teacher who can keep a class laughing while imparting a modest chunk of knowledge.

## How to Use Your DP Apprenticeship to Enter Teaching

Your emphasis in your apprenticeship years, if you want to be a teacher, should be on acquiring the information you want to teach. Exposure to the software that is just becoming popular will open DP training opportunities for you. If you are more interested in college teaching, the actual programming that you do in the corporate environment is not that important. What matters is the fact that you have done it for a respectable number of years. You might find a help desk position useful in getting an idea of the kinds of situations programmers find hard to deal with, so you can better prepare people to face them.

After you have spent a few years acquiring technical skills your company may invite you to teach a class to people within your organization. Make the most of this kind of opportunity. Some corporations have sophisticated in-house corporate education departments, and you might be able to move into one of these if you enjoy teaching.

Corporate training positions can be very satisfying for a person who loves to teach but can't function on a low academic salary. You have all the benefits of being a corporate employee but still spend your time teaching.

If you are interested in teaching, whether in the academic world or in industry, you will immeasurably strengthen your resume by publishing articles in your area of expertise. Articles printed in the trade press or in academic journals go a long way toward establishing you as an authority, whether you are one or not. Writing a book can be useful too, although it is best to be aware that the amount of money you make from a technical book will be tiny compared to what you could have earned applying the same technical skills to consulting. Writing is primarily valuable for giving you intangibles: the respect of your peers, the acquaintance of other specialists you might otherwise never have met, a base from which to effect change, and not the least, the satisfaction that comes from passing on your knowledge. Having published technical books you may well have the extra edge that makes you appealing to DP-training seminar houses and universities.

If running your own DP-training business is your goal then use your time in the corporate world to build the kind of visibility in the company that will bring you to the attention of middle level managers who are the ones with the authority to hire you later to teach. Building up a contact base is probably as important as learning your subjects. Maybe more so.

Needless to say you will have a much easier time establishing a DP-training business in a large urban community that is home to a lot of companies than in a smaller center, but with the expansion of computers into every phase of business, and especially their increasing use by knowledge workers, the next decades should provide ample opportunities for people building careers in DP education and training.

## Selling Programmer Services

If you have good local contacts, a good understanding of the business of programming, and an outgoing personality you may enjoy a career in sales.

Generally you won't find programmers going into hardware sales. Companies seem to recruit students directly out of college and then give them intensive in-house sales training. When companies look for experienced sales personnel to sell computer-related items the emphasis is usually on prior experience in sales rather than experience using computers.

Programmers sometimes are hired to be "sales engineers." These positions are for people who are technical assistants to actual salesmen. The S.E.'s role is to keep the customer happy, by helping with the technical analysis needed to provide a useful system tailored to his needs, and by solving problems that could put the ongoing relationship with the vendor in jeopardy. Additionally, the S.E.'s role is to keep the salesman grounded in reality, by curbing his wilder flights of fancy with technical information. While salespeople are paid a base salary plus commissions based on what they sell, the S.E. receives only a salary.

The only area in which experienced people can cross over into high-paying commission sales jobs is in the field of selling programmer services. These are the salespeople who work for headhunting firms, which we discussed before, and for consulting firms. They are usually paid a draw and commissions on the placements that they make.

Some of the characters who fill these sales positions appear to have gone into DP recruiting straight from selling used cars at the kind of car lots that advertise "E-Z Credit Terms." Quite a few sound and dress like gangsters. Whatever they lack in class however, they make up in the ability to make the sale. Managers laugh about them and tell funny stories about how they call anytime someone sneezes in the parking lot and inquire if the manager would like a replacement for his sick employee, but managers hire from these folks.

Other people who try this kind of work are ambitious young people with training in marketing, nice suits, and a very sketchy knowledge of programming.

The better consulting firms and headhunters, however, draw their salespeople from the ranks of competent programmers. These people have the advantage of being able to screen potential personnel intelligently and place them in positions that make the most of their talents. Some people move into these sales positions after having worked as contractors for consulting firms.

Ambitious contractors who have built up good contacts among both employers and programmers have been able to move directly into running small consulting companies, placing other contractors, and receiving the broker's 20 to 30 percent fee for their efforts. Before the 1986 tax reform this was a relatively simple thing to do; however you now must be scrupulous about collecting, withholding, and paying required employer's payments, such as unemployment compensation, or you could face prosecution by the IRS.

Sometimes entrepreneurs have combined placing programmers and writing software and done both in a small way while building up their businesses.

This is not work for the faint-hearted. To succeed in sales you must have a special knack. You must be able to deal with rejection and have a pretty good understanding of how people function. To place programmers either in permanent jobs or in contracting positions you must have a very good idea of what is going on in the businesses in your area and must always have an ear to the ground for news.

You will also have to become adept at dealing with problems that may come up between your clients and the people they hire. Particularly if you are placing contract programmers you must be able to intervene at any sign of friction and help the programmer deal with the problems that are causing the friction. Otherwise he could be out of a job, and you could lose your commission.

If you want to try your hand at selling programmer services your first job is to get the headhunting firm or consulting firm excited about you! Expect to be tested when you apply and display the same cheerful persistence and tact that you would use in placing others.

The washout rate is reportedly high in this field, particularly in the sleazier companies. In the "help wanted's" you will sometimes see agencies looking for DP recruiters and promising them indecent salaries and trips abroad. Common sense would suggest that starting out by working with the likes of these would be counterproductive. However you may have no choice. One successful headhunter in the Hartford area, whose company has a good reputation locally and is affiliated with a national DP placement network, told me that his company hires only people who have successfully withstood the rigors of starting out with one of the sleazier firms and established a record of successful sales work. The reason for this, he explained, is that it is extremely painful to watch a newcomer learning the trade. A new salesman goes through what he described as a "shock period." The established companies would prefer to hire people who have survived this period and know what it takes to make a placement.[1]

Some experienced programmers have been able to break into sales by working for small local consulting companies. These companies usually avoid the bad reputations associated with many headhunting companies. Your personal contacts are the way to find these jobs.

The rewards for the person who can put up with the constant rejection involved in this kind of work are great. Incomes above $100,000 a year are possible. Since these are sales positions your income directly corresponds to how good you are at selling. Headhunter salespeople usually are paid a draw and commissions on their sales. As mentioned before the headhunting company usually receives a fee of up to 30 percent of a placement's yearly salary. This fee is then divided between the company and the salesman who made the placement according to a formula that varies with the individual company and the salesman's standing within that company. Usually the salesman receives half or less of the commission.

There are several different methods for paying salespeople in consulting firms. Some firms pay a salary and a flat commission for each placement, for example $1,000 for a six-month contract. Others pay their salespeople a base salary and a percentage of the hourly rate that they are billing the consultant out at, typically something near 10 percent of his rate.

However, you should be aware that your earnings in the placement business will fluctuate with the business cycle. When recession

---

[1] Personal phone interview with Mark Jacobs, Senior Consultant, Data Pros, 50 Founders Plaza, East Hartford, CT 06108.

threatens and layoffs begin few companies will be paying you to find them employees, so no matter how successful you are, you should build up a cash reserve for possible hard times.

Recruiters with bona fide, respected headhunter and consulting firms have another career option open to them. If the pressure of commission sales becomes too much for them, they can move into positions as recruiters in the personnel offices of large prestigious companies. The wiser companies that use a lot of DP personnel are already moving toward developing staffs of people who are actually capable of reading and interpreting a programmer's resume, since it is a lot cheaper to pay such people and pay them well than to pay that same money and more to headhunter firms. Some companies are experimenting with developing their own consultant force, too, to bring down consultant costs. If you develop real expertise in recruiting and placing DP personnel but don't want to have to deal with the nerve-wracking hassles of running a placement firm of your own you might be able to set up a very profitable business consulting with personnel departments on how to improve their DP recruiting. There should be a lot of opportunity in this area in years to come.

Again I must caution you that the kinds of jobs we are discussing in this section are open to you only if you live in a major urban area with a large number of programmers working in it. In smaller towns, and cities with few DP shops most DP recruiters work out of regular employment offices and generally have a low level of actual DP expertise. In these cases one recruiter's sales territory may encompass several states. It is only in the major DP centers that you can expect to be able to support yourself by concentrating only on DP placement.

## Using Your DP Apprenticeship to Prepare for Sales

There is no particular background that would lend itself to preparing you for sales better than any other. Probably some team leader experience would be useful. So would any other experience where you are responsible for getting people to work toward a goal together. If you are not able to motivate the people you work with it is unlikely that you will be able to motivate perfect strangers. However the main thing to do is keep your ears open and talk to all the people you encounter in your various jobs. Where did they work before? What was it like? What kind of software did they use? How many programmers were there at that site? Every time you hear a manager's name anywhere, write it down in a small notebook. Save corporate telephone books. The numbers will change but you will have a base to start with. Go to Data Processing Managers Association (DPMA) meetings, and strike up conversations with everyone you meet there. Go to Toastmasters luncheons. Again, anyone you make any kind of connection with who has the slightest chance of developing into a manager should be noted down in your book. If you see that someone has been promoted, give them a call and congratulate them. Your capital will be the people you can call up who will tell you the local scuttlebutt.

An intelligent, capable person who goes into the field of selling programmer services can provide a valuable service both to the programmers he places in jobs they enjoy and to the managers who hire them. You are not in a social service field, it is true. But if you can make your clients and the people you place happy the result for you will be repeat sales and long-term business success.

## One Last Word about Career Paths

Throughout the previous chapters we've stressed that your personality, technical skills, and geographical location will have a lot to do with which career paths you pursue. You can also do a lot to control the direction of your career by paying attention to the information in the next part of this book which focuses on the details of selecting a job since the particular positions you fill in the early years of your career will do more to shape that career than any other single factor.

But like anything else in life your career will be subject to "X-Factors"—forces beyond the control of any one individual. The personalities of your supervisors, the fate of your employers, and your own being at the "right place at the right time"—or conversely, the wrong place—will also have a big effect on your career. In looking at my own career, for example, I have to admit that its shape was really determined by the simple fact that my first manager assigned me to a terminal which was one of the few in the building set up for using the APL programming language. Since I was not programming in APL and the person I was sharing the terminal with was, I ended up giving her the terminal and using one in the office of a Systems Analyst on an unrelated project. This, in turn, led me to spend a lot of time with the Systems Analyst, who, as result of our conversations, asked to have me transferred to work with him on his project, which happened to be the installation of prototype PROFS product. Since I had selected my first job specifically for the exposure to IMS database processing which it offered, this turn of events effectively nullified my original plans, while opening up a whole new set of experiences I had never dreamed of.

You too, can expect a certain amount of random effects in your career.

Then too, the pace of technological change means that none of us can really predict what the programmer's career will look like ten or fifteen years in the future. On the upside, new technologies as revolutionary as the personal computer revolution may emerge, providing yet more situations that call for the skills of talented programmers. On the downside, some industry pundits are suggesting that programming jobs may follow manufacturing jobs to Asia and other places where people can live on fifty dollars a month, leaving American programmers with no work at all!

The moral of this is that each of us in planning our career should expect our plans to be flexible and subject to radical change at any time. You will never, really, be done with choosing your career path! At every phase of your career you should be looking at trends in the broader marketplace, keeping aware of what new forces are coming into play, and considering how they might affect your future.

Flexibility and the constant expectation of change—refusing to let yourself get into a rut—coupled with planning and the determination to take control of your own career, will in the long run lead you to a satisfying career, even if it turns out no to be what you had originally had in mind.

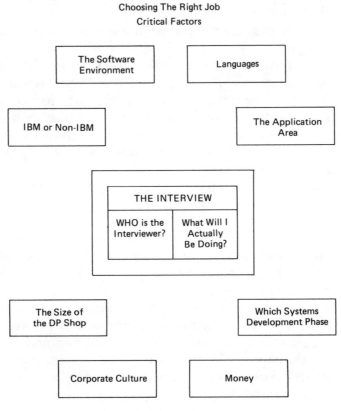

Figure 3

# 8
# *Choosing the Right Job*

The first part of this book was designed to give you an overview of the kinds of career paths open to you as a mainframe programmer. We have not exhausted all the possibilities open to you, but we have covered the pathways taken most frequently by people who have chosen a mainframe data processing career.

My assumption has been that you will start your career by going to work for a middle-sized or larger company and that after five years or more spent in a DP apprenticeship you will be ready to move on into whatever direction you have chosen for your long-term career. Figure 1 facing page 1 illustrates the early stages the programmer must pass through and the optional paths that are open to him after he has completed his apprenticeship.

The decision of which direction to take can only be made by you. And you must be honest with yourself in assessing your interests and your needs. A decision to become a software developer would be foolish if you are a person who rarely comes up with innovative ideas. If you intend to keep your hair in its current spiked mohawk, perhaps you would be ill-advised to choose management—unless you had very good connections in a very unconventional company. It is not the role of this book to tell you which direction to take. I hope that reading the preceding chapters has given you some idea of the directions that are open to you, and that you have gotten the idea that you can take steps at any point in your career to prepare for taking one or another direction at a future time.

The key to being able to go in any direction, though, is to begin at your current situation. The problem for most of us is hooking up this present situation with the future we would like to build for ourselves. In short, most of us know more about the future we would like to have than we know about how to get there from where we are now.

With that in mind I would like to help you develop an approach to evaluating either your current or a potential job, with the aim of showing you how to identify the jobs that will give you the training you need to achieve your chosen career goals.


## Why People Hate Job Hunting

Most people spend a lot more time and energy looking for a new car than they do looking for a new job.

There are good reasons for this. Most of us look for a new job in a state of anxiety, especially if we are not currently employed. If we have no current source of income this tends to obscure any other career goals we ought to have. Most of us take the first job that offers us a salary within the range we have decided we must have.

Many people loathe being interviewed. They hate the feeling of being put under the microscope and examined for flaws. I know of people who have stayed for years in jobs they hated just because they were phobic about the interview process. This is not helped by the fact that some interviewers really do try to trip people up at the interview or grill them with trick technical questions, sometimes memorized from textbooks, which bear little relationship to the job the applicant is applying for.

Finally if you already have a job, the chances are that the forces of inertia will work to keep you there. It is just plain easier to show up every morning in your rumpled suit and do the predictable task you've been doing for a while than to plunge into finding a new and unknown environment and go though the hard work of establishing yourself there. Many people work in jobs that they know intellectually are doing nothing for them in the long run because of this seductive ease.

Most people feel helpless in the job hunting situation. They don't feel in control, and they don't know how to go about getting the job they want. They job hunt when they must, leaving to chance what position they end up with.

I can't make it easier for you to go out and find a new job. Nor am I going to go over the well-trodden subjects of crafting a resume or conducting an interview. There are many of books already available on these and other job-hunting topics.

I can, however, give you a framework for thinking about the different kinds of programming jobs in a down-to-earth and very specific way that can help you decide what kind of job it is you really need. It is then up to you to psych yourself into believing that a job exists that has the characteristics you want—and then go out and find it. You should expect your job hunt to take time. Fundamental to this process is the fact that you are going to have to reject jobs before you find the one that is just right.

I am going to present, one by one, eight factors that you should consider when thinking about a possible job. We will look at each factor to see why it is important in your job selection. We will also try to show how each factor can affect your achievement of your long-term career goals.

I have my own biases. I've worked with a lot of programmers and seen too many of them with many years of so-called experience that have led them only to frustrating dead-end jobs. I place a large premium on keeping as many options open for yourself as possible. That way if the path you have followed turns out not to be as interesting or rewarding as you had expected you will still be able to try other avenues. Nevertheless there are contented individuals who have built careers in highly idiosyncratic fashions that contradict most of the principles I would recommend. My advice is based on going with the percentages. If you are an extraordinary person you can do extraordinary things with your career that the average programmer would not be able to pull off. However, for the rest of us who can't count on brilliance or luck, avoidance of the pitfalls I mention may spell the difference between a a career you consider successful or finding yourself ten years down the line completely burned out.

If you consider the following factors before you go to a job interview you will be best prepared to enter the interview able to ask the questions you need to ask to determine whether this is going to be the job that gets you where you want to be or one that you should pass by.

In some cases you will need to do some homework before you get to the interview to find out facts about the company and to check things out with people who have worked there. In other cases, you will get the answers you need during the interview itself.

At the end of this book you will find twenty-five sets of questions. These questions were selected to show you the kinds of things you should feel free to ask about at an interview. Each of them relates to a topic covered somewhere in the book. Naturally you won't be able to ask all or even most of them, but by familiarizing yourself with the list you should be able to spot troubling signs or, conversely, selling points of a job you are considering. Decide before the interview which of these questions are the most important to you, then make sure that you don't get so carried away by the heady atmosphere of the interview situation that you forget to ask them!

Figure 3 on page 132 graphically illustrates the many elements you have to consider when making a job decision.

Taking the following factors seriously and using them to shape the interview process will give you two advantages. First of all you will be able to exert some control over your future by selecting your job, rather than, like most people, letting it select you. The second advantage is that if you do the research you should do before the interview, you will come across to an interviewer as much more aware than the people you are competing with, and thus, more likely to be hired.

Some of the factors we will cover relate to the nature of the company you are considering, they concern structural features of the company and the more elusive characteristics that make up its personality. Others relate to the kind of work the company can offer you. We will look at the software environment from several different perspectives and we will look at what application you should choose and where a project will fit in the project development cycle. Finally we will talk about the subject of money.

No job is going to be perfect. For that matter, few jobs will turn out to be exactly as they were described at the interview. What you must do is define what factors are the most important to you and try to find a position you are certain embodies those factors in a way closest to what you want.

If you are starting your job hunt fresh out of school and your credentials are far from breathtaking, obviously you cannot afford to be too highly selective. You may well have to do the best you can with whatever you can line up. But you can still have some minimal standards that will keep you from accepting a job that will frustrate all your career hopes. And even if you are beginning with less than a running start don't forget that in two years you may well have an experience level that will open up a broader range of possibilities. You can apply more rigorous standards then.

If you are a more-experienced person, you can afford to be choosier. You must also, unfortunately, be more suspicious. The more qualified you are the more hiring managers will tend to exaggerate and bend the facts to attract you to what they know is a mediocre job. It is all that much more important to come prepared to ask the revealing questions that will expose the truth. And don't analyze just the new job with these factors—look at your current job and current company as well. Be certain that you cannot attain your long-term goals by making minor adjustments in your current situation before committing yourself to making major and irrevocable changes which must, by their nature, subject you to greater levels of uncertainty than you have in a known job.

Building your career is not easy, but you are way ahead of most people as soon as you take the responsibility for shaping that career into your own hands. If you devote to your job search the same energy and hard work you gave to doing well in school and on the job you can find the jobs that will build a lifetime of career enjoyment.

## What You Must Learn at the Interview

Before we look at the factors that define a job, let's look briefly at the interview itself. This is particularly important if you are about to interview for your first job.

When you are in an interview situation you should assume that you will be a bit flustered or "hyper." Since in that state you can't remember very much, focus on the essential: You should try to do is emerge from the interview able to answer the following two questions:

- What is the role of the person I am talking with and what relation does it bear to my possible future position?
- What will I actually, specifically, be doing?

These might seem like obvious questions, but they are not. All too often new hires jump to conclusions about the answers to these questions that lead to real unhappiness when they take the job.

### Whom Am I Talking To?

I wish I had a dollar for every new hire I've met who has told me that he took one job rather than another because he liked the personality of the person who interviewed him for that position best.

This is probably the worst mistake you can make. Any experienced corporate employee has learned that the chances are good you will never again have anything more than a nodding acquaintance with the person who interviewed you.

This is because in most companies the interview is not conducted by the person who will be your boss but by that person's boss. It is the interviewer's job to see you and evaluate you. If he decides to hire you he will then assign you to the team leader in whose group he feels you can make the best contribution.

In some companies you may be introduced to the person who will actually direct your work, and you may get to speak with him briefly, but this is by no means the rule. Even when you are interviewed by a supposed boss the nature of business is that things change. Often by the time you are ready to begin your job this boss has been transferred to another department.

You should always take the time to determine what role the interviewer plays in the organization you are interviewing for. The interviewer will take this as a sign of intelligence on your part. If he pulls out an organizational chart study it with interest, it can tell you a lot about the situation you are getting into. Many applicants are so eager to impress at the interview that they plunge into descriptions of highly technical achievements before determining if the person they are talking to is a technical or administrative person. It is very embarrassing to discover that the person you are snowing doesn't begin to understand what you are talking about.

If the interview is going well and your interest is growing, feel free to ask if you will meet the person who would be your boss. Just remember that there are no guarantees. What you should be looking at is not the individual you are introduced to but his characteristics, what his nature tells you about the organization. Does he seem intelligent? Does he seem harried or overburdened? How does he respond to his own boss? With relaxed friendliness or with wariness and forced joviality? Even if the actual people you get to work with are not the ones you see at the interview, you will usually find that the company's style remains the same.

Rarely, if ever, do you get to meet the people who will be your coworkers. Most companies see no point in having them be a part of the interview process. If you are otherwise favorably impressed with a job opportunity it might be a good idea to ask a simple question or two about the people you will be working with. Keep your questions generic. Are there a lot of recent college hires? Have most of the people in the department been with the company a long time? The only specific question you should feel free to ask is what happened to the last person who had the job you are interviewing for. If that person was promoted into a higher-status job you will usually be told about it. Otherwise you will be told that you are filling a newly created job or given a vague answer.

Keep your eyes open as you walk through the building. Look at what people have on their walls and compare it with what you would have. A place where everyone has posters with cute pictures of kittens is going to be quite different from a place where all you see is trophies, or diplomas. If you see nothing that shows personal taste at all that in itself tells you something about the company's personality.

You might ask whether the pleasant (or not-so-pleasant) offices you are passing are where you will be working. More than once I've been told no, the department I'm interviewing for is located in the basement.

By making no assumptions during the interview process you will save yourself some nasty surprises.

## What Will I Be Doing?

It would seem that you should expect to be told what a job you are interviewing for is all about. But all too often you are not. All too often interviewees jump to dangerous and damaging conclusions.

I mentioned before that the person who interviews you is rarely the person who will be your boss. Unfortunately this means that he rarely knows what you will actually be doing. Frequently the interviewer shares with you his own broad view of the project. This is the view that he must have to run the project. Often this results in the interviewer telling you about the more interesting features of the entire project—and a project can involve up forty or fifty people at all levels. He may mention a new development project that is planned or tell you about a new state-of-the-art technology that the project employs, for example, a network of PC's communicating with a host relational database. Unfortunately the portion of the project he has you slated for has nothing to do with this interesting stuff. It is all being done by old-timers who have worked in this project for years. You may be getting interviewed for a job off-loading boring maintenance tasks from the people who are going to work on these new projects.

Remember that a project manager may be responsible for five or six related areas which he views as a whole. He wants to present the project to you in its most favorable light. The truth may also be that he has no idea what he will have you working on. Often it may take months and reams of paperwork for managers to get permission to hire new people so they often stock up on them while they can, even if they have no specific role in mind. After they have met you and the other applicants, they will decide who they want and what they are best suited for.

Because of this you are in somewhat of a quandary. If the interviewer really doesn't know what he is going to have you do you can't very well pin him down. If you demand specifics he will often tell you something off of the top of his head, but you can be sure that it is not what you will be assigned to when you show up for work.

At other times the job to be filled is very clearly defined. The only thing that can go wrong here is that the department is reorganized, as occurs about twice a year in many businesses, and the job you were originally hired for is eliminated.

Again, your best bet is to look at the broader picture of the project and determine the flavor of what is going on. If you can see a couple of different jobs within the project that would interest you, the chances are that you could eventually get into one of them even if the job you start out with is less than ideal. However if you are shown a terrific sounding job but what the rest of the people on the project do seems pretty drab, be careful, you might easily end up with one of their jobs, rather than the bait the interviewer held out to you.

Finally, if you know anyone who works at the company, pump them for information. Usually the company grapevine can tell you something about the people and the jobs in the area you are interested in.

If you do neglect to ask an important question at the interview you have a second chance to ask, after an offer is made to you. Don't feel you must instantly respond to a job offer when you get a phone call. Instead ask if you can contact the person offering the job. Most companies will be happy to let you phone that person. Then finish up the interviewing process and try to get the answers you need to make sure that the job is for you.

If you get a strong, hard-to-quantify feeling during an interview, take it seriously. You may be picking up on some subliminal features that months of experience will only confirm. Try not to talk yourself into something just because you are desperate to make a change and don't want to have to keep interviewing. None of us gets that many chances to change jobs, and each job you take has a major impact on your future career development. You owe it to yourself to find a job that you feel good about, and finding such a job may take some time.

# 9
# Factors—The Size of the DP Shop

The size of the DP shop where you start your career can have a tremendous effect on the shape of your career—more than you might realize when you start the job-hunting process.

The term "DP Shop" may not appeal to people who like to think of computer programming as a professional occupation. The word "shop" brings with it a certain proletarian tinge. It sounds tough and gritty and has overtones of people doing real work as opposed to the glorified puzzle solving we programmers do. However, this is the term used, particularly among recruiters. What it refers to is the total computer environment of a company, taken as a whole. The important fact to grasp is that as a programmer you need to be more concerned with the size of the DP shop within the company rather than the size of the company itself. Many people are surprised to discover that some large and well-known companies employ only a small number of programmers, while some outfit they have never heard of has many times more.

This is not to say that the size and strength of the company as a whole is not important. It is. You should have some idea of any potential employer's fiscal health as reflected in its more recent quarterly reports. The best job in the world is worthless if the company folds, and this does happen. I know of two situations where companies in their death throes went on hiring binges bringing on board expensive, experienced programmers who were relocated from other parts of the country, in the vain hope of salvaging the company. A month or so later management threw in the towel on the divisions that these programmers were brought in to serve and out the door they went, faced with the grim need to find new jobs in an unknown city.

You should try to work for companies with a history of quarterly earnings, not losses. But don't confuse the size or importance of a company with the size and importance of its DP shop.

The size of the company's DP shop is reflected in two statistics: the number of programmers working within the company and the number of mainframes and minicomputers (not PC's!) that the company has installed.

## How Large Is Large?

One industry that uses a great number of programmers is the insurance industry. What insurance companies have to sell is their ability to track huge numbers of customers, claims, investments, and agents. All these things lend themselves to computerization, and the insurance industry was among the earliest to computerize. A large insurance company can easily have three or four thousand programmers working for it.[1] Some of the largest insurers have more.

At the other end of the spectrum, a manufacturing company that uses computers only for bookkeeping functions might have only twenty programmers or less. As you move down the scale you find a good number of smaller companies, many of them producing products or services with trade names you as a consumer recognize that have mom-and-pop-style DP shops. In such a company there might be three people supporting a minicomputer system that performs billing and accounting functions. These systems often run off-the-shelf software rather than systems designed and coded by their own programmers. Some companies of this size will advertise for a

[1] "Color Me Blue," *Datamation,* January 1, 1987, cites a figure of 3,000 programmmers at The Travelers Insurance Company in Hartford. Aetna has more.

computer programmer/operator who is responsible for running programs, customizing packages, cleaning and maintaining the printers, and maybe even ripping listings off the printer and delivering them. The job title for a job like this might even be "DP Manager."

With the introduction of PC's, computers became available to very small businesses. You often see ads for programmers to work for a small business where the owner bought himself a PC but never figured out how to use it. In this case you are talking about a DP shop of one. However jobs of this type are rarely full time.

The number of programmers employed by a company tells you a lot about the size of its shop, however that, in and of itself, doesn't tell the whole story. The kinds of mainframes in use and the software they are running tends to separate into large systems and smaller systems. A small life insurance company that employs fifty programmers and uses a DOS/VSE operating system running batch jobs on an IBM 4341 computer is a small shop. This is because IBM's mainframe DOS system is thought of as a small systems operating system. Even though it runs on the same family of machines as MVS, DOS provides less function and is usually found in smaller, less technically sophisticated shops. If you rack up a few years' experience in an environment like this you will be thought of as a small shop programmer and might find it hard to switch into a large shop environment.

Along the same lines, you might work for a different small insurance company that had the same fifty programmers and a similar IBM 4381 computer but was running an on-line network with an MVS operating system. Although this machine is not one of IBM's top-of-the-line workhorses it is running the same operating system the workhorses do, and it is the operating system the programmer uses that defines whether he is in a large or small shop environment. The programmer with this experience, particularly if he has had a chance to root around debugging the on-line portion of the system and learn on-line internals, would have no problem at all switching into a job in a much larger shop. In fact, he might be able to get a much better job there than he could have evolved to entering the large shop first because it would be much harder to get the internals exposure in the large shop environment.

A final determinant of the size of a company's DP shop is how many different and dissimilar computer systems the company maintains. A large insurance company that has five hundred people supporting its personal lines insurance products might actually be supporting fifteen different versions of the same system. What I mean by that is that there might be a daily batch system for homeowner's insurance, and a daily batch system for car insurance in a set of states that have similar legislation governing auto insurance, and yet another system for car insurance in the state of Massachusetts (which is a law unto itself) and yet more insurance daily batch systems for individual and for group health insurance. In moving from one system to another you will learn that the systems are all doing the same things in similar ways. They may have all been cloned from the same base system years before. Only the details relating to the business side of the application will vary. Although this is definitely a large shop, compare it to another company which has two hundred programmers in a manufacturing environment. This company might have an inventory system that uses minicomputers in the warehouse to collect data and send it to mainframe databases. It might have computerized accounting systems that run through a large batch cycle with an on-line query system that executives use to track their operations. This company might have floor control systems that monitor and control the manufacturing process and collect performance data on the manufacturing equipment. There may be computer aided design systems (CAD) around, utilizing state-of-the-art hardware and software. It might even have a mainframe document library system used by the company's technical writers for in-house documentation and manuals.

Even though there are fewer programmers in this environment, it is clearly a larger shop since the variety of different computer applications that the programmer could get involved in is much greater.

There are advantages to working in small mainframe shops and advantages to working in the larger ones. Let's look at the good and bad of each.

## The Large Shop

### Advantages of a Large Shop

The best thing about working for a company with large, diversified DP operations is that the chances are that if you don't find your first job compelling, you will be able to find something different within the same company without having to quit and lose all the benefits you have built up with the company. Very big companies sometimes act like collections of loosely associated, smaller independent companies. In big companies like this each individual DP area often has its own distinct personality. This can mean that moving from one part of the company to another can feel like moving to an entirely different company. When I worked for IBM I found that switching jobs within IBM divisions exposed me to radically different ways of doing things. Everything changed when I changed jobs within the company, from the way I was expected to dress to the frequency with which my paycheck was issued. Because of the size of the company the different divisions had substantially different corporate cultures although certain fundamentals, like IBM's famous policy of respect for the individual, were unchanging no matter the location.

For example, in my first job at IBM it was expected that when you received a promotion you would treat your coworkers to something. At lower levels it was donuts all around. As you progressed up the ladder the treats got more expensive and entry into middle-level management could entail contributing (along with others at your rank) to an open bar for one hundred programmers after work on Friday.

At the second IBM location such behavior would have been looked at askance. However in this group you could always expect that the achievement of any project objective would be followed with a company paid luncheon and the awarding of gewgaws.

At the first location dress was casual, and even managers wore suits only if they had an important meeting scheduled for the day. At the second location everyone dressed like the famed IBM sales force. Programmer dress was carefully scrutinized and managers had been known to call programmers to task for wearing what they considered to be "inappropriate" footgear (too casual).

The reasons for these differences lay partly in the functions of the business which the DP areas were supporting. The first location was a factory located in a remote country location. The second was a central marketing headquarters located in a conservative urban center. However these differences highlight that a large company gives you the opportunity to change your environment radically without having to quit. And this means that the reputation you build within the company, your most valuable personal asset, remains undiluted.

Some companies offer geographical diversity. If you would like to move around the country or even go outside the United States to other nations this is a real possibility with such a company. This is particularly true if you select a company that has far-flung operations and does not centralize its DP services. If a company has twenty plants and each has its own independent DP system you have a good chance of moving during your programming career with that company—whether you want to or not. Companies that sell DP services such as large consulting firms or larger software developers also provide travel opportunities for the programmer who proves himself within the organization.

This "advantage" works both ways. When you are interviewing for a job with a company that has widespread DP operations you need to ask some explicit questions about how likely you are to remain at the location you are being hired into. Some companies will tell you that you will be expected to move when and where they need you to and will let you know that the job you are being hired into is part of a project that is going to wind down in two years and free you to move to an entirely different part of the country. Other companies are not so forthcoming, or to put it in a better light, may not be able to foretell the effects that changes in their business will have on where they locate programmers. When Electronic Data Systems of Dallas was bought by General Motors a large number of its programmers around the country suddenly received marching orders for Detroit and Indiana where General Motors plants were located.

Obviously if you are tied to a particular part of the country you would do best to stick with a company that has its DP functions centralized in one or two locations, as many of the insurance and banking companies are. In this case you won't be forced to move or lose your job in the future.

This issue is particularly important if your spouse has a career too. Many companies boast that they have programs to aid spouses when one of the couple is relocated, but these efforts usually boil down to writing up a resume and paying employment agency fees (which you wouldn't need for a professional level job!). If your spouse is also building a career and your lifestyle depends on both salaries, then being forced to move can spell real economic hardship, and generate resentments that can harm your marriage.

If you are attracted to a company because it has programmers working at locations that you find particularly appealing, but you are not interviewing for a job in one of those locations make sure the job you would be getting will give you the skills required at the location you would like to be transferred to. Often companies have radically different skill requirements from one installation to another, and you might find that the transfer you had hoped for is impossible.

Some caution is in order, but I have known programmers who were sent, with all travel and lodging paid, on long-term assignments to Hawaii and London. Many programmers value their profession because it offers them the possibility of living in almost any urban center they choose. The trick here, as with so much else in evaluating a job, is to know what you are getting into before you make your decision.

Besides offering physical diversity, large shops can offer exposure to a much wider range of hardware and software. If you want to develop yourself as a technical programmer you should pay attention to any opportunity to work in an environment where the company has installed (or even better is installing) hardware and software from a number of mainstream vendors, including "Big Blue."

Not only do larger companies have more computers and computer applications installed than smaller ones, they also have more money to throw around experimenting with new approaches. They are more likely to have several development projects going at once. Working within such a company, you might be trained in a state of the art software environment that is being tested at the company before the vendor releases it to other companies. This way you get a jump in adding a potentially "hot" item to your "bag of tricks." Vendors like IBM or Wang choose certain good customers with whom they have a comfortable relationship as "beta test sites." This means that the vendor gives the customer site a prerelease version of a piece of software and then works closely with the company's technical personnel to deal with the bugs that emerge as the software is used. This way the vendor gets to do the final debugging of his software in a real-world environment, and the customer gets to have the most advanced technology first. If you are lucky enough to be associated with the beta test of a product that becomes a success, the dollar value of your knowledge is enormous. You will have the ability to work in almost any company that is thinking of implementing the software you have mastered. If you are thinking of being a consultant you can charge the highest rates for this kind of knowledge.

If you have decided that you want to become a systems programmer you have very little choice except to work for a company with a large shop. These are the only companies that train people in systems programming. Generally, smaller companies have only one or two systems programmers on their staffs and they do not have the resources to train people in systems. Typically they raid larger companies for the people they have trained, luring them with high salaries.

The larger shop with its "cast of thousands" might just have a cast of fifty systems programmers. Usually these companies have evolved training programs designed for applications programmers who have demonstrated technical aptitude in their earlier assignments. If you yearn to be a supertechie then you should try to build your reputation for technical wizardry in a large shop environment where you can be rewarded by being offered this kind of training.

A word of advice is in order before you go this route: you must make sure to get some exposure to Assembly language programming if you want to advance toward the technical side of the house. No matter how good a programmer you might be in COBOL you won't get considered for positions where you learn software internals unless you can demonstrate some exposure to assembly language and dump reading. This is often a stated prerequisite for entry-level tech support jobs.

Large DP shops offer advantages if you have decided that your career goal is to develop into a manager. This is simply because a larger DP shop needs more DP managers than a small one. Large companies with huge bureaucracies also tend to have formalized paths for developing management personnel that include classroom training. Large companies also are forced to pay a little more attention to equal opportunity issues. Although I know of no companies where women DP managers outnumber men, there now seem to be more women managers at both entry level and middle levels in companies that have a lot of management positions.

In a small DP shop you might have to wait until the three current managers quit or die, whereas a large growing DP shop will be creating new projects and new project teams which, in turn, creates new management slots you can fill.

In an earlier chapter we've looked at the advisability of going into DP management, and again I caution you against expecting to ever reach a truly "executive" level coming from a programming background; but if you would like to have a career that leads to middle management the more DP managers there are in a company you work for the better your chances of breaking in.

Large DP shops have other advantages. They may offer better benefit packages (although many larger companies have, in the past few years, been cutting benefits back). A company-matched pension plan might not set your pulses racing when you are twenty-two contemplating your first job, but in fifteen years you might be grateful to know that there is a little something waiting for you when you hit the end of your working years.

Large shops as we've mentioned often have formal education programs. Some have whole education organizations with classrooms and professional instructors whose only job is to teach technical courses. Much of the technical training that can set you up for a career as a supertechie or top consultant is taught in these courses, and often these courses are given to applications people when they've done an especially good job.

*Problems with the Large Shop*

The very diversity and size that makes the large shop so attractive creates some problems too. While the company may teach just those courses you want to take, getting your management to send you to them can prove almost impossible. Managers are not stupid, and they know what is of value on the open market. They are not likely to provide you with a new skill set that will substantially improve your marketability to their competitors until you have proven your loyalty to the company in concrete and time-absorbing ways.

Usually when you are interviewed for a large DP shop the hiring manager will promise you that you will be sent to two or three courses a year. Some companies go so far as to make it a requirement that each employee at a professional level get a certain amount of annual training. Unfortunately what usually happens is that in your first year you get a lot of training in the nuts and bolts stuff you need to know to perform your job. For example, you might get some classes in JCL, or classes teaching you how to use the editor or move programs into production. But when your second year rolls around instead of getting the technical classes you crave you will find yourself going to workshops on "Stress Reduction," "Improving Business Communications," or even "Creative Parenting for the Working Parent." The closest you will usually get to technical classes is a seminar on structured design, which would be great if you were ever permitted to use what you were taught on the job!

IMS internals, PC networking, and other hot topics will probably have to wait until you have given five or more years of service to the company.

The frustrations of working in a large company often boil down to the fact that although everything you might want is right there somewhere, the company is so big that you can never find it. You will need to be very sharp and very much devoted to controlling the direction of your career to avoid being pushed down career avenues that are useful to the company but not in line with your own goals.

This brings us to what is perhaps the most dangerous illusion that people working in large organizations fall into—this is the belief that if you work hard and do a good job with what you have been assigned the company will reward you by giving you the assignments that are the best for developing your long-term career.

Many programmers look at the mechanisms of performance reviews, especially the section where the employee lists his career goals, and assume that the company is dedicated to actively trying to help them attain these goals. As a result, they allow their managers to do their career planning for them. It doesn't work. The company will see that you get the occasional congratulatory plaque, the appropriate rewards banquet, and whatever unfilled job it has available at the moment you are not needed on your current project. In short, relying on the company for career development is entrusting your future to random chance. The company satisfies its short-term needs, not your own long-term ones.

To let a lower level manager steer you to a new job can be career suicide. That is because the company's best use for you is to have you continue doing what you have already done well. This means you will not enlarge your "bag of tricks" or widen your experience in a way that opens more options for your own future. At worst you can become so specialized in some obscure area, of value only to your company, that down the line when the company has moved away from that technology or application, you may be told not to expect advancement because you don't have skills they need. It sounds grim but it happens.

The only person in the corporate environment who is really interested in helping you develop a long-term career is you, yourself. The sooner you accept this and take on the responsibility, the sooner your career will progress.

You can, however, utilize the fiction that the company projects of wanting to build your career to your own advantage.

Your first step must be to work hard and work smart until you have established the kind of reputation that causes you to stick out from the crowd of people at your level. Without this as a basis any strategy can only backfire.

Once you have established yourself you must constantly agitate in a tactful but determined way, asking for specific opportunities you have decided you need. You must be able to demonstrate that it would be to the ultimate advantage of the company to give you the jobs or the training that you are requesting. You must also do as much self-training as possible to show how well invested the company's education dollars will be in you. You must take pains to project a feeling of corporate loyalty and not make snide remarks in departmental meetings. If, like a lot of bright people, you project the feeling that you are too good for where you are working no one is likely to give you training that would be your ticket out!

Finally, when you are due a new assignment let management know what you would like to move into long enough before the change is made so that they can take your wishes into account. Management is often very responsive to well-thought-out requests for assignments because they are unusual. Most workers are confused about what they want and only ask vaguely for "something more interesting" to do. By having a clear idea of the direction you want to go you are making things easy for your managers, as long as you have a realistic idea of your abilities.

You do have to understand the organization you work for and the principles it operates on. No one is going to move you into management six months after you enter the company as a college new hire. Neither are they going to send you to operating system internals class when you have only served one year maintaining a batch system. What you have to do is identify the series of logical steps that leads from the job you have to the job you want, steps that you identify by studying the careers of people in your organization who are doing the things you would like to be doing. Then you can suggest a viable move to management which they can let you make, particularly if you have served the company well and they would like to reward you.

There is another problem you may encounter in large DP shops. It is one that grows out of the way that many large DP shops have organized the work that they have to do. A company that employs three thousand programmers knows it faces formidable numbers when it looks at job turnover. Since such companies often can't afford to pay high salaries, they accept that large numbers of people are going to quit every year. They also accept that they will not be able to recruit and keep three thousand geniuses to work on their systems, or for that matter, even three thousand people who understand programming.

What such companies often do is segment off the work so that low-skill low-salary types can do the bulk of the grunt work while a few highly paid sorts figure out what the grunts should do. This is defensive programmer management. In this situation management tries to order things so that no single stupid programmer can screw up more than a tiny part of the system. This is done by making sure that the same "stupid" programmer has access only to a tiny portion of the system. His job is clearly defined and limited.

In a company organized this way you will often find herds of clerk-like programmers, each assigned the responsibility for a small set of programs. Other departments will have the responsibility for talking to the user group and defining the requirements for program changes. Other departments will have the responsibility for creating the JCL that runs the "stupid" programmer's code or defining the files his on-line program updates. Other departments might even write the I/O modules that the "stupid" programmer uses to retrieve and write his data. The poor old "stupid" programmer gets to do one thing: he changes the code in his assigned modules exactly the way he was ordered to and passes it down the line.

While this system might allow companies to employ people of limited ability as programmers and pay them poorly while still keeping their systems afloat, it creates an environment that is painful to work in not only for the poor slob on the bottom, insulated from ever learning more than the minimum amount needed to keep his job, but also for the more talented programmers throughout the organization who have to function in an environment where only the minimum is ever expected from anyone.

If you are an ambitious, intelligent programmer interviewing for a job in a company that employs a large number of programmers, be very certain that you are not falling into this kind of trap—even as a supervisor. The fact that you have terrific credentials that demonstrate your ability and intelligence is not protection against finding yourself consigned to a job designed for the "stupid" programmer described above. This system often produces managers of such limited technical abilities (having never themselves been trained in anything more than the minimum needed to do their jobs) that the hiring manager may not be able to interpret or understand the implications of the facts stated on your resume!

If you do fall into a job like this as your first job right out of school you are in serious trouble. You will learn a tremendous amount about a few specific programs. You will not get software exposure. You won't get to observe the systems development cycle, and you won't even learn the business side of your application. At best you will learn how to read detailed specs provided by a systems analyst. And if this is your first job you will have to stay a year because there is usually no way you can change jobs until you have gotten a year of experience. I have seen very bright people spend two or three years doing nothing but updating rate tables in a single set of insurance programs. I have heard of team leaders whose technical skills were so limited that could not read a link map (that was another department's responsibility), and I have worked (briefly) in one company where the standard answer to any question was, "Well, maybe there is some way to do that but we wouldn't know, we're just dumb [company-name]-oids."

You need to avoid these situations but how can you? Well start out by looking for the telltale signs of the dead-end job.

- Are there a large number of programmers all working for the same project in an single large room or other physical environment that reflects uniformity?
- When you look at the organizational chart for the group do you see a customer interface group, an I/O group, a database group, and an on-line group all listed as part of the application group? (It would be okay to see database support and on-line support appearing in a separate technical support ladder but not under

the same lower-level management.) Of course you might not see a chart that lists these groups even when they exist.

- Does everyone on the team do the same thing? In a better shop each person in a department will have responsibilities that are quite different from his coworkers. The similarity will be that they are supporting the same user group.
- Will you be responsible for developing your own specifications for enhancements or is this the task of a higher-level person? In the best jobs you will do the specifications and the design yourself for a project as well as coding and unit testing.
- Are there a lot of contractors on the project? This does not always mean trouble but often a cluster of consultants is a sign that the company has had trouble retaining employees in this area.
- Will you have direct contact with the user group? If not find out why not. In the better jobs you are trusted to communicate with the users. In the worst you are forbidden to talk to them.
- If you are in a batch environment are you expected to understand and create your own JCL? If you are told not to worry your little head about it, flee.
- Does the interviewer ask questions that show that he cannot understand the technical stuff you have listed on your resume? This is not relevant for college students who often have weird software listed that they picked up in college. But if you have been working with fairly standard stuff in the business world and get the feeling that you are losing the interviewer when you explain what you did in a previous position, this is a pretty good sign you might not be very happy in any assignment he might give you.

Some judicious talking to people you meet at work about where they used to work or where their friends work can often inform you about the worst places to work in your area. But don't be surprised if your friendly neighborhood headhunter tries to sell you one of these as a "wonderful opportunity."

However, if you do your homework and ask the right questions at the interview you can find a lot of positions in large shops that provide a terrific boost to any mainframe programming career.

**The Small Shop**

There are two very different environments that make up the population of small shops. The first kind is the small mainframe shop. This is an environment that runs low end versions of the same mainframe families that the larger companies do. These computers usually use the same operating systems as the large shops, although not always. There are some operating systems that are used exclusively by small mainframe shops, most notably DOS/VSE. Usually these shops occur in retail companies or smaller manufacturing concerns. However you will occasionally find a small bank or insurance company running this kind of system. Often the company started out having a service bureau doing their data processing. As hardware became cheaper and easier to buy some of these companies took over their own processing. Companies of this size are often attracted to packages. These are programs that outside vendors provide that can be used with a small amount of customizing. Some small shops do develop systems for their own use from scratch. But as a rule major development does not occur in small shops, it is too expensive.

*The Minicomputer Shop*

The other kind of small shop is the minicomputer shop. These use intermediate size computers, larger than PC's but smaller than what are usually considered mainframes. The two major minicomputer families are the DEC VAX family which traditionally were used in scientific, engineering, and other number-crunching applications and the IBM System/34, System/36, and System/38 family which were designed for business applications and often are programmed in the RPG family of languages or use off-the-shelf packages like MAPICS, IBM's manufacturing package. A host of other vendors also supply minicomputers for small shop use.

The programmer who begins his programming career using one of these systems may well find that he is limited to working on them in the future since there seems to be an invisible wall keeping these programmers out of the larger IBM mainframe jobs.

This is not necessarily a problem. There are plenty of minicomputer jobs available. IBM claims to have sold 160,000 of its System/36 and System/38 minis and there are a great and growing number of VAX systems in use around the country and the world. The important thing is to be aware that if you take one of these jobs you will find it hard to cross over into mainframe programming later. Nevertheless, there are several positive reasons for pursuing a minicomputer programming career.

## Advantages of the Small Shop

Almost everyone who has worked in a smaller shop has said that the best part of the job was the friendly, intimate atmosphere. If large corporations can be like big cities with different neighborhoods and a lot of traffic, a small shop company can be very much like a small town. In a small shop you may often have a nice summer picnic and a big Christmas party which you might actually enjoy since you recognize everyone there. In a small shop, too, you know who is in charge at all levels since there is a simple management structure to deal with and not as much moving around from department to department.

For many people the more personal environment of the small shop is its major attraction, outweighing the career advantages available in the larger but more anonymous big shop.

The smaller mainframe shop offers some specific advantages to people who are just beginning a programming career. Many of these small mainframe shops run the same software that the larger shops use. What they don't tend to do is compartmentalize the programmers as much. Since they have fewer programmers to work with they cannot afford to limit their scope of action the way that the larger companies often do. What this means for you as a starting programmer is that in a small mainframe shop if you have responsibility for a set of programs you will be expected to talk with your user when they have any problems with those programs or want changes made. You will probably get to do your own analysis and design in consultation with more experienced programmers. You will do coding, testing, and creation of your own JCL. You may very well get to go into the operations area and walk the staff through any procedural changes you must make to a system. This breadth of exposure is invaluable. You may very well get to do a little of everything in the first few years if you work in such a shop.

Another benefit to the new programmer is that you will usually be kept very busy in a small shop environment. This might sound like a strange advantage, but it is not unusual for new people to be brought into huge shops and then find themselves sitting around for weeks or even months, waiting for something to break so that they can get to work fixing it, with nothing but busy work meanwhile to keep them occupied. This is probably the most boring situation you could ever end up in, and it is a lot less likely to occur in a smaller shop that has a tight manpower budget.

In the smaller shop you may end up feeling a greater sense of accomplishment. You will usually get to see "your" users using "your" programs. People from other parts of the company often will know who you are and what systems you support.

Best of all you can have all of this in the smaller mainframe shop with the assurance that if you want to move to a larger shop it is possible to do so, as long as your mainframe is using one of the operating systems used in the larger shops—VM or MVS. If you are in a DOS/VSE shop it might be a little harder to convince an MVS manager to hire you, but it could be done.

### Special Advantages of Minicomputer Shops

In many parts of the country you may find one undeniable argument in favor of working in a minicomputer shop: it's the only kind in your town! If you want to live in a rural area the chances are that there are a few good-sized local companies that use minicomputers. Mainframes are rare in the boonies. If you were planning to move to the mountains or some other bucolic locale you should investigate whether minicomputers are the dominant computer form. That in itself could make minicomputer programming the career of choice for you.

Another reason you might choose to go this route is that you find minicomputer applications that are more interesting to you than the standard business fare which runs in the larger shops. I saw one job in Dallas that involved programming a minicomputer for a small air freight company. If you were an aviation enthusiast, this might have been your dream job! The programmer here worked in an office right on the runway of a mid-sized airport. Pilots were in and out all day while their planes idled on the tarmac outside the window.

If you are interested in working for nonprofit companies, smaller computers might make sense too. Instead of enriching a profit-hungry corporation you could use your programming talents to improve the service at your library or administer the funds for a charity. If you don't want to work for big business it might be a good idea to specialize in smaller systems.

A minicomputer career offers the same entrepreneurial possibilities that mainframe careers do, both for software development, in developing turnkey systems, and in consulting.

One woman programmer I spoke with a few years ago built up a flourishing RPG consulting business, which she operated out of her home. She told me that the owners of the smaller businesses that used these systems tended to be much more flexible about letting her work part time or on an unconventional schedule than were the larger firms. She found it ideal to do consulting for minicomputer systems while her children were little. This is not a trivial advantage. Most mainframe consulting requires you to work rigid employee-like hours, and it is often difficult to manage if you are trying to make time for small children.

This kind of consulting can be more entrepreneurial than mainframe consulting, too, because it is easier to build up a personal relationship with the proprietors of smaller companies than to try to stay in touch with the herds of ever-changing corporate managers who make the hiring decisions for consultants in large firms.

## The Disadvantages of Small Shops

There are limitations imposed by the smaller size of the small shop. The very intimacy that makes some small shops so appealing can make others hell. Negative personalities or abrasive management styles have a greater impact here. If your DP manager is a stinker you can't just switch departments to get away from him. You may have to quit. Likewise if your user group is a total pain in the neck you are probably stuck with it if you want to keep your job. It is very important that you choose a small shop that has a personality compatible with your own. A friend of mine used to work in a small mainframe shop where the boss took all the programmers out once a month to a restaurant that featured all-you-can-drink lunches. For some people this was heaven. However a different person could have found this very confrontational.

The other main problem is that the chances for promotion and rapid salary development may be limited. If there are only a few DP managers in a company it is going to take a lot longer to break into management. If there are few development projects you won't be able to get experience with new technologies just coming into the marketplace. In the worst case situation, where you have a small shop whose systems are mature, you might get almost no technical experience at all, since the company sees no reason to spend money enhancing what it sees as satisfactory systems, or the trend may be toward letting users do their own programming either with PC programs like dBASE III or Lotus 1-2-3 or with fourth-generation products like FOCUS.[2] Finally, most small shops cannot afford to pay high salaries.

The last reason more than any other is the reason that most programmers I've met cite for leaving smaller shops. For a small company, keeping overhead low is not an abstraction. It is often the difference between survival or bankruptcy. Remember, programmers are overhead! As a result, many programmers leave the smaller mainframe shops for rich large companies awash in waste and fat, where they spend their lunch hours telling their buddies how much better the small shop job they used to have was.

[2] Frederic G. Withington, "Managing Your IS Pros," *Datamation*, October 15, 1987. This article (published after my chapter was written) discusses the disadvantages of working in the smaller shop from the perspective of the small shop management and offers some ideas on how to keep small shop programmers from leaving.

# 10
## *Factors—IBM Vs. Non-IBM Shop*

As important as the size of the shop you choose, is the question of whether or not the job your are considering is in an IBM shop. This is particularly true when you take your first job. This factor more than any other has major implications for your long-term career.

When we speak of an IBM shop we are not talking about what logos appear on the boxes in the computer room. The computers in use might come from any number of vendors. What we are talking about, as programmers, is the operating systems that these computers use. In the mainframe world there are two kinds of hardware vendors: those that produce machines that run IBM-compatible software (the so-called plug compatibles like Amdahl) and those that provide machines that have their own unique architecture and operating systems. Digital Equipment Corporation, Honeywell, Wang, Hewlett-Packard, and Unisys are all examples of the latter.

### IBM's Role in Your Future

The salient fact to contemplate as a programmer entering this world is that IBM has, for the last twenty years or so, maintained a market share of somewhere near 65 percent of all mainframe sites. When you add to this the number of plug compatible machines out there running IBM-style operating systems only a small sector of the market is left to be subdivided between the various competing non-IBM compatible mainframe vendors. From a software perspective, therefore, the majority of the places where you as a mainframe programmer could be employed are IBM shops.

*Datamation* reported in July of 1986 that there were some 10,817 IBM and plug-compatible mainframe sites in the United States.[1] It is hard to get exact figures on market share for different vendors. *Datamation* runs an annual user survey that is respected as a gauge of who is using what in the areas of hardware. In one survey *Datamation* found that 60 percent of these IBM shops run large systems (the 308X family of computers and 3090's) and another 13 percent run the smaller 43XX series mainframes (which often use DOS/VSE).[2]

It is only common sense then to realize that if the majority of mainframe programming jobs are to be found in large IBM shops the programmer who gets his training in one of these is ensuring that his skills will be marketable in many shops other than where he got his training.

If, on the other hand, you get your initial training in a shop that uses non-IBM-compatible software, you may very well find your skills in demand, but only in another city. Worse, you could be thrown a nasty surprise if the vendor whose systems you have mastered decides to get out of the mainframe business. The IBM Corporation, whatever your feelings about its products or its methods of doing business, is not about to go out of business very soon. This cannot always be said of other vendors.

If you choose to go into a non-IBM shop you owe it to yourself to research the company that makes the system you will be learning—determine its market share and what industry watchers think of its prospects. Read all you can about it in the business and computer trade press.

Another thing you might do when interviewing with a non-IBM shop manager is ask whether the company has plans to convert

---

[1] Hersh Wiener, "Software, What's Hot and What's Not," *Datamation*, July 1, 1986, pp. 50-62.

[2] John W. Verity, "Datamation/Cowan Mainframe Users Survey," *Datamation*, May 1, 1986, pp 67-74.

to IBM systems in the near future. You might be surprised to find out that this is the case. Many companies would like to be able to take advantage of the enormous amount of third-party software that has been developed to run in the IBM environment such as powerful database packages and the fourth-generation languages. In spite of the cost of conversion a constant trickle of non-IBM shops convert every year. If the company you are considering is about to embark on such a conversion try to determine what your role would be. Would you be stuck maintaining some elderly but vital batch system which would be the last to be converted or would you work on the conversion itself? How would you get IBM software training? Will the company send you to vendor classes (a good way to learn) or expect you to pick things up on your own (a lot harder if your shop is short on IBM systems old-timers.) Often these projects are staffed almost entirely by consultants who leave when the conversion is through.

I have participated in only one conversion, and that was one from an IBM DOS/VSE to MVS operating system, which doesn't cross vendor lines. However my experience there was that the conversion process is probably the worst way to learn a system. This is because in a conversion most of your effort is directed toward the operating system interface. You need to rewrite and restructure JCL for batch jobs and change your access method interfaces. If you were working with COBOL programs (or other high-level language programs) the only changes you would make to them would be in the file definition statements and the I/O statements which vary from vendor to vendor and between operating systems. This is rote work in which you never really look at the function of the program itself. The only programs that would have to be examined in depth would be those written in low-level assembly language. A neophyte would never be given the task of rewriting one of these.

Thus the chances are good that if you start out your career participating in such a conversion effort you will do a lot of rote work and have little opportunity to understand the subtler features of the system. In the conversion I worked on we managed to successfully convert an actuarial system without ever really looking into what any of the programs we converted did. We ran them before conversion, made the necessary changes, and ran them again. When the old and new outputs matched we were done. The occasional glitches we encountered were caused by changes in sort parameters and other

JCL level control cards and rarely necessitated understanding the code. Do you need this kind of experience early in your career?


## The DEC Alternative

There is only one vendor company that is generally reckoned as posing a serious threat to IBM's mainframe hegemony and that is the Digital Equipment Corporation (DEC). Traditionally IBM dominated the business mainframe world while DEC built up a solid customer base selling minicomputers used for number-crunching applications like scientific programming and engineering.

While "Big Blue" concentrated its efforts on building and maintaining the best sales force in the world, DEC traditionally had a somewhat lackadaisical approach to sales, basing its strength on its product line's demonstrable superiority of design. By 1986 DEC machines commanded 52 percent of the market for minicomputers used in scientific and engineering applications while IBM machines accounted for only 25 percent of these.[3]

However industry watchers are agreed that DEC changed its approach to marketing in the mid-eighties and sharpened up its sales force. More important to you as a programmer, DEC extended the size of its computers upward. Although technically its VAX family of computers are minis, it is possible to buy a cluster of eight VAX CPU's which is as powerful as smaller mainframe systems. And DEC did not stop there. DEC is aggressively marketing upper-end machines to the corporate business users who until now were strictly IBM customers. Not only are they selling them, but they are providing experienced programmers who go into the client's shop and show him how to get the most good out of his new VAX system.

Ætna and John Hancock of Boston are two large insurance companies hitherto entirely within the IBM fold that recently signed up for VAX systems, events which made it to a cover story in *Business Week*.[4]

DEC's machines have always been favorably compared to IBM's by those knowledgeable in systems architecture. In addition, the DEC VAX machines represent a family of machines ranging in

[3] Datamation Mainframe User's Survey, op. cit.

[4] *Business Week*, "The IBM-DEC Wars: It's the Year of the Customer," March 30, 1987, p.86.

size from desktop units to virtual mainframes, that all use compatible operating systems. This means that networking these machines is easy and that code developed on smaller VAX systems is easily portable to larger ones. IBM's different-sized systems, on the other hand, have a history of being utterly incompatible and applications often have to be rewritten to cross from one hardware family to another to another.

Given the strength that DEC has been able to demonstrate over the last decade, the appeal that its larger systems are beginning to have to nonscientific users, and its estimated 16,000 to 20,000 installed systems in North America,[5] you have nothing to lose and a great deal to gain by getting your initial DP training in a business application area that is using the VAX.

## What About the Rest?

I have one warning for students coming out of university computer science programs. These students often have done their work on non-IBM systems in school, either because the university bought a system that was better adapted to scientific applications than IBM's mainframes or because they were constrained to order a system from a low bidder—which IBM will never be. I have seen cases in which students coming from these environments have picked up from their professors a snobby tendency to look down on IBM's systems as clumsy and intellectually inferior.

As an example of this kind of professorial attitude, when an experienced programmer friend of mine wrote a paper describing MVS internals for an operating systems class at the University of Vermont the professor gave her a low grade and told her that no operating system could possibly function the way that the one she had described did. He only sniffed when informed that IBM's MVS operating system did and refused to change her grade.

The student who emerges from this kind of environment may turn away from working in an IBM shop without realizing how precariously he positions himself for the future. Unless you have an engineering background, you are taking a career risk by working on an obscure vendor's systems, or even, perhaps, on any that are not provided by IBM or DEC.

[5] "Software, What's Hot and What's Not", op. cit.

The strategy that is probably the safest in the long run for the business mainframe programmer is to get your start in an IBM shop and then, if the opportunity presents itself, move to a different vendor's system. The reasoning behind this strategy is simple. There are enough people trained in the IBM environment so that managers do not feel they should have to provide basic software training when they recruit supposedly experienced people. The experience that they are paying for mainly boils down to familiarity with the Byzantine intricacies of JCL, CICS, and the popular databases.

Companies running non-IBM shops however are accustomed to having few trained people to draw upon to fill open jobs calling for experienced people. They face the alternatives of paying expensive relocation costs or training an experienced person from an IBM background.

Another factor to consider is that it is often much easier to learn a non-IBM vendor's software. In order to be competitive with IBM they have had to design sleek, easy-to-learn systems since no company but IBM could get away with selling systems embodying the levels of confusion that IBM users have grown accustomed to.

Most non-IBM systems don't have JCL or they have something a lot simpler providing the same function as JCL. They also make it fairly easy to create on-line applications. For example, developing an on-line application for a Wang VS system involves mastering about ten minutes worth of straightforward information as opposed to the hours you must spend pondering before you can do the smallest development project in a CICS system. You will find that if you have a solid grounding in IBM operating system-based software your options are almost unlimited since most managers are familiar with IBM's software product line and will recognize what the acronyms on your resume represent in terms of experience.

Unfortunately it does not work the other way. If you had mastered the internals of GCOS, Honeywell's popular operating system, few IBM shop managers would have ever even heard of it. And if your experience centered on Burroughs DMSII database package your resume would probably hit the trash can when you applied for an IBM-based database job, no matter how good your skill level—although your skills would be in great demand at shops that had these vendor's products installed.

If you would like to master non-IBM software and are starting out in an IBM shop pursue all opportunities to strengthen your understanding of systems and of internals so that you develop a theoretical understanding of how systems work. If you have only a cookbook understanding of how to display an on-line screen it will be much harder to work in a new system. However if you understand the underlying processes that are taking place when you display your screen, then you should have no problem picking up how to do the same thing in a different environment.

If your future plans include intercompany mobility, software development, or consulting, you would probably be advised to stick with an IBM shop as a beginner. The time to broaden your experience is when you have assured yourself that you have a solid basis for future employment.

If you do choose to work for a non-IBM shop be sure that you are entering a stable, sturdy company that can offer you years of long-term internal career growth. If you have proven yourself in the company and enjoy working there then the hardware and software you master will be of little consequence in your career development, at least within that company—and should the vendor's systems be removed you will be trained in whatever takes their place. Another successful approach is to master the intricacies of the applications you encounter, the weirder the better. In this case you will be building a strong applications background for yourself to rely on that might bail you out if the vendor you have specialized in proves unstable.

# 11
## Factors—The Software Environment

Once you have gotten a year or more of experience, an interesting thing begins to happen when you look for a new job.

No one cares what your grade-point average was in college. Few interviewers even care if you attended college. No one is concerned that you are an efficient programmer or write elegant code. For that matter, no one ever looks at your code. No one cares either that you came in twenty-three times last year at 3 A.M. to fix production abends or that you got promoted to associate programmer before anyone else in your training class.

What they do care deeply and passionately about is whether you know DB2, CICS, IDMS, FOCUS, IMS/DC, and a host of other acronyms that make up the alphabet soup describing the experienced programmer.

These acronyms are the names of best-selling software products used in the mainframe world and this alphabet soup (or stew if you prefer) is the single most important factor defining your usefulness to a potential employer. Sometimes the alphabet soup alone is all you will see in a job description for an opening advertised in the Sunday classifieds. If you visit a headhunter he will very often run down a checklist several pages long asking if you have experience with each of a large number of software products and how much. If you apply for a consulting contract the match between the acronyms on your resume and the client's job description is all that will get you the interview.

Because this factor outweighs all others and because it is just as easy to learn how to use software that is in great demand as it is to learn software no one is interested in, it is of paramount importance that you are able to put some useful acronyms on your resume.

## Why Is Software so Important?

There is a simple reason why hiring managers consider the acronyms on your resume the single most important factor in evaluating you for a position: These acronyms indicate the software environments that you have worked in. They reflect real hard-won experience acquired hour by hour working with arbitrary, balky, and sometimes out-and-out absurd program products. More important, they represent knowledge that cannot be acquired intuitively. No matter how smart you are you cannot be productive in an on-line or database environment without having first absorbed a large body of trivial but essential details, each one of which can bring a program to its knees.

As we've discussed earlier, most students come out of school thinking that the programmer's main skill is writing programs. After a few months on the job most programmers come to realize that writing programs is the easy part. The hard part is understanding programs written by other people. The software environment is a set of infrastructure programs—programs that are bought by systems departments to provide the tools that the working business programmer uses as a foundation for his own programs.

This software environment includes programs that fall into several families. In one group there are the operating systems. Operating systems are the complex sets of programs, usually supplied by the companies that sell the hardware, that direct the flow of applications programs through a mainframe and make sure that each program as it executes has the resources such as files and printers that it requires.

Associated with the operating system there are a number of file access methods. Access methods get your programs the records they need from data files that are organized in different ways. More complex methods of storing and retrieving data are called database management systems. These are sets of programs that use complex indexes to provide the ability to rearrange the relationship of data independent of the actual files the data is stored in. Database management software may include data dictionaries and application generator software. Data dictionaries centralize information about the data contained in a great number of files used for many different applications. Application generators streamline often-required functions, such as reporting and full-screen database inquiry, so that instead of having to code an entire program every time a new report or screen is needed the programmer can feed parameters to a generic, all-purpose master program that produces the customized output.

In addition to these kinds of software, the software environment also includes teleprocessing programs that control networks of terminals for on-line applications and the software that the programmer uses to design and display on-line screens.

Finally there is a whole set of software tools whose only function is to simplify the job of programming itself. In this family we find full-screen editors, some of which are as complex as a programming language in themselves. These let the programmer create and modify his source code, although VM/CMS's XEDIT editor goes way beyond this and can be used to develop full-screen applications. We also encounter session managers, such as TSO or ROSCOE, the programs that provide the on-line session environment which the programmer uses to develop his code. These environments often include interpreter languages that enable the programmer to code up "quick-and-dirty" tools for himself and his users. There are also interactive debugging aids that let the programmer observe programs he is testing while they execute in both batch and on-line modes. Using one of these, the programmer can stop a program, examine storage values, and even change program logic on the fly.

Some of these infrastructure programs are simple to understand and use. Others are not. The older, more-established ones are the worst. They were developed at a time when customers expected computers to be difficult to work with and little or no attention was paid to designing "user friendly" interfaces. On top of that, no matter how well designed these programs were when they started out, twenty years of quick fixes and got-to-have-it enhancements have obscured their logic.

What all these pieces of the software infrastructure *do* have in common is that they are entirely arbitrary. This means that while similar types of software usually provide similar function, they do it in whatever way their own particular designers decided to program them. For example, most editors provide you the ability to do a global change. That is, they let you change a character string into a new character string everywhere that it is found in a file, using a single command. However if you are using IBM's ISPF editor you will have to type in at the top of the screen "CHANGE 'FIELDA' 'FIELDB' ALL" to globally change the string "FIELDA" to "FIELDB" everywhere in the file. If you were to move to a system that uses IBM's VM/CMS operating system and the XEDIT editor instead of ISPF, the command above would only generate an error message. To do the global change in that system you would have to know that you must type "C/FIELDA/FIELDB/ * *". The only advantage you might have as an experienced programmer confronting a new editor is the knowledge that some sort of global change command probably exists somewhere in the editor software. But locating it in an unfamiliar environment could easily take you ten minutes or more.

The example above illustrates a very minor difference between two similar software products. When you venture into dealing with database management systems or on-line software the differences in how you accomplish similar functions become enormous, and it can take weeks or even months to master the details.

Managers hiring what are supposed to be experienced people don't want to have to pay for those days and weeks of training, and it is precisely for this reason that they are so picky about what software you have already encountered and learned in detail.

Employers do expect to spend a certain amount of their DP budget on training classes. But almost universally they want to reserve these classes as rewards for loyal employees. If they are going to have to pay to train someone it does not make sense to them to bring in an outsider who has not proven his worth to the company. The only exception to this is, of course, the college new hire who must be trained in some software in order to be productive, since colleges rarely provide training in the software generally used in the business world—and as we have mentioned, many companies won't bring in college hires for this reason.

### Getting Software Training

All this should make it clear that your first job represents a never-to-be-duplicated opportunity. It is often the only time that a programmer will receive software training that substantially improves his employability—if the software environment of his first job is well chosen. After the first burst of training most programmers will find that they have to wait several years before they receive any further software training that is of value for building their resumes, and that training is usually awarded, if it is awarded at all, only to the programmer who has been a star performer using the first training he received.

The reluctance of managers to train new people in valuable software skills is so strong that you should be very cautious whenever an interviewing manager holds out the prospect of immediate software training to you as a lure. The sad fact is that the only time managers will condescend to provide training to an experienced person at the start of a new assignment is when one of two situations exists. The first case in which training might be offered is when the company is using some obscure software products unknown outside of the company. These might be home-grown products. If some misguided manager let a local genius write his own operating system or teleprocessing monitor fifteen years ago, the company may have such a huge investment in the code that rides on top of this software that it must continue to support it, even though maintaining home-grown code can be of the worst nightmares imaginable. Home-grown software seems to be an occupational hazard found mostly in large, bureaucratic companies with more money than sense, and large, often idle, programming staffs.

If a manager promises to train you in "on-line internals" make sure that it isn't the on-line internals of JUNQUE written by Joe Smith in tech support. The theoretical mastery you acquire by learning a home-grown software product is useful to you personally in enhancing your understanding of how systems work, but unfortunately it doesn't buy you anything when you go out looking for your next job.

The second situation in which you might be offered training is when a company is using vendor software provided by a vendor who has a very small market share. In this case you might be looking at an opportunity, but then again you might not. In a case like this you might have the chance to learn something that is used outside of the company interviewing you, but the chances are that you would have to look long and hard for other companies that have this product installed and are looking for programmers who know how to use it.

Often vendors struggling to break into the software market will provide cheap, or even free, classes to companies that install the software, to encourage them to use the product. The products in this category may turn out to be fourth-generation languages (4GL's) which are a hot area of expansion for software vendor firms. These 4GL's provide features of computer languages, database management, full-screen application generators, and even spreadsheeting and statistical analysis. They are still relatively new in industry, but between 1983 and 1987 the number of mainframe sites using one of the three most popular 4GL's grew from 7 percent to 22 percent.[1]

If your resume suggests to an employer that you might be a good candidate for training in a brand new software product that he is just installing (and where the courses are cheap), you might be offered training at the start of a new job. In this case it is important that you do a little market research of your own. Read the surveys found in the trade press to find out how many companies are using the software you would be getting trained in, and find out what industry watchers think the long-term prospects for the product are.

If hiring managers are not going to train you in the mainstream software that could mean money in your pocket and a wide choice of career options down the line, what can you do?

The first thing you can do is decide what kind of software exposure you would like to have, based on your future plans. Identify the components you would like to be able to put on your resume. The rest of this chapter can help you with this. Having done this, get the best entry-level position you can find in a company that has an installation featuring the components you want to learn. As we've stated before, if your credentials at entry level are not breathtaking you may not be able to be very picky about the job you take first, but

---

[1] Willie Schatz "The Gauntlet is Thrown, RAMIS Challenges Focus," *Datamation*, May 15, 1987, p. 36.

if your first, or failing that, your second job puts you in an environment where the software you want to learn is installed and used by a large number of programmers, you can do a great deal on your own to learn it even if you are not immediately assigned to a project that uses that software.

There are several ways to do this. First of all, you must build up a reputation for competence doing whatever it is you were assigned to do. The next thing you should do is locate the manuals for the software you want to learn and browse through them at any opportunity. Sometimes when new versions of manuals come in the old ones are thrown away. Ask if you can keep some of these back issues for your own use. Although they may not have the very latest features described, you can learn the heart of the product.

Get to know people who do work with the software you are interested in and ask if they can let you have old copies of listings of programs or applications that use the software. These old listings are worthless to them and can give you the concrete examples you need to look at to learn the software. Finally, let these people know you are interested in moving into their area. When a position opens up they might even suggest you.

You should also take advantage of education benefits your company may have. Many companies will pay for work related courses. See if you can take relevant technical school courses and get your tuition covered. And finally, after you have worked for your current manager for at least nine months, and done a terrific job for him, let him know that when it is time to move on you are ready to move into the area that uses the software you want to master.

## The Well-Rounded Resume

There is no prescription for the "right" software combination for your resume. You can have a terrific career specializing in a single product by learning its internals and becoming the resident guru, or you can flourish, especially as a consultant, by having a broader, more superficial exposure to several popular software packages.

If you are planning to go into management you might never have to learn any of the "hot" packages at all, but might just demonstrate business skills and leadership working in a so-called dead-end software environment and rise on the strength of your management skills alone.

My experience would lead me to suggest that the safest approach is to try to get exposure to a popular product in each of the three major software families: an operating system, a database product, and on-line software. To be utterly well-rounded you might want to add to the foregoing list mastery of a leading fourth-generation language. If you have this kind of well-rounded software exposure your family will never starve and you will always be able to find work. Furthermore you will have a good idea of what the world of business data processing is all about if you choose a noncorporate career path.

The rest of this chapter discusses, at greater length, the three categories of software that are the most important to the programmer in terms of the actual products that you will encounter in the IBM shop environment. I make no claims of being unbiased. In fact I admit I have very strong opinions about many of these products, opinions that are shared by many other programmers but which may contradict what you hear from other experienced folks. I urge you to learn what you can from this book and supplement it with what you learn from those other people so that you can best decide what products *you* would enjoy working with the most and which are likeliest to lead in the career direction *you* want to follow.

I have confined myself to covering only those products found in the IBM software environment that have the largest market shares and apologize for the many fine products I have had to omit.

Remember, too, that business conditions change and today's hot item may suddenly become tomorrow's dud. By the same token, new products can appear whose success can radically change the marketplace. A case in point is the history of IBM's DB2. If this book had been written in 1985, DB2 might not have even been mentioned, as it was used almost nowhere. Now, as a result of aggressive marketing by IBM, software mavens in the trade press are calling it the "COBOL of the 1990's."[2] And its effect extends beyond the mainframe world. Its data manipulation language, SQL, is being implemented in a multitude of vendors' products. And not only in the mainframe world: it is becoming a PC standard too, and those PC

[2] Ralph Emmett Carlyle "DB2 Dressed for Success," *Datamation*, March 1, 1987, pp. 59-62.

developers whose database products do not offer SQL compatibility are facing rocky times ahead. Since the software marketplace is subject to revolutions like the emergence of DB2, the message is clear that the wise programmer will continue to scan the trade press to keep constantly up to date with the software universe. *Datamation's* annual Mainframe User's Survey is a good place to begin your research, but you should modify what you read there with supplementary information about your local DP marketplace that you pick up from the local grapevine.

The following paragraphs are provided as an aid to you in beginning to analyze the different software products you may encounter. It is intended to help you organize your thoughts so that you can begin thinking about what software you want to specialize in. In no way should what follows be used as a substitute for your own research into the current market.

## Operating Systems

IBM and plug-compatible mainframes generally run one of three IBM operating systems, MVS (including MVS/XA), VM, and DOS/VSE. If you are thinking of becoming a systems programmer you will need exposure to the systems internals of these operating systems. As a systems programmer you will be responsible for installing the operating system and tailoring it for your installation. You will update it with fixes and new releases. You may also be responsible for tuning it. This means making it perform as efficiently as possible, and in order to do this you will have to learn to work with a number of performance monitoring programs such as SMP. You may also need to learn how to read systems dumps to troubleshoot problems that are occurring at the systems level to determine whether you can fix them yourself or need to bring in vendor personnel to deal with them.

A subgroup of system programmers are specialists in telecommunications software. Telecommunications programs are not, strictly speaking, part of the operating system, but are programs run by it; however they are always maintained by systems programmers. The VTAM terminal communications program is one such program in the IBM environment. Telecommunications programmers design, set up, and maintain networks of terminals, printers, and other remote devices. They must be familiar with data communication protocols. These are the conventions that devices use to communicate data back and forth and ensure that the data is not changed in the process. Common data communications protocols are SNA, Async, and Bisync. Telecommunications programmers must also be familiar with methods of monitoring network performance and debugging network problems.

If you are going to be an applications programmer you will know far less about the operating system. Many applications programmers only know how to modify canned JCL that they have copied from another programmer. It is not necessary to know much more to survive, however for each of the main operating systems there is a further level of systems knowledge that the applications programmer can pick up that will allow him to shine. In particular an understanding of how the operating system handles I/O (input/output) and how to trace I/O problems in dumps is invaluable to anyone with pretensions of being a technical heavy.

Let's look at each of these operating systems in detail.

**MVS (IBM CORP.)**   MVS is the predominant operating system used by large IBM-style mainframes. MVS/XA, its latest incarnation is the latest in a series of OS operating systems that IBM created beginning in the 1960s for its third-generation computer, the IBM 360. The OS development project was one of the most expensive software development projects ever undertaken. In spite of spending billions, IBM ended up with a clunky system. MVS is a batch-processing system. Its primary interface with the outside world is JCL (Job Control Language), an antiquated set of statements that tell the system where to find the files it needs and where to put new ones it creates. An enormous number of enhancements have been made to MVS over the years to allow it to communicate with a host of devices and with other systems and, most recently, to use high-core addressing, which substantially increases the amount of memory that programs can address. Phenomenal numbers of programs can run simultaneously on an MVS system, which often is made up of several CPU's linked together. MVS systems are where you find the largest database applications and networks comprising hundreds of terminals, but the system is in no way elegant.

In response to the need for on-line programming in this batch environment IBM came up with CICS and IMS/DC which are two separate software products which are alike in that they both are batch programs that control terminal networks and thus, in a round-about manner provide an on-line system. Because MVS is basically a batch system nothing is simple when it comes to programming for these on-line environments, compared to other operating systems designed from the start to incorporate on-line processing.

The main thing that you need to know as an applications programmer working with MVS is how to use and understand JCL. JCL is associated with batch programming and batch programming is often perceived as unglamorous and less than state of the art. However there are an enormous number of batch systems around and if you are interested in creating software or becoming a contract consultant, a knowledge of MVS JCL is very useful.

Used in the JCL batch environment are various utility programs such as sorts, merges, catalog management routines, and file manipulation utilities. Some of these are IBM products, such as the IEBGENER utility used for moving and copying partitioned datasets. Others are sold by software vendor firms, such as Syncsort, which sells a popular sort. Knowing how to use these can be very useful to you. Unfortunately just about every installation you work in will have a different set of these utilities installed, and your favorite might not be available.

If you are working in an MVS environment take advantage of any chance to get training in dump reading. It is not strictly necessary to do this. You can function as a high level language programmer without understanding how it is done. A product called Abend-AID sold by Compuware Corporation of Birmingham, Michigan, which many companies have installed, just about reads dumps for you. This product takes the pain out of analyzing simple abends by locating the source of the problem for you but it can do only so much. MVS dumps are complex and contain a wealth of information beyond what Abend-AID interprets, which can be of great use when you are faced with a pesky abend where your registers have been blown away or weird things are happening to your files. Some time spent mastering MVS dump reading can let you really stand out in a crunch.

Programmers on MVS systems often use a session manager called TSO. When people speak of TSO they are usually really talking about ISPF/PDF which is an IBM software product that runs in the TSO environment and provides a menu-driven program development facility. Using ISPF under TSO the programmer can edit and browse sequential files and update programs as well as submit batch jobs. There are further products which in turn run under ISPF such as Pansophic's Panvalet and Compuware's File-AID which are not IBM offerings but are provided by other vendors and extend the power of ISPF. File-AID extends the features of ISPF to VSAM files and Panvalet provides a library control system for source code libraries. TSO itself includes a primitive interpreter language called CLIST with which it is possible to develop simple on-line applications that run in the TSO environment. Using CLISTs you can sometimes provide your user with a user-friendly tool that enables him to remain blissfully ignorant that he is in actuality building JCL or editing control files.

Most hiring managers will insist that you have previous JCL experience before hiring you in to a batch MVS jobs. However they usually will not care that you don't know TSO and ISPF, unless the job is a tech support one and involves using CLISTs and doing ISPF dialog development, jobs which are a tiny proportion of the MVS jobs available. This is because many MVS programmers use other session managers such as ROSCOE or Panvalet's own front end, or else they have done MVS program development using a VM/CMS system linked to an MVS machine on a network.

**DOS (IBM CORP.)** Mainframe DOS, or DOS/VSE was put together by the IBM Corporation when they first brought out their third-generation 360 computers in the 1960s. It was created because the OS operating system took much longer to develop than the company had anticipated, and they needed to get *some* operating system running in their shiny new machines quickly if they were going to sell them. DOS was simpler and less powerful than the eventual OS operating systems. IBM had originally intended to migrate their customers to OS once it became available. However many customers were quite happy with DOS and saw no reason to invest in expensive conversions to an MVS operating system that, with more systems overhead, would be more expensive to run than DOS. DOS/VSE is usually found running on smaller mainframes now, such as the 4300 series computers.

DOS, too, is a batch system with its own JCL which is different from the OS JCL used in MVS. At the assembly language level it has a different I/O and system command macro set than the OS macro set used by MVS. The file definitions are different for the high-level language programmer, but not very. DOS systems run CICS for on-line application development and use VSAM files. They usually do not use powerful databases that soak up a lot of systems resources. There is a CICS-based development facility, called ICCF, which is sometimes used as the session manager on DOS systems, however, many DOS/VSE systems currently run under VM and use VM/CMS's powerful tools for program development.

If all your mainframe experience is with DOS systems you may not be able to move easily to a larger MVS system since you will have to learn the infinitely confusing MVS JCL from scratch, as well as a host of other system details.

**VM/CMS (IBM Corp.)**   VM was developed by a very sharp group of people within IBM who used it as a tool to help them develop operating system products. VM was designed to allow them to test an operating system without having to re-IPL an entire computer every time they wanted to test a new operating system load. VM was used within IBM but was not marketed to customers until someone realized that it could be a good aid in helping their customers migrate from the DOS systems they were stubbornly clinging to the larger and more expensive MVS systems. This is because what VM does is take one real computer and logically divide it up into any number of virtual (that means pretend) machines. Each of these virtual machines is configured with virtual (pretend) printers, disks, internal storage and card readers, and the like, and, most important, can be IPLed (started up) with any operating system that is resident on the real systems disks. Thus a single VM machine can simultaneously "host", that is, run, a DOS virtual machine running DOS programs side by side with an MVS virtual machine running OS programs.

To top it all off IBM provides a very powerful "native mode" operating system for VM which can also be IPLed into a VM virtual machine. This operating system is called CMS and is the best thing IBM has ever designed. (Excuse me but I am a hopeless CMS bigot.)

CMS is exciting because unlike other IBM operating systems it is designed to be an on-line operating system. Throw out your JCL. CMS has an extremely powerful editor called XEDIT and several interpreters, called EXEC languages and REXX which work together with XEDIT to enable you to produce what are for the mainframe environment extremely sophisticated interactive applications.

VM has low system overhead. It is so well designed that 90 percent of the time you don't need operators to tend it. It runs comfortably at a 99 percent CPU utilization which would kill MVS. And it is especially well adapted for networked applications. It even has a delightful set of assembly language macros which allow you to do things like read an entire file in with one I/O. With all these terrific features you would think that IBM would be marketing it like crazy. But historically this has not been the case. CMS competes too well with other products IBM has a stake in maintaining, and rumor within the company was that management more than once tried to cancel the VM/CMS project.

Within the IBM Corporation itself most development programmers do as much of their work as possible on VM/CMS systems that are networked together and are provided with a powerful electronic mail network-cum-database called PROFS. These programmers working at IBM have access to a great number of internally developed programs to perform a wide range of functions, and new ones are constantly being added. A very small percentage of these programs eventually make their way out of the IBM internal programming shops and appear as new features in new VM/CMS releases.

However if you are going to use VM/CMS at a company that is not IBM itself you may find that the CMS environment is a lot less exciting.

Note for example that a graph in the September 7, 1987, issue of *Computerworld* showed that at that time 62 percent of VM systems were used to host DOS/VSE, a further 7 percent hosted old OS/VS1 systems, while 14 percent hosted some version of MVS. Only 15 percent ran VM/CMS as the main guest operating system.[3] What this means is that in most places where you will encounter VM you will use only a fraction of its features, probably being limited to using its editor, XEDIT, to modify source code destined to run on DOS or MVS. As VM will merely be hosting other less appealing operating systems, you will have little chance to explore VM's power. Very few companies outside of IBM itself develop applications based on

---

[3] *Computerworld*, "Data View; VM Distribution," September 7, 1987, p. 23.

VM/CMS and very few programmers outside of IBM seem aware of the bells and whistles that VM/CMS provides.

It is a shame that the many programmers working on VM/CMS systems are insulated from the rest of the powerful software that is in place when they log on to CMS, since you can have more fun programming in the CMS environment than in any other IBM system available, and, incidentally, get a great deal of work done.

In most cases then, when you are interviewed for a job where you are told you will be using CMS, you would actually be just working in an MVS or DOS environment. The employer will teach you the basics you need to use VM/CMS to get the work out, but if you want to go more deeply into working with VM/CMS you will have to go into a tech support group. Even there you might not learn much. VM/CMS allows you to tailor many of its utilities so that VM/CMS commands look and behave the way you want them to, not in a single fixed way like most systems software does. You can even easily develop your own system commands by the way. However, as an example of how little system programming departments understand VM/CMS, at one very large insurance company using VM/CMS as the front end for thousands of programmers, the systems programming area set up a system command meant to be used for looking at output listings, which are read-only files, with an option that allowed you to add lines to the listing, but not one that let you view more than the first 600 lines of the listing. This rendered the utility virtually worthless, since most listings are several thousands of lines long, and as a result nobody on the system used it. Instead, incoming programmers wasted valuable time learning a tedious line-command-driven output display utility, developed (of course) in-house. A one-line change could have fixed the utility and probably saved the company some money!

If you do work on a VM/CMS system make use of the excellent on-line HELP facility which reproduces the entire COMMAND and MACRO manual. You can learn quite a lot about how to use the system using these help screens. In addition you can teach yourself how to use the interpreter languages, a wonderful feature of CMS, by printing off several of the CMS commands which are written in these languages and using them as examples.[4]

---

[4] For example, print off the FILELIST EXEC, a system command to manipulate files on different virtual disks.

There is some hope that VM may become more widely used in the future. The 9370 minicomputer recently introduced by IBM can use VM but not MVS. This computer was introduced to provide a minicomputer which is compatible with the larger 370 style computers, as the System/38's are not, and if it is successful many more people may become familiar with VM and VM-based application development.

## Database Management Systems

In theory the job of a database management system is to manage a set of files. In practice just about every so-called database system also provides some kind of on-line interface and application generator software. Some of the products routinely discussed in trade magazine articles about databases are not marketed as database packages but as fourth-generation languages. This seems a bit confusing and is. So lets start at the beginning.

Before we look at the more popular mainframe database products let's start out with a discussion of IBM's VSAM. VSAM is not really a database—it is an IBM file access method, the only commonly used one in MVS and DOS which allows you to randomly retrieve and update records. (The other access methods are sequential, except for DAM, Direct Access Method, which is little used today.) The reason we must look at VSAM is that VSAM is what most places use that do not use a database package. Many homemade databases are constructed of VSAM files. In fact most of the database management systems sold today are constructed of VSAM files too, although you do not need to understand VSAM to use them (unless your index pointers get blown away.) You will often see ads requiring VSAM experience.

After discussing this bare-bones database tool, we will turn to the popular, and valuable, database packages.

**VSAM (IBM Corp.)** VSAM (pronounced vee-sam) is a file access method. It allows files to be written in either a sequential or an indexed manner and allows the creation of secondary indexes for indexed files.[5] If you have ever used indexed files in another vendor's

_____

[5] Although few batch COBOL programmers realize it, it can also read files backwards, but unfortunately, this is not implemented in the COBOL VSAM interface.

environment you will be appalled at how confusing VSAM can make things.

VSAM files are defined not in JCL or in the program like other kinds of IBM files, but in a special VSAM catalog which is addressed using a set of utility programs called IDCAMS (pronounced eye-dee cams). These utilities must be used to create, delete, or print VSAM files and are documented in the worst set of manuals IBM ever put out. VSAM, in addition, communicates with the programmer by means of error messages so terse that it is almost impossible to understand them unless you have them memorized. Finding explanations of VSAM error messages in manuals is an exercise in frustration. Typically your message will inform you merely that "ERROR 97" occurred and, after that, you are on your own. If you are lucky you may be able to locate the manual in which the error message is explained, but there is a high probability that the explanation for the error message will be as incomprehensible as the message itself.

Defining VSAM datasets involves understanding a lot of parameters that few programmers ever master. To make it worse there is definitely a right way and a wrong way to define VSAM files and doing it wrong causes significant performance deterioration.

Fortunately for you as a programmer, since few programmers outside of systems areas understand VSAM no one will be shocked or upset if you ask for some help with VSAM, even if you are supposed to be an experienced programmer. The control statements for IDCAMS jobs are passed from programmer to programmer in most shops and rarely are you expected to be able to create your own. I sometimes suspect that only one set of IDCAMS jobs has ever been written from scratch and that all the programmers in the world have been copying copies of that original ever since. A few years of VSAM experience will make you better at debugging it, but it does not seem to be a hot, got-to-have item for your resume.

What you *do* learn when an interviewer tells you that you will be working with VSAM files is that you will *not* be learning a more sophisticated database management system.

**IMS (IBM CORP.)**   IMS is IBM's database behemoth. It is a hierarchical database where information is organized in a top-down fashion. This means that in order to get at a piece of information you are interested in you must retrieve high-level information first, then retrieve the next logically defined level, slowly working your way down to the level where your information logically resides. IMS itself is a region controller program, a giant load module under whose control and in whose storage other application programs run.

DL/I is the name of the set of commands you use to navigate through the hierarchical IMS database. To make things more confusing, you can have a DL/I database running under CICS in which case I believe it is no longer called IMS but just DL/I, although the access commands work the same way.

I was told by a friend who used to work at IBM's Palo Alto location that some of the programmers there had a picture of a bramble bush hanging up in their offices captioned "IMS Internal System Logic." It is likely. IMS has developed by accretion over the years. What this means is that the original design kernel has so many layers of enhancements superimposed on it that it has grown from an initially complex system with a lot of overhead into a performance monster.

You will find that IMS is often found in large companies that got into database technology very early in the game and who can afford to lavish system resources on this resource hog. IMS means huge.

In most cities I've lived in there are always advertisements for programmers with IMS experience to work as contractors. I used to think that this was because IMS was a rare and valuable skill, which to some extent is true. However I have come to find out from talking to ex-IMS programmers that some of the volume of advertisements reflects the high turnover rate of dissatisfied programmers leaving casts-of-thousands IMS programming shops which they perceived to be sweatshops. I don't know to what extent that is a local or universal phenomenon.

In the mid-1980s IMS's market share decreased, reflecting companies' conversions to other systems. In 1982 34 percent of sites surveyed by Computer Intelligence Corp. of La Jolla, California, had IMS installed as their database. By July of 1986 this had dropped to only 20 percent.[6] More significantly, when managers were surveyed about their plans to bring in new database systems only 4 percent surveyed by *Datamation* in May of 1987 planned new IMS systems

---

[6] Hersh Weiner, "Software, What's Hot and What's Not," *Datamation*, July 1, 1986, pp. 50-62.

compared to 29 percent who were looking to bring in DB2.[7] IMS suffered significant losses to a competing database product, Cullinet Software Inc.'s IDMS, in the 1980s. All in all, IMS may very well be the wave of the past for the database programmer. Not that IMS is going to disappear: the billions that have been invested in the development of huge IMS systems make that unlikely, but few new systems are likely to be developed under IMS in the future. It is quite likely that doing IMS-to-DB2 conversions will be a viable way to make a living as a consultant or software developer in coming years.

If you do interview for a job in an IMS shop be warned of a nasty trick employers pull. Aware that many people would like to learn a valuable skill, they will tell you that you are going to be working in an IMS environment and can "learn IMS." However what you will often discover is that while you are working in an IMS environment all the actual IMS interfacing is done by database administrators or by a separate department whose task is to create I/O modules for applications areas to use. In this case you will be working with black boxes and will be writing the identical code you would have written in a non-database environment, completely ignorant of the specifics of really using IMS.

**DB2 (IBM Corp.).**   IBM inflicted IMS on an unwary world when it was pretty much the only game in town. Over the intervening years a group of lean and hungry competitors developed database products that were simple to understand and required less system overhead to run. By the early 1980s IBM was not amused to discover that several of its competitors, especially Cullinet with its IDMS product, had carved out healthy and growing market shares for themselves. IBM's answer was to unveil its long-awaited relational database, DB2, which uses the SQL data access language.

Although DB2 began with a modest market share, within a relatively short period it became obvious to industry watchers that it could become the next big thing. Most important was that IBM threw all of its marketing muscle into getting DB2 into as many mainframe sites as possible. In the second half of 1986 IBM gave DB2 away free for six-month trial periods and soon after claimed to have sold between 750 and 1,000 licenses. IBM used both the carrot and the stick. Besides giving away free licenses, IBM hinted that DB2 might be-

[7] John W. Verity "Mainframe Users Survey: Tough Times for IBM," *Datamation*, May 15, 1987, p. 69.

come a requirement for installing MVS/XA or VM/XA systems at some future time, as system-generation information for these systems might be defined in a DB2 "repository."[8]

By May of 1987 *Datamation's* "Mainframe Users Survey" reported that while only 6 percent of IBM mainframe sites had DB2 installed at the time, a whopping 29 percent of those sites planned to install it in the coming year and an additional 15 percent planned to install SQL, the data access language used in DB2. At the same time, IDMS, IBM's strongest competitor, was installed at 16 percent of all IBM mainframe sites but managers only had plans to install it in 9 percent more.

As a result of this, there developed an almost instantaneous demand for people with DB2 experience, a demand that should stay strong. By 1987, DB2 training was advertised as bait in ads in my local paper and all the consulting firms were begging for people with DB2 experience.

At that time most of the DB2 projects installed were still in some form of pilot or testing phase. DB2 was still going through its final shakeout and a lot of people were waiting to see how it performed over the long run before committing large-scale development projects to DB2 or beginning to convert major existing systems. The history of IBM's introduction of the PL/I programming language, another "better mousetrap," and its failure to catch on in the business world because of stubborn problems could, after all, be repeated here. There were, for example, mutterings about DB2's "leaky security." It seems that DB2, designed for ease of use, was a bit too easy to use when it came to accessing data that a user was not intended to be able to get at. It was also extremely difficult to create an audit trail within DB2, experts said.[9] These were by no means trivial flaws to corporations that tend to be hypersensitive about data security issues. So in spite of all the signs pointing to its success, the saga of DB2 was by no means over.

Another minor issue is that DB2 was apparently designed by people with advanced degrees in computer science. I infer this because DB2 manuals use a vocabulary quite alien to the language of the common or garden-variety programmer. The concepts that the language is describing are, of course, the same old programming

[8] "DB2 Dressed for Success," op. cit.

[9] Jean S. Bozma "IBM Slow to Remedy Leaky DB2 Security," *Computerworld*, September 28, 1987, p. 12-13.

concepts we old-timers know and love, but a certain amount of mental retraining is necessary to get used to it. This too might be a factor in whether it catches on.

**IDMS (CULLINET SOFTWARE, INC. WESTWOOD, MA.)**    For quite a while IDMS had the largest market share of any of the non-IBM database packages according to several surveys reported in *Datamation* in 1986 and 1987.   Its share was something like 16 percent of all database sites, or about 1,104 surveyed sites.[10]  Dave Litwack, at the time executive vice-president of Cullinet, claimed in print that 2,000 sites had ADS/O (and thus IDMS) installed.[11]

This should tell you that IDMS must be a very attractive product, and it is. IDMS in its original version is a network model database which is a lot more flexible than the hierarchical model. IDMS also has a relational database called IDMS/R which, in 1987, was installed in from 10 percent to 15 percent of sites using IDMS.[12]

IDMS databases use an access language called DML. You may also encounter a utility called DMLO which allows you to navigate through an IDMS database on-line, viewing and modifying it as you go. IDMS sells an application generator called ADS/O which is a set of utilities which allow you to create sophisticated multi-screen interactive applications that run in the IDMS/DC environment. IDMS also provides a powerful data dictionary called IDD.

The only question you should ask yourself before committing to IDMS is what other potential employers in your region use it. Although it does have a solid installed base if you are tied to a geographical region your shop could be the only IDMS one around, posing a problem if you want to job hop. However this could also be true for any of the other databases discussed here, since few towns have many installations large enough to need to use these database products.

### Other Non-IBM Database Management Systems

Outside of IDMS in 1987 no non-IBM competitor had a share of the database market that was greater than 10 percent. The exact market

---

[10] "Mainframe Users Survey", May 15, 1987, op. cit. The previous Datamation "Mainframe Users Survey," May 1, 1986, showed IDMS with a 20 percent market share in IBM 4300 (smaller size) mainframes and 19 percent of IBM 309X (larger size) mainframes.

[11] Karen Gullo, "Steady as She Goes," *Datamation*, January 15, 1987, p. 37.

[12] "Software What's Hot and What's Not," op cit.

share of the many small contenders ebbs and flows from year to year. In 1987, for example, the leader among these was FOCUS (Information Builders) which is a fourth-generation language package that includes a database among its many features. FOCUS is part of a group of 4GL's which, proponents claim, can cut down on the ongoing expense of maintenance for existing systems as well as holding down development costs. These 4GL's seem to be catching on. *Datamation* reported that the number of sites using one of the three main 4GL's tripled in the period spanning 1982-1987. The other two 4GL contenders are RAMIS (On-Line Software International) and NOMAD (D&B Computing Services). However, the market penetration of these is still small. *Datamation* reported that according to a 1986 survey RAMIS's market share was only 4 percent of database sites and NOMAD's share was less than 1 percent. [13]

Other database products that have a small but tenacious hold on the market are ADABAS (Software AG), DATACOM/DB (ADR), TOTAL (Cincom Systems), and SAS Institute's System 2000. There are other fourth-generation languages to consider too, most notably ORACLE, the product of the Oracle Corporation of Belmont, California, whose fortunes took a sudden upturn in 1987 because it was selling a mature PC database product that used SQL and could communicate with mainframe DB2 systems.

So how important are these tools to the programmer concerned with building up his software arsenal? The word on most of these later databases, or 4GL's, seems to be that there are not enough people trained in using them in the pool of available programmers to allow employers to be fussy. Knowledge of one of these would be a plus if you wanted to work for a company that was using the package, but if only four hundred sites in the entire nation have a package installed, and many of those sites have small pilot projects, you aren't going to find very many of them.

I would treat these low-market-share databases as a nice extra for your resume. However, many of these are installed in large companies that, for the most part, run the mainstream stuff. I would advise trying to get experience in the database used by the majority of the companies in your area that you would like to work for, before committing to something that might, after all, be only a management experiment.

---

[13] "Software What's Hot and What's Not," op cit.

## On-Line

When 99.9 percent of managers working in IBM shops talk about on-line they mean applications that are running under CICS or IMS/DC. As mentioned before, many of the database and 4GL software packages include nifty on-line application generators that can allow you to quickly design and code on-line applications. But this is usually not what interviewing managers are asking for when they ask if you have "on-line experience." VM/CMS programmers may also have used XEDIT and REXX along with DMS/CMS (all IBM products) to develop sophisticated on-line applications. But for most business programming, on-line refers to high-level language programs tortured to conform to the requirements of IBM's aging heavies, CICS and IMS/DC.

For some reason many people have the idea that working on on-line systems is much better than working on batch systems. On-line systems do have one tremendous advantage: they are usually turned off in the evening ensuring that the on-line programmer will not be called up at 3 A.M. and forced to drive downtown to fix a program abend. This is not to be sneezed at. On the other hand, the frenzy that occurs when an on-line system comes down in the middle of the productive morning hours is something else again and the level of hysteria from irate user managers and the nervous inquiries of your own management as to when it will be fixed can be just as hard to deal with as midnight calls.

From a processing standpoint, though, many so-called on-line systems are simple data collection systems used by clerical personnel. They allow users to fill in screens with information that is used to update some files on-line and then often shipped to batch systems for further processing. On-line data collection systems can be extremely dull to work with since their main function is usually editing data and giving error messages. In my experience the batch side of a data collection system can sometimes be much more interesting to work on. However there is no denying that there is a snobbery about being an on-line programmer, whether it is deserved or not.

The truly interesting on-line systems I've encountered are those that are directed to knowledge workers rather than clerical people. Systems that are used by investment analysts, planners, middle-and upper-level managers, and other professional people can have quite sophisticated on-line sides. These systems must be user friendly.

While you can impose just about any system on a hapless clerk you are forced to provide a lot of understandable error messages and recovery loops when you are programming for middle managers.

The more sophisticated and truly interactive an on-line application is, the harder it becomes to implement using CICS or IMS/DC. As a result it is often in development groups that are working on this kind of system that you find application generators, 4GL's, and PC networks being tried out, since all of these facilitate the development of complex multiscreen on-line applications. You may also encounter non-IBM hardware and software in situations where particularly innovative on-line solutions are being tried. Wang's systems have a very friendly, full-screen interface, for example, which lends itself to quickly developing on-line programs.

The Catch-22 here is that if you master the most popular on-line software packages, CICS or IMS/DC, you are ensuring yourself a constant supply of on-line assignments working on the more boring on-line systems. If you go for the more interesting on-line applications you might end up with a resume full of hard-to-transfer (let alone explain) skills. I've done both and find that I infinitely prefer working with the complex and challenging nonstandard on-line systems; however, I have had to scramble to add the standard stuff to my resume to ensure that I can work.

**CICS (IBM CORP.)**  CICS is a TP monitor. Basically it is a huge batch program that controls terminals, thus providing on-line capability. If you are used to creating on-line programs in a different environment where displaying a screen is a pretty straightforward activity, you will find the initial complexity of CICS baffling. Interesting things happen in the CICS environment, many of them seemingly beyond your control as an application programmer. Other tasks running in the same CICS region (it's called a platform) can stomp on your program's storage and there is not much you can do about it except to stay friendly with tech support.

CICS programs have to be designed in something called "pseudoconversational mode." This means that unlike every other system you have ever used, you can't just display a screen and wait for a response. No, in CICS you have to exit your program every time you display a screen after dropping CICS a note telling it what program to call when you get a response. This is because CICS really is just one big program running all the applications on the platform as subtasks. There are many other odd features that you will have to learn to be able to write on-line programs in CICS.

CICS has its own subset of alphabet soup. There is a distinction between macro level CICS and command level CICS. Macro level was used in older systems. It gave you a large number of assembly language macros to work with but also enabled you to really screw things up, or so the old-timers have told me. The newer systems use command level. Since, under MVS/XA, you cannot run both types of CICS together, the macro level seems to be disappearing. Command level CICS gives you a set of commands which you imbed in your source code. The source module is then run through a CICS translator before it is compiled. This translator turns it into incomprehensible gibberish that includes CICS internal names and parameter values that now appear in your source code. When this step is complete you compile your program as usual.

To further complicate things, your screens can be displayed using something called BMS (Basic Mapping System) or you can use another set of programs called DMS. There are several ways to build your screens too. You can code them up using BMS macros or you can use a utility called SDF, which lets you draw the screen and define the fields and their characteristics on-line.

Unless you have a good understanding of how on-line programming works in the IBM 370 world you will find it hard to just pick up CICS. Because of this, employers often hold out the promise of a CICS class to lure in new employees. Here again you need to exercise caution. Often you will be told that you will be working in a CICS environment only to discover that all the CICS code is maintained by a specialist and you are just doing gruntwork. The worst abuse I've encountered along these lines was the installation where interviewees were told that they were going to be working in a CICS environment only to discover that they were in a tape-based batch shop where the editor they used to develop their programs was ICCF, an editor which is program running under CICS.

In the CICS environment you might encounter a product called InterTest (On-Line Software, Inc.). This is an interactive debugging aid which is very handy to have. It allows you to run your CICS program and stop its execution at a set place so that you can examine storage. It has a very good set of help screens that can teach you how to use InterTest without needing a manual.

If you are interested in tech support you should be interested in any opportunities to learn CICS internals. CICS requires herds of systems folk to support it and debug it. If you enjoy systems work, CICS work should be around for a while.

**IMS/DC (IBM Corp.)**   IMS/DC is a piece of IMS. It allows you to display screens when you are running under the control of the IMS region. IMS is transaction driven, and so IMS/DC gives you a set of transactions that you use to display and retrieve screen information. There are formats you use to send screens, and formats you use to receive back the entered data. The lowest level of IMS/DC is pretty brutal to work with so IBM has promoted something called ADF which can simplify the process. Many IMS systems have been converted to CICS, a trend which is likely to continue.

### Can You Fake Software Experience?

When I was little my mother taught me never to lie. As a result I don't think I could ever just come right out and claim I have worked with a product I've never seen. However, after several months of having my resume thrown out because the people reading it did not have enough experience themselves to comprehend what skills my nonstandard experience represented, I did start rephrasing my resume so that it more accurately reflected what I really could do. Many programmers follow a similar strategy.

The problem is that if you have good technical skills there are a lot of software products that you can master in about ninety minutes, since the new products closely resemble other products you have worked with. Unfortunately people whose experience has been limited to a single software environment rarely understand this and may reject you for a job that you could easily fill with distinction.

I've seen people try to fake skills in things they really had no experience with and look like fools. I have worked with not one, but two, characters who claimed to be IBM 370 Assembly Language programmers when it was obvious that they were not. While it is true that you can pick up a new high level language pretty fast if you know a couple of others, assembly language coding is a whole different magnitude of complexity and not something you can pretend to know. Both of these guys got canned.

I've heard of a young woman who claimed to be an experienced COBOL programmer (a consulting firm employee consultant) who was greatly confused when Abend-AID informed her that she had a S0C 7 data exception. This is something any COBOL programmer in an IBM environment would have encountered in the first two weeks of training. (She was not canned however, so strong was the local demand for programmers!)

I was also told, by the team leader who had hired her, of another consultant who was baffled by her inability to get a programming change to take effect. The team leader looked over her shoulder and saw that she was making her changes to the program's compile listing, not to the source code itself. When this was pointed out to her, she said that she *still* didn't see why it wouldn't work!

These were people who really were out of their depth; however I have met people who faked CICS experience and pulled it off. But in every case they were experienced professionals who knew enough other software to have a very good idea of what sort of things were going on in CICS even if they did not know all the details. They also claimed only to have "light CICS experience," a phrase that will cover you the first time you do something really dumb.

Since each company uses software products a little differently than other companies do, you may actually have good experience with a product and find it installed a bit differently in a new surrounding. Because of this, even experienced people are given some leeway to make mistakes at first.

If you have a good understanding of systems fundamentals and have worked in several software configurations you may be able to exaggerate yourself into a rewarding job that lets you use software you have always wanted to learn.

If you have this kind of background you will not be doing the employer a disservice because you really will be able to do the job, often better than a person who has only rote learning experience and doesn't understand the why's of what he is doing with the software.

The key thing to evaluate, when considering a situation like, this is the following: What skill level does the hiring manager really need? If a manager is asking for IDMS experience because he wants someone to design an IDMS database from scratch this is probably not the place to extrapolate from your experience with XYZ Corporation's homemade FEEBLE database package. However, if he is looking for someone to maintain existing programs you might be perfect for the job. In this case you will be making small enhancements to existing programs, and the chances are that you will rarely even have to touch the portions of the code that do the database calls. You will have time to read the manuals and look at the existing programs to learn how to do things in this environment. In a case like this your exposure to database concepts and your ability to hit the books should pull you through.

Another question to ask is whether there will be some skilled people around as a resource, or whether you will be on your own. Clearly, if you are going to be teaching yourself new software as you go, you will want someone to be there who can answer your questions or help you when you get stuck .

With the brighter managers you won't have to stretch the facts to get a position like this. They should be able to understand what you have already done and know that at a certain point a data processing professional can learn just about any new software easily, bringing to it the valuable experience of previous years. The chances are that you would be happier working for a manager who had this kind of intelligence too. But if you can't find one of these and are forced to exaggerate, make sure that you know enough about what you are claiming to know to be able to learn it quickly.

# 12
## *Factors—Watching Your Language*

Strictly speaking, computer programming languages are just another part of the software environment. However, since they are probably the single most important form of software that the programmer works with, we will consider them separately here. There are many different computer programming languages. Basically they fall into three groups. At one extreme are the "low-level languages." These are low level not because they are inferior in any way, but because they are the closest to the internal machine language that the computer actually processes. These low-level languages are called assembly-level languages or assembler for short. The assembler you are most likely to encounter in the mainframe business world is the IBM 370 assembly language which is used by the 43XX family of computers and the larger, top-of-the-line 30XX computers.

The languages in the next group are generally called "high-level languages," because one statement in one of these languages is translated by a program called a compiler into many low-level machine language statements. This group includes COBOL, PL/I, and

Fortran, which are all used in the business world, as well as a host of other languages that are taught in colleges but rarely used in mainframe programming, such as BASIC, PASCAL, C, LISP, and ADA.

All of these have their own exclusive syntaxes, but, with the exception of APL which is used in mathematical modeling applications and LISP which is used for artificial intelligence applications, they are conceptually similar. This means that if you are familiar with one it is not too hard to pick up another.

Unfortunately, as is the case with so many of the items constituting your software experience, hiring managers do not always understand that this is the case and will rarely hire you to work in a language that you have not coded in before—in a business environment. Hiring managers rarely consider school exposure to a language to be real experience. This is because too many college students get credit in college courses for giving correct answers on exams rather than for producing complex debugged code in the language being studied.

Most recently a new group of languages has emerged. These are called fourth-generation languages or 4GL's for short. This term covers a hodgepodge of software products, ranging from report writers to full-screen application generators to databases. The overriding concept in all fourth-generation languages is that the programmer should not have to code over and over again the common logic of similar programs. However fourth-generation languages differ in what parts of the coding process they automate.

Let's look more closely at the different languages you are likely to encounter in the mainframe data processing world when you go on your job hunt, and let's see what strengths and weaknesses they can contribute as you serve your data processing apprenticeship.

## COBOL

COBOL, as any college student knows, is absurd. It is wordy. The version used in most businesses has no in-line perform and no case statement. You can't address individual bits worth a damn. COBOL, however, is the industry standard. There are currently an estimated

[1] Karen Gullo, "Steady as She Goes," *Datamation*, January 15, 1987. p. 37.

70 billion lines of COBOL in use worldwide[1] and programmers are adding to that total even as you read these words. COBOL, therefore, is not likely to go away.

The main reason for COBOL's dominance is its relative simplicity. It is almost impossible to do something tricky in COBOL. While this means that it is often impossible to do something that you as a programmer would like to do, when you finish coding a program it is very likely that another person will be able to understand what you have done—even if that person is not very bright. Contrast that with a language like APL with an instruction set so powerful that a single line can perform an entire engineering application, but where the only sure way to modify a program is to rewrite it from scratch, because it is just too hard to understand existing code!

Other advantages of COBOL are that it is easy to learn and that there are many programmers who are familiar with it in the pool of available workers.

Most college students rightfully disdain COBOL, preferring instead the elegant block-structured languages that they used in their college classes. However, the majority of the jobs you encounter will use COBOL, so you might not even have a choice of alternatives. If this is your situation, console yourself with the thought that several hundred thousand other programmers around the nation (and thousands more around the world) are putting up with the same inefficiencies as you are, and that you will never have trouble finding another COBOL job. If you have any intention of working as a contract consultant you will almost have to have COBOL somewhere on your resume since the vast majority of consulting work calls for COBOL programmers.

Currently the American National Standards Institute (ANSI) an organization that exists to set standards for wrenches, tires, and COBOL, has come up with a new, improved standard defining the features that COBOL compilers must support. This version is called COBOL 85 and remedies some of COBOL's more obvious deficiencies such as the lack of an in-line perform. However it is not compatible with the earlier COBOL 74 which is in use in most businesses and requires a conversion to be undertaken on old code before it can be used on it. As a result, adoption of COBOL 85 has been slow. I personally have never seen it in use.

Since COBOL is so widespread it has been worthwhile for software developers to develop productivity tools for COBOL programmers. Most commonly you will find debugging aids used in the workplace. XPEDITER (Application Development Systems) is a popular example of one of these. It is a product that allows you to run your COBOL program on-line in a TSO or VM environment, stopping it at a prespecified address and examining or changing storage values or logic flow at will. Other software has been developed to analyze existing COBOL programs with an eye to simplifying maintenance and yet others to straighten out "spaghetti code." These later, more sophisticated tools in the late eighties had only begun to penetrate into the market, but showed signs that they could catch on in the coming years. There is also a kind of fourth-generation language called a code generator, which itself writes COBOL programs in response to parameters coded by the 4GL programmer.

## IBM 370 Assembly Language (Also known as BAL and ALC)

Once upon a time when dinosaurs roamed the earth and computer time cost a whole lot more than programmer salaries, people wrote programs in assembly language because they could be written to run at maximum efficiency and optimize system utilization. Assembler programming is hard. It is what a programmer friend of mine calls "work for crazed dwarfs working in pairs." When you program in assembler you move every bit and byte yourself, set every switch, and control every loop. At the assembler level you are writing code that reflects what the machine can really do.

Assembler programmers as individuals tend to be somewhat quirky. I've noticed in particular a widespread refusal among assembler programmers to spell English words the way they appear in the dictionary. This stems I assume from the assembler programmer's deep admiration for logic.

As little as ten years ago there were enough assembler programmers around to constitute a snobby subculture in industry. But because the expense of maintaining assembler programs can become prohibitive and because there has always been a shortage of programmers capable of dealing with assembler's level of complexity, a large number of companies have converted their assembler programs to COBOL. Company training programs for new programmers used to routinely include a few weeks of assembler instruction for all trainees. Nowadays that is becoming rare. Assembler training is given only to programmers destined to work on assembler systems. While it is true that most college students study "Assembly Language" in college courses, the approach in many of these courses is theoretical: the student may actually write his own assembler, but rarely encounters the IBM assembler used in industry or learns its quirks. This means that an awful lot of programmers who work in the IBM environment are pretty fuzzy about what that environment looks like at the lower level. It also means that newer COBOL programmers are not receiving the training they need to be able to interpret program dumps. This lack of exposure to assembler is a shame.

It is particularly a shame if you would like to be a quality technical programmer—not because you would like to work at doing maintenance or even development in an assembler environment. You probably wouldn't. Developing assembler code is so time consuming compared to developing the same code in higher-level languages that almost no companies anywhere do it. (The exceptions are a few smaller shops where fanatical assembler programmers have risen to positions of managerial power.) Even some code that appears to be written in assembler, such as IBM's source code for many of its systems products, is actually written in a higher-level language, (IBM's is called PL/S), and then run through a translator that turns it into assembler code. No, the reason you would like to be exposed to assembly and to get some hands-on experience with it is that assembler language introduces you to what is really happening underneath all that snazzy syntax that the higher-level languages, databases, and on-line software provide. It enables you to understand what the machine is really doing.

When you have worked with assembler programs for awhile you develop the skills you need to be an effective debugger in higher-level language environments. The chances are that you will rarely have to look at I/O blocks and registers, but when things really do go haywire on a system it is nice to be able to understand what you are looking at. If you ever get to look at an assembler program that is doing screen I/O you will start to understand all the odd features of the higher-level software you have been using for on-line too. Without an understanding of how programs function at the assembler level, it is unlikely that you will ever be able to develop good software designed to serve the tech support community.

There exist several levels of assembler code. Some elderly business systems that were developed in assembler in the bad old days use assembler exactly as if it were a high-level language. All the fields you will encounter are addressed with label names and the program flows in an orderly series of branches. There are even things known as structured coding macros that allow the assembler programmer to code with IF, THEN, and PERFORM statements.

The most challenging (and interesting) assembler code is a lot trickier. In this code, which is generally found performing operating-system-type tasks, fields are referred to only as offsets from addresses stored in registers, and branch table logic is common. Complicated instructions like the BXLE are used for purposes not immediately apparent to the neophyte and complex macros are used for such functions as handling system interrupts, performing waits, and other operating system functions. It is not at all uncommon to spend five or six hours reading and attempting to understand two pages of this kind of code. It puts hair on your programming chest.

There do remain some assembler applications around, especially in on-line systems. If you have aspirations to go into tech support or to master software internals you should try to get some assembler exposure in your first couple of years on the job. Take advantage, too, of any courses the company can offer you in advanced dump reading. Try to find an environment that is a mix of higher-level language coding and a small set of assembler programs, since you would be best off avoiding the totally assembler system. The chances are that an all-assembler system is the company millstone. It will be maintained, but just barely, and no enhancements of more than a few lines will ever be planned for it. The best situation would be one where you had some assembler subroutines in your system performing sophisticated I/O or bit manipulation routines.

If you have plans to be a software developer you owe it to yourself to master assembly language programming for PC's. Even though you will probably not develop your software in assembly language, there is a good chance that you will need to understand your PC at the level that assembly language addresses in order to add some bell or whistle to your product. If you are accustomed to mainframe assembly language the transition to the PC assembly language is not that difficult.

## PL/I

I love PL/I. It is a high-level language designed for mainframes that possesses a sophisticated bag of tricks. It is a block-structured language similar in many respects to C and PASCAL and it has a whole set of built-in functions. You can use a subset of PL/I to write code that is very similar to COBOL or you can use a different subset and write code that is much more like FORTRAN. Using PL/I after COBOL is like taking a spin in a Toyota after driving a tank.

Unfortunately, PL/I was introduced to the business world with a lot of fanfare and then fell flat on its face. Rumor has it that since it doesn't own the rights to COBOL (which was developed, as you could deduce from looking at it, by a committee), IBM decided to come up with its own language, which it hoped to make the industry standard. The first compilers delivered to the business world had egregious bugs, I'm told. Worse for its long-term prospects, it was hard to teach PL/I to programmers accustomed to the simpler COBOL. Thus, although most colleges continue to teach PL/I, it is only encountered in a small number of business data processing environments.

However, this should not necessarily deter you if you do encounter an opportunity to program in PL/I. You might be looking at an interesting job. Its powerful instruction set allows the programmer a high level of control over program storage, almost as much as assembler does, and so any application that needs to do bit twiddling or fancy string manipulations will find PL/I very useful. Often, therefore, you will find PL/I used for applications that are more technically challenging than the usual business fare. However this is not always the case. Some companies simply adopted PL/I as their company standard years ago and have stuck with it. If you discover a PL/I job try to determine whether it reflects the former or latter situation.

If you do work in a business PL/I environment it never hurts to have an occasional look at a COBOL program. Most places with PL/I systems have a few elderly COBOL programs left over from before the invention of PL/I. If you can program in PL/I, COBOL will seem ridiculously easy for you to pick up. Therefore if you are ever stuck for a job, saying that you had responsibility for some COBOL programs might get you into a COBOL environment if that is all that is available. Your only real problem will be that when you try to do all the spiffy things you used to do in PL/I in COBOL you will find out you can't. It's like having a limb amputated.

## FORTRAN

Fortran is almost exclusively used for scientific applications and is often run on Digital Equipment Corporation's VAX family of computers. I have rarely encountered it being used in the business data processing environments I've been in, and my impression is that although most students study it in college, FORTRAN is used mainly by people whose backgrounds are stronger in the engineering or scientific aspects of the application being programmed than in programming itself. For example I have met people doing programming for actuarial systems in FORTRAN, but they were in training to become actuaries, and I have met FORTRAN programmers working in the oil industry on oil exploration systems but their backgrounds were in engineering, not programming.

### Ada

Ada is a new language cooked up by the Department of Defense. It is required for programming done on certain military contracts. However the trade press reports that it has not currently caught on in American industry outside of aircraft and defense systems. [2] IBM has announced that it will provide MVS and VM Ada compilers for mainframes, which some analysts think may lead to more business development being done in Ada, but it is hardly taking the business world by storm. Although Ada has experienced slow commercial acceptance in the United States, *Datamation* reported in 1987 that 85 percent of Ada applications in Europe are commercial (without giving the actual number of these applications which might be very small) and also says that the language has found acceptance in Japan

---

[2] Edith D. Myers "What the Countess Didn't Count On, Ada continues its slow march to the DP world, but can it shake off the DOD image," *Datamation*, February 1, 1987, pp. 32-33.

(Does it give a competitive edge?). I suspect that most of these applications are not mainframe applications.

If you do get an opportunity to work in Ada, you 'd better ask yourself how comfortable you would feel working in the defense industry since the chances are good that you will be doing just that. You should also be sure that you can qualify for a middle-level security clearance since most defense contractors won't let you into the building without one.


## APL

APL is the hands-down winner for the title of weirdest language ever produced for computers. Its inventors were brilliant, no question about it, but clearly did not live in the same world as the rest of us. This is readily apparent to anyone who has ever programmed on an IBM terminal that has an APL keyboard option. APL's inventors (sophisticated mathematicians) did not personally think much of the standard typewriter keyboard. So they designed their own, assigning to many keys strange Martian-looking symbols and Greek letters, and just to be different, assigning some familiar characters from the standard keyboard to keys different from the ones on which they usually appear. If you ever hit some random keys on your terminal and find yourself stuck typing in this bizarre character set you know whereof I speak.

What those Martian characters stand for in APL is a set of operations so conceptually advanced that no other programming language has ever provided them. For starters you can perform a string of operations on each and every member of an array simultaneously. You can string operations together too, so that their effect is cumulative rather than sequential. This allows levels of deviousness that, as I mentioned earlier, can result in code so dense not even the person who wrote it can untangle it when it needs to be enhanced. Among APL programmers at the Burlington IBM plant, it was standard methodology to throw the whole program out and rewrite it from scratch if an enhancement was really needed—it was much faster.

APL is rarely coded by garden-variety programmers. Like FORTRAN, it is usually the province of engineers and statisticians who encounter problems in their professional life that make such deviousness necessary.

If you are hired to write APL you may very well not be going in as part of the company's usual DP establishment. It is more likely that some user group whose members have a mathematical cast of mind have become disgusted with waiting for corporate information services to answer their work requests and have gotten the budget to hire their own programmer—you.

This can mean a dead end job for you if you are not trained in the user's area and intending to make that area your career path, rather than programming. If you are hired in this way you will not be able to move easily into other DP jobs within the company. In fact if you are hired into a user group as their pet programmer you might find yourself a pawn in the ongoing user/MIS battle, which is not a fun thing to be.

## Fourth-Generation Languages

This term covers a multitude of products, some relatively popular and others quite obscure. (See chapter 11 for some statistics on the market share of the more popular 4GL's.) Originally, a fourth-generation language was defined to be something a step beyond the so called "procedural languages" in which everything had to be spelled out step by step. The idea was that with these 4GL's you would no longer need programmers to do the programming. You would give your user group a quick class, and they would then log on and design their own report-extracting routines or design full-screen interfaces for themselves, thus off-loading from programming departments a lot of the work caused by having to constantly reprogram reports and screens that the user said he wanted but hates when he finally sees them delivered.

The reality is that most users don't *want* to log on and create their own report-extracting routines. (The ones who do often migrate into systems jobs anyway.) Furthermore, in order to provide the flexibility that users demand, the designers of 4GL's had to add feature after feature until the 4GL's became as complex as programming languages. As a result many now require good programming skills of the person who is to use them effectively. That's because, although they streamline the coding process, you still have to understand the coding process itself to be able to get results out of a full-featured fourth-generation language.

The more successful 4GL's like FOCUS and RAMIS provide a database with full inquiry capabilities and the ability to design full-screen interfaces. FOCUS also provides advanced statistical functions.

Other 4GL's you might encounter include MANTIS, NATURAL, PACBASE, NOMAD, SAS, and ORACLE. An important fact to remember about all of these is that unlike most computer languages where many different competing companies provide competing compilers, these 4GL's are owned by the companies that produce and sell them. Thus the fate of each 4GL is tied closely to the fate of its owner. If the company loses interest or lets the quality of its customer support deteriorate the way Martin Marietta did when it owned MANTIS, the language's customer base can quickly shrink. Thus there is a certain amount of risk to you as a programmer in committing yourself to becoming a specialist in one of these 4GL's. If the company that owns it goes belly-up you could be out of a job.

On the other hand, industry appears to be warming up to the 4GL concept after several years of waiting and seeing. *Datamation* estimated in 1987 that the top three 4GL's, FOCUS, RAMIS, and NOMAD, would be found in 22 percent of IBM mainframe sites by the end of 1987, which was up from only 7 percent of those sites in 1983.[3] Since few programmers are trained in using these 4GL's there is a constant demand for people experienced in them. If you plan to become a contractor, experience with one of the more popular ones could be very valuable.

If you are at the point in your career where you have worked with one or more of the older programming languages long enough to be able to claim them on your resume then you might well consider taking a job that uses a popular 4GL. Read up in the trade press and find out whether the installation base of the 4GL that you are considering is growing or shrinking. If the 4GL seems to be well-established then adding it to your bag of tricks can only be to your advantage, especially if you have a firm base in the other forms of software that we discussed earlier.

However, if you are looking for your first job you should be very wary. You want to learn the fundamentals and these packages are set up to bypass the very technical knowledge that you want to

[3] Willie Schatz, "The Gauntlet is Thrown, RAMIS Challenges FOCUS," *Datamation*, May 15, 1987, p. 36.

acquire. As a new hire you might find yourself simply filling in the blanks to produce boring user reports, rather than learning the interactions that make up a complex system. The best thing for you as a beginner is to stick close to the more traditional language environment. If you can do this and simultaneously pick up some exposure to a popular 4GL, then you have probably found the very best situation of all.

## Junk

There are a number of so-called languages to be found in the programming world, the knowledge of which is entirely useless to you as a programmer. These are one-of-a-kind languages, which the company either bought or developed itself in some misguided phase of its DP life. These languages are often, technically, application generators, akin to the fourth-generation languages we just discussed. However, unlike the ones discussed earlier, they are not industry standards, in fact they are rarely used anywhere outside of the department that has them in place.

Companies that have made investments in such languages are always looking for people to work with them because most programmers, quite wisely, want nothing to do with them. For a trainee straight out of school to get involved in one of these is utterly foolish. The skills you acquire working with these "languages" have no value outside of the department in which you learn them. Nevertheless in environments where these are found, it is not at all unusual to find a few new hires blissfully unaware that they are going to have a very nasty surprise when they go to get their next job whether in a new company or the same one they are currently in.

If you interview for a job and are told that the company has its own operating system, TP monitor, or full-screen interface which they wrote themselves, or that they have their own language which they use for all the development in a particular area, run, do not walk, to the nearest exit unless you have three or more years of experience in some standard technology and can afford the luxury of fooling around with this stuff.

I am not, by the way, saying that these languages are not interesting to learn or fun to use; they often are. I know what I am talking about here, having mastered not one but two of these monstrosities. It is just that they do not contribute to any future growth in your career. Also be warned if you are considering a job that uses in-house software, the chances are very good that there are no manuals (or else very deficient ones) and that debugging any code you produce is going to be challenging in the extreme. Tracing is often impossible. Frequently your only recourse when problems emerge is to sit at the feet of the guru who wrote the language and hope that he can be persuaded to make time in his busy schedule to meditate on its internals until he remembers a known bug. If the guru has left the company you may be well and truly in the soup.

## RPG

RPG is a family of languages that are generally used on IBM's System/34, System/36, and System/38 minicomputers. There are two RPG's currently in use, RPG II and RPG III. RPG started out as a 4GL type of language. It is table driven. What the RPG programmer does is fill out a series of forms specifying different things he would like to have occur at specific places in a canned program flow. For example, the canned program has times when calculations are performed, so the programmer indicates on a calculation form which calculations should be performed at what time. However as RPG has been enhanced the canned program has become increasingly complex and it is now a quite-powerful, if somewhat odd, language.

The minicomputers that use RPG are usually found in two types of installations. A large number are in small- and medium-sized manufacturing companies. Many of these use MAPICS, IBM's manufacturing software. The other places they are found is in large corporations where they have been networked in with mainframes to provide distributed processing. For example, in IBM's Burlington plant a warehouse-tracking system used bar code readers to scan product coming into and leaving the warehouse. The information read by the bar code readers was processed by a System/38 programmed in RPG, which produced summary files that were transmitted up to a mainframe and run through batch programs which added the information from the bar code system to an IMS database.

The vast majority of RPG programmers work in the smaller shop environment. In the warehouse application described above the RPG code was not written by a programmer who had years of experience in RPG but by a mainframe PL/I programmer, knowledgeable in the IMS database, who had picked RPG up through a course.

If the newspapers are anything to go by, there is a steady demand for experienced RPG programmers to work in smaller shops. Possibly the major challenge for RPG programmers comes from PC's. As PC's increase in horsepower and decrease in price they may take over some of the work traditionally done on the Series/3X machines. However so many companies have a hefty investment in RPG systems that it is unlikely that it will go away soon. So is unlikely that ex-RPG programmers will be standing in bread lines. If worst comes to worst you might be able to make a living doing RPG to dBASE IV conversions!

## PC Programming in the Corporate World: C, BASIC, and Pascal

Increasingly, programmers in a mainframe environment are using PC's to provide user front ends to mainframe applications and to create networked systems which may or may not communicate with mainframe-based databases. While you will almost never find the kind of programming for PC's that you read about in PC magazines[4] going on in corporate IS departments, you will increasingly encounter mainframe-related PC programming opportunities.

Thus you might very well be hired into what appears to be an MVS IDMS mainframe environment only to find yourself programming in some variety of BASIC or C as part of an effort to develop a subsystem that collects data at a distributed processing node and then ships it up to the host system.

This is not necessarily bad. But there are still a lot more jobs for mainframe programmers in data processing than PC programmers. There are also enough hobbyists around who can work with BASIC so that finding someone to program in it is not very hard. As a result contracting rates for PC work are often much lower than the corresponding mainframe programming rates. I know of one highly experienced programmer who had worked only in BASIC for a PC

---

[4] Mostly the programming of snazzy utilities and general purpose packages.

vendor firm who was forced to contract out for $10 an hour. The reason for this was that the only companies interested in having PC programming done in the part of the country where he lived were small proprietorships who blenched when told of usual contracting rates.

In spite of all the furor that has surrounded PC's in the last few years you will often find that a company with hundreds or even thousands of mainframe programmers will only have a handful of full-time PC experts. These will usually be clustered into something that for some reason seems to be named the "info center." These PC programmers' task is to support the people in the company who have been given PC's, usually managers who use them for creating spreadsheets, schedules, memos, and the ubiquitous pie charts. These info center programmers hook up systems, respond to problem calls, and evaluate software purchases for the company. They may also help users set up databases and spreadsheets using off-the-shelf products like dBASE III or Lotus 1-2-3. They may also configure and install Local Area Networks (LANS). This is a tech support type of job. These programmers rarely are called upon to develop PC software themselves. There is so much on the market that companies find it cheaper to buy stand-alone PC software off the shelf.

There do not appear to be very many technical PC jobs outside of these. In fact when applications programming departments are preparing to develop PC segments of new systems they rarely go outside their organization to hire in someone whose expertise lies in PC work. Instead, in every situation I have ever seen, they find experienced mainframe programmers in the organization who are PC enthusiasts in their time off and make do with them, or else train experienced mainframe programmers. This is again because it is the mainframe knowledge—that managers cannot find on the open market—which must be understood if networked PC systems are going to communicate effectively with existing mainframe databases, batch, and on-line systems.

You can confirm the difference in demand for PC as opposed to mainframe programmers by comparing the relatively empty help wanted pages in PC-oriented *Infoworld* or *PC Week* with the corresponding pages in the more mainframe-oriented *Computerworld*.

People who have tried to make careers as strictly PC programmers tell me that the biggest problem they have encountered is that most programming jobs for PC programmers are to be found in struggling software companies, which tend to be highly unstable. In these companies you can easily lose your job either when the company folds or when it becomes highly successful, since success often attracts the attention of other software firms which acquire the original firm and either move its programmers across the country or lay them off and use their own staffs.

If you do intend to diverge into PC programming you will have to read constantly to keep up with what is happening in the PC universe and with PC languages. Unlike the mainframe world where a small number of entrenched products dominate, it appears that today's hot compiler or database for PC's can easily be tomorrow's junk.

PC programming, for the mainframe programmer at least, looks like yet another item, like the 4GL, which belongs in the "nice-to-have-as-an-extra" category. It is a terrific plus if you have a solid base in mainframe software and programming, but puts you in a risky position if it alone is your only marketable skill.

If you intend to become a software developer, however, you really should try to become familiar with C, which is emerging as the preferred language for PC software developments.

The C language is, to put it mildly, sparse. In a manner reminiscent of APL it allows the clever programmer to pack a lot of function into a single line of code. Whether anyone other that its author can interpret that line of code a few years later is another question. C also allows the programmer to drop to the assembly language level when necessary, a powerful feature that IBM gave its company programmers years ago in the language that IBM operating system developers work in, PL/S. (Unfortunately IBM never saw fit to distribute PL/S to the rest of the world.) If you do use C to develop your own software which you intend to support for more than a single release, you would be well-advised to steer clear of being too clever in your use of C and you should make sure that you write and document your code in a manner that will allow it to be maintained by a less-than-genius programmer. It is unfortunately true that the most brilliant code is often the hardest to extend because only its originator, usually promoted to higher and better things, can figure out how it does what it does.

Although mainframe C compilers are now available for mainframes, the small number of experienced programmers who are comfortable working in C ensures that C will not take the mainframe world by storm very soon, and the programmer who works only in C is most likely to find himself working in a mini or micro environment for some time to come.

Much of the work for C programmers is to code C applications that run under some version of the UNIX operating system, an operating system developed by Bell Laboratories. The U.S. government is a strong proponent of UNIX where many departments are required to use it and UNIX is routinely touted as the next big thing in mainframe DP, but to date has not penetrated business computing beyond scientific and engineering applications where it has fanatically enthusiastic users.[5]

As PC's grow in power and complexity it will become increasingly difficult to program for them. If you are lucky enough to have been able to learn software internals for mainframe operating systems there looms an even greater career opportunity for you in PC product development working with the newest generations of PC's which are capable of multitasking and sophisticated networking. There are terrific software development opportunities for programmers familiar with the solutions used in mainframe software to handle the technical challenges posed by these new features. As the PC's become more powerful, software vendors are striving to give their PC products the same features found in mainframe fourth-generation languages and databases and to enable the PC software to access these mainframe databases and make use of the data retrieved from them; consequently the hunt is on for programmers who can do this. But once again it will be your mainframe experience rather than any skills specific to the PC environment which are of the greatest value to you here. You can see that this is true by noting that Ashton-Tate, developer of dBASE III, a prominent PC-DOS database, recruited large system developers like Moshe M. Zloof, creator of IBM's Query By Example product, when faced with the need to develop a far more complex SQL-compatible OS2 product.

[5] See Computerworld Spotlight, "Unix Climbs Corporate Ladder," *Computerworld*, October 26, 1987, 16-page pullout section following page 74.

# 13
*Factors—*
*The Application Itself*

Up until now we have talked about the company you will work for and the hardware and software environment in which you will do your programming. Now it's time to get down to the part of the job that many programmers give the least thought to: the application they will be doing their programming for.

**Your "Second Career"**

Unfortunately no one hires programmers because they want to see interesting technical problems solved or so that they can marvel at elegant code. No, businesses bring people in to solve what they see as business problems and the area of the business that your programming efforts are going to address makes up the application area.

This might sound pretty basic, but many programmers go through life as if the application they were working in was irrelevant to their career. They choose a company because it has a good reputation or offers excellent compensation, or because it offers a lot of DP education and the opportunity to work with state-of-the-art hardware and software. What most don't seem to give very much weight to is that in programming for a specific application area you are going to find yourself spending a tremendous amount of time learning the business details of the application. In fact, if you are going to be a good applications programmer, in many cases you are going to have to know almost as much as your user does in order to help him design the system that he really needs.

There is little difference between the skills needed to write a file maintenance program in an IMS database environment used by an insurance company and those needed in an IMS database environment used by a widget maker. But there is a tremendous difference, I find, between thinking about insurance all day compared with thinking about inventory control, real estate investments, electronic mail, or hospital patient tracking, all applications areas in which I have worked. If you would rather think about patients lying in bed getting better treatment as a result of the pharmacy management system you are writing than think about the formulae used to rate drivers in a specific risk pool, then the benefit of the extra money you might make working at an insurance company might be canceled out by the boredom that daily contemplation of the minutiae of insurance can bring on.

Since many programmers begin in one applications area and never move out of it they often are unable to separate their feelings for the application area from their feelings for programming. Many of the programmers I've met who tell me that they feel burned out in their careers appear to be people who are bored by the application areas they have mastered.

Therefore when you are looking for your first job you must think carefully about the application you will be working on, since you can expect to learn a tremendous amount of trivia about it in the years to come. In fact, you should treat the application area as your second career!

## Applications Families

Applications tend to fall into families, and after you spend four or five years working in a single family of applications you may find it hard to move out, particularly if your experience has been centered on systems analysis which is heavily applications oriented, as opposed to more technical concerns. However it is a lot easier to move into a new applications area than it is to move to a new software environment.

The one exception to the above statement occurs when your applications area and software expertise merge together in the case where you are working intensively with a widely used applications package. Examples of this are insurance programmers working in companies using Life/70 or LIFE-COMM, which are life insurance packages sold by The Continuum Company, Austin, Texas, banking programmers using software from HOGAN, and manufacturing programmers using MAPICS, a manufacturing package developed for System/3X computers. In this case your value to a potential employer is not just your applications knowledge but your very specific knowledge of how these software packages work. Thus the impact on your career of taking a job where you learn one of these is stronger than application level decisions usually are.

Sometimes applications are grouped by industry. You will see advertisements for insurance programmers or banking programmers, even though the software environments may be quite varied from one insurance company to another, because in many insurance applications the level of technical skills needed is low but it is very important to understand fairly complex insurance concepts.

Manufacturing applications form another related group. These range from robot control to cost accounting but again, many employers value your applications experience here as much as your technical background.

The fact that you suspect that your programming skills are by far your most important asset will not make much difference if the manager interviewing you has worked only in manufacturing himself and doesn't realize that your insurance experience has taught you how to design and code just about anything that needs input definition, processing, and output definition.

Other times you will see applications grouped together by their function within a company rather than by industry. For example, accounting applications, billing applications, and office automation applications will be grouped together since it is assumed that if you have worked with accountants in one situation you can work with them in another. Yet another specialized set of applications are the scientific applications, including engineering ones, and CAD/CAM, computer-aided-design and manufacturing. For these, as we've mentioned, your applications knowledge is often the major qualification you need, since in order to do program definition in these areas you need to be able to understand the kind of highly advanced mathematical or engineering concepts you would only have learned by getting the same training as your users.

Choosing an application that is harmonious with your personality is a key factor if you want to find yourself happy fifteen years into your career. It is just plain harder to work with people who are talking all the time about things that bore you! If you treat the application as secondary you run into another source of strife: conflict with your user.

Misunderstandings and out-and-out bad feeling between the user of a system and the programmer are so widespread in business data processing that many people assume that it is just a natural outcome of having programmers try to support people who are not interested in understanding programming. However often the real problem is the programmer's deep dislike of the very thing most central to the user's life: the application.

If you are interested in your user's field of endeavor you will be much more likely to listen closely to him. Furthermore you will be more likely to think the details of his system out in terms of how it will appear to him. This enables you, in effect, to save him from himself during the all-important system design phase. The programmer who can say to a user, "This screen that you said you wanted here is going to be a real pain in the neck because you will often want to look at it when you are in the middle of this other screen here" will not have to redo the screen flows late in the project after customer testing, which is when the customer unused to using a computer system may first discover the problem. The only way that the programmer can come up with this kind of useful suggestion, though, is by having a very good idea of how the user thinks when he is doing his work. And the only way I know really to get that understanding is to be interested enough in what the user does that it is fun to walk in his mental footsteps.

In contrast, the programmer who is bored by the application (and, by extension, by its practitioners, the users) will often spend just enough time with the user to get the rough specifications for a project before running back to the systems department where he can begin doing what he enjoys—programming. When his program is done and demonstrated to his user, the chances are that the customer will not be satisfied with the end product and will explain in a testy way all the things that ought to have been put in the program in the first place. The programmer feels cheated because, for crying out loud, he did just what the user told him, and the user feels irritated because programmers can never get anything right!

It is very hard to do good work for someone you consider to be a boring jerk. For this reason and because it is very unrealistic to expect your user to understand the problems that the programmer must deal with, you will do the best work, and the work that is most highly praised by your user, when you work in an area that captures your interest.

If you intend to become a software developer who provides packages for businesses you can see that the applications area you learn in your DP apprenticeship years will either strengthen your ability to come up with a viable product or hinder it. You are not going to pick up applications knowledge at the depth necessary for creating a successful product except by working in that application in a business environment. So you must be particularly careful to choose an applications area you enjoy and one you are prepared to spend several years mastering.

About the only people who can ignore applications completely are systems programmers. This is because in their case the application is programming itself. If you find yourself the kind of person who seems to find just about all applications uninviting, but who loves working with computer systems, you probably should take the steps necessary to move into a tech support area as soon as you can.

When you are interviewing for a new job you should pay a lot of attention to the way the interviewer handles his discussion of the applications area. It will give you some clue as to whether you are looking at an environment in which most of what you learn will be application-related or whether technical programming skills are being called for. I have had interviews with DP managers who sounded much more like users than programmers, going into great detail about the business aspects of the system they were developing. In contrast I've worked for other managers who hadn't an inkling of how users would actually use the system they were building but who obviously had very sophisticated technical skills. It is very important for your future happiness that you find a good match here.

But a word of caution: This doesn't mean that if you love to fish you must work only for a boat manufacturer! We all have our little oddities. You might not, for example, have ever thought of yourself as a person who enjoys accounting. But you may get tremendous satisfaction out of balancing your checkbook or preparing your own tax return. If so then you may find working in an accounting or financial application quite tolerable.

I myself have always enjoyed the working with manuscripts and as a result have always enjoyed any work that created attractive documents, whether the application was word processing software or just a humble report writer. I also enjoy thinking about real estate and therefore found working on a real estate investment system much more interesting than working on an insurance system in the same company, although to many people the demands of the two might have seemed very similar.

So here again you will need to spend some time taking inventory of your proclivities. You must ask yourself whether you can live with the application area you are thinking of entering. If everything else about a job seems terrific except the application involved you might give yourself the benefit of the doubt and take the job, in the hope that the programming component will outweigh the application itself. But if you find yourself hating your job, before abandoning programming entirely you owe it to yourself to try to move into an entirely different applications area. You might be surprised at what a difference a switch like that can make.

# 14
## Factors—Your Place in the Systems Development Cycle

Somewhere among your college computer science courses you undoubtedly studied something called the systems development cycle. Your textbook detailed an orderly process by which the user's original need was analyzed, designed, coded, tested, implemented, and maintained—in that order, with neat demarcations between each phase.

In real life, particularly in companies whose primary business is not software development, the life cycle of a system is a lot messier, and it is often difficult to tell at what "phase" a project really is. Nevertheless you need to understand where a system is in its overall life cycle, before taking on an assignment with it, because here, too, is a factor that can have some important ramifications in the development of your career.

Because college courses tend to focus almost entirely on the creation of new systems, most new college-trained programmers tend to glamorize "development" and shy away from "maintenance." Development is seen as the opportunity to do something new and exciting, preferably with state-of-the-art techniques. Maintenance, on the other hand, is viewed as scut work, propping up old programs at best, an inferior kind of work to be avoided if at all possible.

Hiring managers know this. As a result almost no interviewer will ever tell you that the job you are being hired to fill is a maintenance job. He knows that to tell you this is to fatally discourage your interest in a position he very much needs to fill. Instead he will characterize what you will be doing as "small development projects" or perhaps that useful catchall "enhancement."

## The Hidden Benefits of Maintenance

The new programmer who buys the stereotyped view of maintenance versus development may actually miss out on the jobs that could best prepare him for his career future.

Why is this so? Let's look at what experienced programmers know about "development" and "maintenance."

Working on new software development projects can provide terrific career advantages—for the experienced programmer. However, for a person fresh out of school, development groups can be the worst possible environment in which to make a start. This is true for a number of reasons.

First of all, college courses generally focus on teaching the student how to write individual programs. Even courses that are titled "Systems Analysis and Design" usually present you with an oversimplified system for which the student writes five or six interrelated programs, often working alone, or, in a more enlightened class, with a few like-minded classmates. This exposure leads to new programmers' entering the work force with the illusion that they understand systems design and have some experience in it.

The reality, of course, is that real business systems consist of hundreds of programs with a multitude of interactions. And most new systems have to relate to other, older, company systems that are already in place. In order to be in a position to work on designing even a small part of such a system you must have several years of experience that will enable you to understand this kind of large intertwined system—not only how it functions, but the long-term issues it will face, such as data integrity, security, and the ability of your system to be easily modified so that it can adapt to the changing nature of the company's business needs.

How do you get this experience? Not by writing small pieces of code assigned by an experienced systems analyst on a true "development" project. The new programmer becomes a professional by working on existing systems in a way that allows him to observe these large systems as they function. In short, the very best training for becoming a systems designer is doing maintenance on older, in-place systems.

In my first year as a trainee a small part of my job was responsibility for a system that maintained secretarial mail logs. These mail logs were stored on a mass storage device (MSS). One day this mass storage device malfunctioned, erasing the index to the volume our master file was on. The operator who tried to restore the volume from the master file backup had his mind on other things. Thinking he had completed the restore he carelessly answered a system prompt with a response that told the system to destroy the index to the backup volume! At this point I received a phone call from the operations area telling me that my master file had been destroyed. Naively I told them to load the tape backup for the file, only to be told that there was none. The file had *only* been backed up on the MSS volume that the operator had destroyed. Since it turned out that once the index is gone on an MSS volume no device on earth can recover the contents of the volume, I had no recourse except to spend the next week calling up each of my users, one by one, and after explaining to them what had happened, try to convince them that they really didn't need the data that they had stored in this system after all.

Many of them insisted that they did. So for the next few months the data entry department was busy keying in a new master file reconstructed from the users' latest printouts. What made this particularly sensitive was that this system belonged to a user group which our department was trying to sell a far more complex and sophisticated system that would handle not only their mail logs but all of their intracompany correspondence!

This experience, with a system that was entirely in maintenance mode, probably taught me more about data integrity than anything else ever possibly could. Years later you can be sure that any system I have design responsibility for has frequent and religiously observed backups taken. And I don't take just anybody's word that the backups are being done—I check it out myself. Not only that but I am always interested in knowing what mechanisms the system contains to enable files to be reconstructed should other integrity problems be discovered. Any new system I design, for example will not erase its transaction input files two days after they run through batch (in a system with no meaningful journaling!) as one system I've seen did—designed by people whose experience had been mainly in new development.

In the maintenance environment you will constantly experience episodes of petty disaster, which gradually teach you the principles of good file structuring, good program design, and good operations procedures. That many of these will be teaching you by bad example is irrelevant. The lessons will be indelibly inscribed on your mind.

Maintenance experience will train you to think in terms of daily operations. It will sensitize you to the kinds of procedures that cause problems with operations personnel. It will train you to develop code that is easy to maintain, for example, code in which similar modules use identical paragraph names for similar functions. It will teach you to leave room for expansion in your files so that you are not faced with the need to go through tedious file conversions affecting many programs every time your user has a new idea. Most important, it will sensitize you to the fact that if anything can go wrong on a production system, it will, especially if you are trying to give management a demo!

In contrast, programmers who go directly into development groups from college have no way of understanding the huge number of changes that even the best-designed systems will undergo in coming years. And, having had little day-to-day interaction with the people who use computer systems, they also often fail to appreciate just how hard it can be for their users to *use* the best-designed systems.

They tend to think that if they do a terrific job using all the enlightened principles they learned in school, the system won't need modifications in the future. If you've been paying any attention to the rest of this book I think by now you will agree that this is not, in fact, the case.

Experience in maintenance also gives the programmer insight into the communication problems we've mentioned earlier: the problems that arise when the user attempts to explain to the programmer what it is that he wants the programmer to do for him.

The experienced maintenance programmer has learned that, in most cases, the user can describe only a part of what he wants, since much of what he needs he assumes will be provided in the system, simply because it makes sense to him for it to be there. The experienced maintenance programmer in working on a series of smaller changes and fixes has come to understand better the way his user group thinks and the way they use their existing systems.

## The Pitfalls of Development

Maintenance is starting to look a lot better, isn't it? I think so.

You should be very suspicious of any organization that would bring in new hires and put them on true systems development! Very few would. What they are more likely to do is put new programmers into jobs on development projects where their task is to code small sections of code to rigidly designed specifications provided by more experienced systems analysts.

And this, I can assure you, is where you really encounter scut work. The new maintenance programmer usually finds himself in an environment where staffing levels are sparse and he is encouraged to do as much as possible on his own. He must design solutions to users' immediate requests for modifications; he must develop a test environment; and he must test his programs well enough to ensure that he is not roused from a warm bed at 3 A.M. by a hot systems abend. Often the maintenance programmer develops a good relationship with the user group personnel whose system he supports. The so-called development new hire may often spend months doing nothing more than writing COBOL modules following detailed specifications written by more experienced people and testing them with data supplied by others. Often this development programmer has no idea what his modules do in the larger system. He may not even get to participate in the next steps of the testing cycle, the integration and systems tests.

And this is if all is going well on the project. Many programmers I've seen hired into development projects have not even been given the opportunity to show off their coding skills. Instead they have found themselves sitting at their desks for long periods of time with absolutely nothing at all to do! This is caused by another characteristic of development projects that is seldom covered in college systems development textbooks: true development projects have a major flaw from a career standpoint. They are frequently canceled. This cancellation often occurs after anywhere from three months to two years have been spent on the project. Sometimes they escape cancellation but suffer catastrophic shifts in direction and major reorganizations that result in everything the programmer has done up until that point landing in the trash.

This is a natural part of systems development, since in the process of doing competent analysis and design in a certain number of cases the analyst will demonstrate that it is going to cost a tremendous amount of money and effort to achieve what the user has asked for, and the user, who after all has to pay for it, will decide that the project isn't worth what it will cost.

In a well-managed project this decision should occur at the high-level design phase. But life does not imitate systems analysis textbooks. Since many managers demand that programming start before the analysis phase is truly complete it is not at all unusual to see a project canceled only after the programming departments have coded (and tested) enough of the system for the customer to see a demo and get a hazy idea of what the system will actually look like. It is all too often only at this point that the user realizes that the system as it has been designed (and often signed off on by himself) omits some absolutely vital feature (which he may have forgotten to mention in the design phase) without which the system is, from his perspective, junk.

It is at points like this that managers scurry around trying to find ways out that leave everyone looking good (every manager of course) and programmers find themselves with time on their hands.

It is no picnic for any programmer to see his work get thrown away, and I know of one development programmer who wrote programs for five solid years without seeing a single one ever get to implementation. But for a new person with no track record in the company, it can be devastating. You could easily find yourself at the end of a year with the company having nothing whatsoever to show for yourself. Since raises and promotions come as rewards for having demonstrated your worth to the company a situation like this leaves you with little leverage. Your chances of having something to brag about are a lot better working in a maintenance environment.

The programmer who demonstrates real talent and a flair for handling the routine insanity that maintenance represents, builds a strong reputation within the company. This is what can lead to joining the quality development projects—and to joining them in a design role too. Furthermore, if that maintenance programmer is you, and you have been paying attention to what is going on in the company around you, you should have a pretty good idea of who in your organization is likely to lead a successful development project and who is not. This may protect you from even getting involved in the development projects destined to crash and burn.

If you are seriously considering joining a development group the most important thing you should do is look at the people leading the project and assess how good their grasp of matters is. I'm referring here to the managers, not the programmers. In my experience the development projects that were the most destructive to programmer careers were those heavily influenced by middle managers who had weak or nonexistent technical skills. It is these managers who force programmers to waste time trying to modify outside vendors' software to serve purposes it was never intended for. It is these managers who fall for the timesaving gimmicks that almost always result in horrendous time losses, and it is these managers who, worst of all, exhort the troops to follow structured development methodology, but force them to dispense with walkthroughs claiming there is no time for them, particularly at the most important systems design phase.

If you are interested in development you should be warned that there are some managers lurking out there who are real losers. If you ever become a consultant, many of the assignments you will have as a consultant will be to clean up the devastation left in the wake of one of these. As an example of exactly how bad it can get I know of one project that managed to reach its fourth year without written specifications. The different portions of this project had been assigned to managers who were in different warring chains of command and therefore under no pressure to get along. Each group designed its part of the system without having to have it reviewed by the others. The upshot was that a few months from implementation this system consisted of a front end that collected data and put it in a logical order, a database interface that destroyed this logical order, a database that stored the data using logical relationships which were not those used by the report writer routines which accessed it, and finally, the piece de resistance, an almost incomprehensible homemade application generator (the details of which resided

only in the head of one person whose strong point was not communication) which attempted vainly to compensate for the rest of
the system's destruction of data. Since the dominant concern of each
manager was to defend his section of the system against the
managers in the other groups, programmers unlucky enough to be
lured to this project quickly learned to keep their heads low or look
for new jobs.

Contact with a development project such as this one is unlikely
to do much for your career. It is because you are not in a position to
know anything about the people in charge and the history of a project
in a new company that joining a development team can be so
dangerous, even to the experienced programmer.

It is somewhat cynically said by the old-timers that the time to
join a development project is when the end of the project is in sight.
Usually by this time the project's originators are gone, having taken
the blame for all that went wrong throughout the project's life cycle,
and the people who take their places can continue to blame their
predecessors for anything in the system that is not what it ought to
be. Besides that, they get to enjoy the glory of reaching implementation and the corresponding banquets and awards. Sadly, experience
would tend to bear this out.

Having said all this, I urge you to look with fond indulgence on
the interviewer who promises you that a new job is "60 percent
development and 40 percent maintenance." He knows it's not true.
You know it's not true. But at least you can feel better knowing that
in entering the typical maintenance shop which experts acknow-
ledge makes up 50 percent to 80 percent of all programming environments, you are placing yourself in a very good place to spend your
DP apprenticeship.


## Maintenance Losers

There is really only one kind of situation in which maintenance may
not offer you the benefits detailed above, and you should try to avoid
it at all costs.

I'm talking about the "casts of thousands" maintenance environment, which I described earlier, where management has had to
hire a large number of poorly trained people. In this environment
the maintenance programmer's assigned task may be to maintain a

tiny portion of a large system and his area of exposure tightly limited. In this case a programmer usually does not get to learn the larger system his programs are part of, neither does he get to deal in an ongoing manner with users. Coding off of other people specs in an isolated cubicle is not the way to develop a career that goes anywhere. Make sure when you look at a maintenance job that it is one where you do your own analysis and design and that you are not merely the coding arm of a more experienced person.

The other thing to look for when choosing a maintenance/enhancement kind of job is to get that job on a system which offers a rich complexity of function, and ideally, good software exposure. Even if your original assignment is not in the more interesting parts of a system, you are way ahead in the long run if the system you start out on has a database, an on-line function, distributed processing, or some other such things going on in it somewhere. This is because no matter where you start out in this kind of system, by demonstrating competence you can usually move into the more interesting parts of the system.

Not only that but you can often claim it's necessary, for example to learn something about the database to design adequate test data for your program changes. Or you might show that you have to learn how the on-line side works in order to make an enhancement to something in batch. The richer a system you are working on is, the more you can learn without having to job hop within or outside of the company.

# 15
## *Factors—Corporate Culture*

You might find a job that allows you to learn a tremendous amount technically, pays you reasonably well, exposes you to an application you find interesting, and yet still leaves you seething with frustration at the end of every working day.

The reason for this is that, in addition to all the factors mentioned previously, there is another major factor you must consider, one that is much harder to describe. What we are talking about here is what students of business are coming to call "corporate culture."[1]

Anyone who has worked for a number of companies can tell you that no two companies are the same in how they feel. Each company has what might be described as a personality. This personality is reflected in obvious things like the way that the company promotes, whether they promote from within or prefer to bring in outsiders, and how they motivate, whether the emphasis is on giving rewards or causing fear. It is also reflected in a host of smaller

---

[1] Terrence E. Deal and Allan A. Kennedy, *Corporate Cultures: The Rites and Rituals of Corporate Life*. (Reading, MA: Addison-Wesley Publishing Company, 1982). This book put the phrase into common use, I believe.

details—whether managers eat lunch with the people under their control, how workers are treated when their children are sick, the availability of pregnancy leave, and whether you must inform your manager anytime you leave your work area or are considered responsible enough that such scrutiny would be demeaning.

Sometimes the corporate culture is consistent throughout the company. Other companies are made up of many subcultures and you might find that moving from one department to another feels like changing companies.

The important thing for you to realize is that the corporate culture and the way that the people in the corporation manifest this culture to each other will have a tremendous amount to do with whether or not you like working for the company. Your chances for success are much higher in a company whose personality is congruent with your own.

Here again I've found that often programmers who are feeling burned out are suffering not because they are ill-suited to their jobs, but because they have assumed that various features of this own particular corporate culture are present in all companies. Unsuited to this particular culture they begin to feel hopeless.

It would be impossible to detail all the different kinds of corporate cultures you might encounter. Instead what I will attempt to do in this chapter is describe some of the more extreme polarities, the extremes that you might encounter as you move from company to company. I will try to show how each type of corporate culture affects the nature of the programmer's role in that kind of company. I hope this might help you define elements of the corporate culture that is in place in a company you are considering. For the more experienced programmer contending with burn out, it might help you recognize the hallmarks of the dominant culture in the company you work for, allowing you to take some comfort from realizing that some of what irks you about being a programmer might better be thought of as what irks you about being a programmer working in your current corporate culture.

## The Macho Shop

In a macho shop people brag about how they brought in their sleeping bags and slept under the desk all week—if they slept at all—and got the project completed by its deadline. People in macho shops will also brag about how they had to cancel their vacation plans at the last minute, or how they were back at their desks the day after their wife had the baby (or two weeks after they had one themselves!).

Macho shops are by no means staffed only by men. I've known plenty of women who flourished in this kind of environment. For the outsider such shops can seem baffling, especially when the outsider discovers that these people are not being paid any more than their compatriots at other, more humane, shops. In fact the managers in the macho shop sometimes realize that a certain type of individual is so well rewarded by being given the opportunity to prove how tough he is that no further rewards are necessary, and rewards, including raises and promotions as well as the corporate gewgaws and free dinners other companies provide, may be few and far between.

If you come into a macho shop prepare to work like a slave. Often in the macho shop management has calculated that employee overtime is cheaper than rewriting aged and limping systems. In the worst situation you will be promoted to an "exempt" job class, one in which the company is not required by labor law to pay you overtime for overtime hours worked, and then find yourself on call one or two weeks a month for systems that are guaranteed to abend every night.

Being on call for this kind of system is horrendous. What it means, in a shop such as this, is that the phone will ring at some excruciating hour of the night, and you will be told that the system has encountered some problem, usually an abend. This will occur night after night, and each time you will have to struggle into your clothes and drive to work to look at sysouts (printouts generated by the system), since no one in operations will be capable of giving you a clue as to what went wrong. Or, instead of having to come in, you might just have to answer questions at forty-minute intervals throughout the night, every night and Saturday and Sunday. Some companies will even give you a beeper, conferring it as if it were a great mark of honor so that you have absolutely no excuse for not being there when needed. After a few weeks of this you will probably begin to hallucinate from lack of sleep. Your judgment will be impaired and you will begin to appear demented.

A gentleman I once worked with who was known for his sense of humor once substituted the phone number of a well-known headhunting firm for his own on the on call-list, as a hint, perhaps, of what the company could expect if they called him too often. This is not a strategy I would recommend.

Being on call is not a feature particular to macho shops alone. As a programmer you should expect to be on call at various points in your career. The only way to avoid it is to work only on on-line systems that come down in the evening or on development projects that don't make it to implementation. For anyone who ever deals with batch systems, it is part of the job. This is particularly true if you have been responsible for making a lot of changes to the production system recently or if a development project you have worked on finally goes live. There is a certain thrill in being in the data center while the city sleeps, but where corporate culture comes in is in how often you are on call and how difficult it is to repair production problems when you are on call.

When you interview for a new job you should feel free to ask how often you can expect to be on call and you should listen closely to the answer. Some programmers are afraid to ask because they don't want to appear lazy to the interviewer. However a brutal on-call system can be a source of misery to a programmer who does not get ego gratification from proving his toughness through exposing himself to endless hardship. It can also wreak havoc with your family life.

The macho shop manager will tell you that "of course" you will be on call once a week, or one week every month. It is part of the job, and he's proud of it. The nonmacho shop manager will tell you of the steps that management has taken to minimize as much as possible the need for being on call. He will brag about the high quality of his test system and how it ensures that system changes are tested in an environment so like the production system that production abends rarely occur. In contrast, in the macho shop people actually brag about not even having a test system!

In a more humane shop operators are trained to solve JCL problems, and if they can't solve the problem themselves they are trained to give the programmer, over the phone, the information that might help him pinpoint the problem. The operators in such a shop are also allowed to make changes according to what the programmer tells them over the phone. In the macho shop, in contrast, the operations staff rarely speaks English and are unable to locate systems messages on an output listing, making it necessary for the programmer to drive in to look at the listing himself. The humane shop nowadays will provide on-call programmers with portable PC terminals enabling them to log on to the system from their bedrooms thus making a trip in unnecessary. In the macho shop money is not wasted on such frivolity. In fact don't be surprised if you are told that it is simpler just not to go home the nights you are on call since you will only have to turn right around and come back in anyway!

Overtime is the other big issue that defines a macho shop. In a macho shop you are told that overtime is expected, with the hint that people who go home after a mere forty hours of work are sissies. If you work in this kind of shop you will receive this message not only from management but from your coworkers who will be decidedly hostile if they see you heading home at 5:00, even if you have completed all your assigned work.

I urge you to feel free to ask at an interview about a company's attitude toward overtime. You will have to live with the answer. If overtime is not something that you want to handle as an everyday rather than as an every-so-often thing, it is better to know about it up front.

And don't be afraid to turn down a job (particularly if you already are employed) because of the overtime demands. There do exist companies in which the ongoing need for overtime is considered a sign of poor planning by management. You might just be happier in one of these. Some managers have found that programmers who work fifty and sixty hours a week every week for long periods of time produce sloppy work that requires even more effort to fix, or that the long-term effect of this kind of schedule is constant job turn over, as people "tough it out," but secretly look for other, less Spartan environments.

There are individuals who flourish in the macho shop because of their own values and personality makeup and who would be miserable in what they would perceive as the lax environment of a "country club." The key here of course is to know your own personality and what you would be happy with.

## The Political Arena

Most people, when asked, claim that they hate office politics; they just want to do their job. In reality of course people vary greatly in the degree to which they enjoy the game that politics represents.

As a new hire you will probably be shocked at the extent to which "politics" rules what happens in any company; and to a certain extent, becoming aware of the real role of politics in business and learning how to work within the framework of politics is part of moving from being an inexperienced trainee to becoming a seasoned professional. I urge all people new to the business world to read Betty Harragan's excellent primer *Games Mother Never Taught You*.[2] Although this book is addressed primarily to a female audience it is the best guide to the world of business for the unsophisticated I have ever seen and illuminates many of its rules. Technical people tend to be very logical and have a lot of difficulty with the artificial, but very important, rules that are followed in the game of business. To the technical person they often seem like fripperies that make it harder to get the job done. As a result of this outlook, often the brightest technical people ignore important business game rules and set their careers far, far, back.

For example, you need to understand that the placement of offices relative to other offices on a floor is really a code that tells you people's relative positions within a company. Otherwise you might choose an office with a nice terminal that is so far from the rest of your work group that it signals that you are "out of it." You need to understand the signals you send out with your office decor, so that you don't express your individuality in a way that subtly signals you are not a team player. Most important you need to understand the concept of the team and what you must and must not do when functioning as a team player, so that you do not find yourself in a position analogous to that of a catcher who stomps out to the mound and pitches the ball himself since the pitcher is doing such a lousy job.

Technical people often make the worst mistakes because they fail to take politics seriously, and their reward is to have power withheld from them because they have demonstrated themselves to those in control as being dangerously unaware.

What all this means is that you are going to have to deal with a certain amount of politics anywhere you work, since what politics really is is the codified, ritualized ways people have evolved to enable them to function in groups.

[2] Betty L. Harragan, *Games Mother Never Taught You, Corporate Gamesmanship for Women*, (New York: Warner Books, 1978).

But there are politics and there are *politics*. Companies vary widely in the extent to which playing politics is the company pastime. In a company in which politics have been minimized there are well-publicized standards guiding all managers and employees, and which, most importantly, everyone knows.

A wooden desk or a corner office might be the signal that you have attained a certain level of power in the company, but it is clear to all people in the company what you have to do to get that wooden desk. In a well-run company what you have to do to get that desk is to do your assigned task well and demonstrate initiative, identifying and solving problems without needing to have them pointed out to you—when they fall within the scope of your current position.

In a company where politics has gotten out of hand, nothing is straightforward. The company may be riddled with mini-empires and little fiefdoms. Workers in such a company will tell you that the only way to get ahead is to ally yourself with the winning group in the ongoing power struggle. In such an environment it is not at all unusual to hear workers exchanging conspiracy theories to explain otherwise inexplicable management moves.

In a place where allying yourself with powerful individuals has taken the place of demonstrating competence as the method for getting ahead the person who is not adept at political maneuvering is in for a grim time. In this kind of situation people routinely shift blame for project failure onto the backs of powerless scapegoats—often the unwary technical person. Chains of command may be complex and functionally very difficult to understand, reflecting as they do not a simple scheme for getting jobs done, but power alliances forged over many years.

If you have never worked in this kind of place my description probably sounds extreme and exaggerated. But I warn you that they really do exist, and if you should stumble into one you must watch your step. Most importantly, pay attention if more than one person tells you early in your career in a new company that politics is the name of the game there. One or two complainers are the norm in most departments, but if three people tell you that something is going on—it usually is!

The environment in which politics is the most likely to get out of hand is the company where managers and employees are not moved around every few years to new jobs. Current management theory suggests that this kind of movement is a good idea because it keeps people from getting overly possessive about the things they work on and coming to feel that they "own" a particular project.

The worst company I've ever seen in terms of politics was one in which managers managed the same department for ten or fifteen years and programmers remained in the same departments for similar periods of time. A system in this company was not just a system, it was Joe Smith's system, and any suggestion that something could be improved in the system was interpreted as an attack on Joe Smith, causing him immediately to rally his supporters and those who owed him favors to resist all change. Not surprisingly this company had in place some of the stupidest systems I have ever seen in business.

The key thing to remember as a programmer in this environment is that decisions will never be made on the basis of technical expertise and common sense. Nor will your personal career progress because you are excellent at what you do. Instead you will see foolish decisions being defended because of who made them, and those who are the best at making friends with petty autocrats will be the ones receiving the promotions.

Good management minimizes politics for politics' sake and also minimizes the impact of personal relationships in the workplace. But I know people who flourish in an environment of shifting alliances and nefarious plots who would probably find an environment where only programming was going on very dull.

You will not be able to determine the political atmosphere at a potential job site from the interview, I caution you, since absolutely no interviewer will tell you that his company is ultra-political. So don't make a fool of yourself by asking.

The only way you can get some idea about the role of politics in a company is by talking with people who have worked in that company. If you are looking for a job in a town where you have lived for awhile you have probably already heard things that should tell you something about what a company's corporate culture is like, particularly its internal politics. The mistake that people make is that they don't take seriously the things they are told, or they think that they can somehow be immune when entering a politicized environment because they themselves intend to stay out of politics.

If you are a member of a minority or other group that is prone to being discriminated against, you should pay particular attention to this kind of thing. If you hear that a company makes it hard for women or blacks, and hear it more than once or at most twice, take it seriously—there is probably something to it.

If you are looking for a job outside your home territory, it is harder to gauge this. Try to find someone, through friends or old school acquaintances, to talk to about the company before you leap into a job with an unknown company, particularly if it involves relocation.

The penalty for getting in over your head in a company where office politics rules is to find your career completely stymied, because no matter what you do you get mediocre evaluations and no raises. In the worst case you might even get fired.

## Emotional States

Companies have very different emotional climates. Some places are pressure cookers where people are obsessed with deadlines and emotions run high. People yell at each other in meetings. Doors slam and people burst into tears at their desks. This sort of situation can result when management, for whatever reason, gets out of its depth and makes impossible demands on the people working for the company.

A different emotional situation is the one where there is an ever-present undercurrent of grumbling and complaint that rarely breaks through to the surface but subtly poisons the air. Ironically, you will often find the grumble-heavy environment in companies that treat their employees very well. Aware that they probably can't duplicate their present salaries or working conditions elsewhere, employees sometimes feel trapped by the very job security other people would love. Because they feel trapped they mutter and complain, knowing that they are not about to do anything about it.

This grumbling may be conspicuously absent in a high turnover situation, since the people who would be the ones to grumble don't, they quit. If a company has a lot of "lifers" (people who have put in ten or more years with the company) or employees who are close to retirement and merely waiting things out, you might have trouble fitting in as a young, enthusiastic, tear-up-the-world sort. If might be worth taking a look around a potential job site to see if there are other people your age or if you would be in a distinct minority.

Not all emotional states are necessary pathological. In some places people just take things *very* seriously. In this kind of environment everything is very, very important. You don't joke around here, nor do you play space invaders at your terminal when things are slow. Three-quarters of the things that cross your desk are labeled "Confidential" and woe betide the person who leaves without locking up his cabinets. In a contrasting environment you might not fit in unless you could come up with a *better* game than space invaders for your confreres to play, and a person without a sense of humor would be at a distinct disadvantage.

I know of one shop where you would have to really enjoy boating and fishing to fit in since those subjects dominate all conversation that is not directly work related. There are even places that feel like "singles" shops and in contrast, shops where no one ever goes out for a drink after work because they all have to get back to the kids. While I would not advise you to take a job simply because you shared the same interests as the other people who worked there already, there is no question that you are more likely to enjoy working if you are in an environment with people who have interests, beyond programming, in common with yourself.

## The Sweatshop

The sweatshop is similar to the macho shop, except for one difference, in the sweatshop the employees share the common condition that they are working there because they do not believe they could get jobs any place else.

Some sweatshops hire people whose credentials are in fact, so poor that they probably could not get programming jobs anywhere else. In return for hiring them and training them the sweatshop offers low wages and and the opportunity to do endless work. You should be wary of employers who actively recruit people with no DP credentials. A few years ago one well-known company actively sought out college students with no DP background and got them to sign a contract obliging themselves to work for the company, anywhere the company pleased, for a term of three years. If the programmer broke the contract he was liable for some $9,000, which the company claimed represented the cost of the "education" he had received. If the programmer was relocated during this time he signed a further contract that made him liable for all relocation costs should he and the company part ways—including if the company should fire the programmer. On the salaries this company paid it was very hard indeed to save up the money to pay these fees.

This same company also made people hired in from headhunter firms responsible for paying back the headhunter fees the company incurred in hiring them if they left the company within a year. This was true even if the company fired the individual, which they were prone to do, and I know of one case where a fired individual who had worked for almost a year at the company was legally sued for the headhunter fee after he was fired. The enforceability of these contracts varies from state to state, but remember when dealing with any large corporation that a large company can afford far more expensive legal services than you or I can.

A company that operates like this thinks nothing of massive forced relocations, compulsory permanent overtime, and may use tactics that verge on intimidation to keep programmers in line. And of course, when employees can't quit, there is little incentive to give them raises. People who left the company described above after their three-year contracts were up told me that they easily doubled their salaries with the next job.

I have even heard of some sweatshop companies turning to third world countries in the search for programming bodies. A coworker who had immigrated to the United States from India, told me that he had been contacted by a group of programmers from India who were in great distress. They had been recruited by an American retailer, and offered salaries that were very impressive to them by Indian standards: salaries that were under $10,000 a year. They had been brought over to America where they found out these salaries were not enough to support the most meager of life styles, and they were being kept in barracks and forbidden to have telephones.

With business's penchant for exporting American jobs to third-world countries where small children will work for pennies a day doing the work that American workers get paid union salaries to do, you do have to wonder if this is the beginning of a new and frightening development. After all, there is probably no reason why smart people starving in Central America and Asia could not be trained to write COBOL!

Lest you dismiss the above as paranoia, consider an item that appeared in *Computerworld* in 1987,[3] noting that a company called

---

[3] *Computerworld*, "Management Eyes Chinese Workers", September 28, 1987, p. 79.

The China Professional Resources Consortium was planning to supply English-speaking mainland Chinese contract programmers either on-site in the United States or in Chinese development shops and that "a large insurance company" and "a large financial services concern" had expressed interest. The president of the company stated in the article that these programmers "typically earn about $33 a month." 'Nuff said.

As a programmer you want to avoid the sweatshop if you have any other alternative. If you have resolutely avoided getting any training in programming and a sweatshop offers you your only chance to break in, go ahead, it might beat carrying air conditioners up and down stairs for a living. But if you have any credentials at all why do this to yourself? In particular do not, repeat not, sign any contract ever that makes you liable for money if you leave or are fired. This is setting yourself up for serfdom. Decent companies do not charge employees for education either, no matter how great it is supposed to be, so don't fall for that enticement either.

I would also give a wide berth to any company where programmers have been actively trying to unionize. I have great respect for unions and what they can do for their workers. However unionization only becomes an issue in programming shops when things are very bad indeed, since the shortage of skilled programmers for the last decade has meant that dissatisfied programmers can and usually do vote with their feet. Unionization attempts occur in situations where programmers are being intimidated, where long-term employees are having their benefits stripped away, or where programmers who have a stake in the company have become the targets of other exploitative behavior and there is no reason for you to get involved in a situation like this.

## The Country Club

The country club is very different from the environments we've discussed so far in this chapter. Here management has addressed the problem of high employee turnover by making the project fun. I worked at one self-proclaimed "party project" where we had free donuts every Wednesday morning, provided by the company. Not only that, we had a birthday party once a month, a Halloween party complete with costumes, and all-you-could-eat shrimp and champagne when a project milestone was achieved. At Christmastime I found a little Christmas stocking filled with candy at my desk, compliments of management. I also got a personalized thank you note when I did something out of the ordinary as well as a lovely key chain with my initials on it when our project went live. I might add that I was not even an employee on this project, just a contractor!

Not surprisingly, I, and the other people on the project, loved working there, even though the tasks that had to be done at this phase in the project's life cycle were at best routine and at worst, drudgery. There was such a good team spirit in place with all the festivities that turnover was almost nonexistent. People stayed because they liked being there. I myself returned as a contractor later on, turning down the opportunity to take a much better-paying contracting assignment at a macho shop.

Management also made the attempt to give employees the education and opportunities to learn new skills that they wanted. When overtime was required, which was quite often, as this was the last stage of acceptance testing of a large project, management paid for pizza or brought in brownies. More than that every effort was made to see that the overtime that was worked was the minimum amount humanly possible.

I suspect that the dollars spent on shrimp and donuts in this project were saved over and over again by the dollars not spent training new people in that system.

At another company in a different part of the country everyone got Friday afternoon off when daylight-saving time was in effect. That company gave generous Christmas bonuses and turkeys to its employees. Along with these frills the company also provided generous raises and gave programmers the opportunity to take on as much responsibility as they could handle.

The only way I've ever found to locate places like these is by talking to coworkers about other places they have worked. Nobody advertises "Free Donuts and Parties" in the Sunday Classifieds. Keep your ears open and you might be able to find a convivial environment which might restore your feelings of fun in what you do. On the other hand, again, you must know your own nature. Perhaps the limited technical nature of the work available in such an environment would outweigh the team spirit for you. Or you might even have to accept that you were not comfortable working somewhere where people tried to have fun during working hours!

## Physical Environments

On a slightly different tack, as a prospective programmer facing your first interview, you should be warned about the physical environment that you might encounter and how to interpret it. The sad fact is that many programming environments appear pretty grim to the neophyte. You will often be given a desk in a cubicle (familiarly called the "cube") which is defined by paneled fabric walls. Usually you will not get to sit anywhere near a window or have your own office until you have achieved some administrative rank, at least that of team leader.

Although you might be getting paid thousands more than a manager in the user department you are supporting, you will not have the physical perks they do, simply because most companies reserve physical comforts (and that includes natural daylight) as rewards to be distributed to managers. There is some range of variation to be found. While some highly paid programmers work in sub-basements, some new hires have their own offices with doors that close. In the latter case it is usually because the programmers are part of a small department associated with a user group that has heavy customer contact and thus needs impressive office space.

Since the programming shop is usually not a stop on the tour of the premises given to prospective clients, most programmers work in unimpressive office environments reminiscent of (because they are derived from) the accounting clerk environments of the past.

If you are interviewing somewhere that has particularly luxurious office space this may well be a signal that the programming effort going on here is unimportant. Perhaps it is a very small part of what the division you would be programming for does and that is why the office space is a reflection of the user's other functions. Often the places where you will find a lot of programming activity along with the kinds of diversity and training that lead to a bright future are housed in a drab, more traditional type of programmer work space. My first job, which was a terrific learning opportunity, was housed, because of a space shortage, on the second floor of a building in a tiny shopping center, directly over a supermarket.

# 16
## Factors—Money

No discussion of your career would be complete without touching on the subject of money. Whatever other gratification you receive from your job, the salary that you receive for doing it has got to be a major part of your motivation in showing up day after day. Traditionally, programming has been a field that has offered very good salaries to its practitioners, especially when you take into consideration the amount of training needed to qualify for the job. An intelligent programmer with a degree from a two-year technical college can make a salary in the mid-$30,000 range after just four to five years on the job. According to the *Wall Street Journal*, four-year graduates in Computer Science in 1987 were starting work at an average salary of $26,364.

This compares very favorably with many disciplines which require long years of expensive graduate study to qualify for entry-level positions.

This is not to say that programmers in the long run are ahead of those in other fields. Programmers usually see dramatic salary increases in their first five years but find that they hit a salary limit eventually, beyond which they cannot progress in the corporate world without going into management. While an accountant, for example, might start at a lower salary and have to work in the lower salary range for several years in the corporate environment, he can eventually become a CPA and make a much higher salary than most programmers ever see.

The programmer who wants to make more than $50,000 a year is forced in most cases to become an independent consultant or a software developer, or to turn to DP sales. Only a handful of programmers who work as employees ever make more than that amount in industry.

While you will have to face the problem of a ceiling on your earnings somewhere in your career, in your early years your biggest challenge is to make sure that you are paid the most that a person with your skills doing your kind of work is entitled to. Many people new to the corporate world are shocked to discover that people far less qualified than themselves are making better salaries. There are reasons for this.

## Your First Salary

The salary you are offered when you take your first real job is extremely important, particularly if you would like to build your career in that company and not leave it. That is because companies are bound by formulas which specify the maximum salary increase any employee can receive. In some companies these formulas are explicitly stated. Other companies claim that they don't use formulas, and that all salaries are awarded according to merit, but the experience of old-timers in these companies contradicts this. In one such company, in fact, a friend of mine had responsibility for the computer program that did budget planning for the DP area. This program had a series of routines that multiplied current salaries by percentages to estimate future salary needs. The percentages used were precisely those that the old-timers had told us were used to arrive at raises, with appropriate calculations introduced to estimate a range of performance ratings.

What this means is that no matter how good a job you do as an employee of a company, your manager can only give you raises that fall within these percentage ranges. Thus, no matter how high your performance evaluations, you might find yourself paying dearly over many years for a moment of naivete at the job interview.

Sad to say, many people coming to the marketplace for their first professional job prepare themselves for every facet of the job interview, except the question that will certainly be asked by the interviewer: "How much do you want?"

Some interviewees are afraid that if they appear too interested in money they won't be offered the job.

Others, accustomed to the school system where you generally get the grade that you've earned, assume that they will be offered the best salary possible because of their qualifications.

When the student who had a 4.0 average discovers over lunch one day that the big mouth down the hall from him whose credentials are nowhere near as impressive as his own started out at a salary $3,000 higher than his it is a nasty, but illuminating, surprise.

There is no easy way to come out on top on the money question. If you ask for an amount that is way out of line with what the company starts people at, you might indeed lose the job. On the other hand if you ask for an amount that is less than the hiring manager had planned to offer, he may offer you a little more than you asked for to make you feel good and reserve the rest; after all, you said you didn't need it.

How then can you figure out what the appropriate figure to ask for would be? Well, obviously you must, once again, do some research. We'll look first at how you can approach determining the correct amount to ask for as a new hire entering your first job. Then we will examine the slightly different issues you must deal with as an experienced programmer looking to change companies.

### Determining the Range for Your First Job

The kind of salary range that you can expect to find in a DP job will be affected by several factors. The industry your job would be in is extremely important. Some kinds of companies make more money than others and as a result can pay their employees better salaries. According to *Datamation's* annual salary survey (which we will discuss further), the industries that tend to pay above-average salaries are transportation, utilities, DP services (consulting shops), and non-banking financial services (brokerages and investment firms). At the other extreme are programming jobs in the academic world, which pay the lowest salaries.[1]

The second major determinant of what kind of salary you can get for your first job—but not necessarily for any future one—is your educational level. The lowest starting salaries are paid to two-year college graduates, the next higher to four-year college graduates, higher still are the salaries paid to people with master's degrees in a computer-science-related field, and finally at the top are the salaries paid to those with Ph.D.'s. While this sounds as if having a master's degree would be a great idea, as opposed to having an associates degree, you must remember the extra years spent in school earning that degree balance against the salary increases you would have made had you been working each of those years as a programmer. You might be surprised to find that in many companies the people with the two-year degrees are making salaries quite close to the people with master's degrees after five or six years. This is because the salaries at that point in your career are affected much more by the quality of your experience and the job class you are in rather than your educational attainments. After five years the competent person with the two-year degree may well have been promoted beyond his more educated coworkers.

There is only one real problem you might encounter if you do not have at least a bachelor's degree though. If you have a two-year degree you should make sure to inquire at the interview whether the company has a policy that requires employees to have a four-year degree in order to rise to certain job classes. Some companies limit management jobs to those with this kind of degree. Others do not seem to pay much attention to educational attainments in their promotion policies.

Many programmers I've met consider a master's degree in computer science, particularly the business-oriented master's rather than the engineering-oriented one, to be an almost worthless credential. It is true that it will get you several thousand a year more when you are hired in from school (if you know how to negotiate), but if you acquire a master's degree while you are already employed by the company where you would like to remain it almost never is grounds for a salary increase.

[1] Parker Hodges, "*Datamation's* Annual Salary Survey," *Datamation*, September 15, 1986, and August 15, 1987.

You rarely see a master's degree listed as a necessary qualification in ads for any jobs except low-paying part-time college teaching jobs! This may be in part because so many university master's degree curricula are out of touch with the reality faced by people working in the programming field, and the courses that the student takes in these master's degree programs do not significantly increase the contribution he can make to a business.

The situation is different for those with Ph.D.'s who can make salaries of $75,000 a year in the research facilities of blue-ribbon companies, but these salaries reflect the scarcity of people able to get through these rigorous programs.

One place to get some idea of realistic salaries for entry-level programmers is in the trade press. Magazines periodically publish salary surveys. *Datamation's* comes out annually, so does *Computerworld's*. The salary figures you will find in the *Datamation* survey come from the responses of a large number of *Datamation* readers, including management, around the country. The figure you are interested in looking at when you are starting out is the average salary for junior programmers in your region and industry.

My reaction to *Datamation's* numbers over the years has been to think they looked a little bit low. This year's figure for starting salaries was a good $7,500 lower, for example, than the figure my newspaper recently reported was the average offer to college graduates in computer programming. I would suspect that the true figure might lie somewhere in between. The salaries of people I've known in the field have tended to be higher than those in the survey too. But then again I've never known anyone who actually sent their salary information in to *Datamation*.

Look at these salary surveys and supplement what you find there by listening to what students a year ahead of you claim to have been offered. Everyone in college loves to brag about their salary offers, and some may even tell the truth! You can also ask friends who work in the industry what they think the range for starting programmers in their company might be. But please—be aware that it is extremely rude to ask people what their own salary might be. Confine yourself to talking about ranges.

An important piece of the salary equation doesn't show up in the dollar figure that you see listed in the surveys or hear quoted when the recruiter calls you with a job offer. An additional "salary" consideration is the package of benefits the company offers. The company's benefit plan deserves a long hard look before you make up your mind to take a job. In the old days most companies offered very similar benefit plans and many paid the entire cost of health benefits. But that is changing. As the costs of these plans escalate, companies are forcing employees to cover an increasingly larger share of the benefits' expense, or else they are offering employees a choice among benefits, rather than the whole set. For example, it is not at all unusual to have to pay $70 or more a month for family health benefits. Other companies make new employees wait ninety days before they are even eligible to receive benefits or exclude existing pregnancies. If you have a family, the difference between a completely company-paid plan that covers all your health expenses, and one where you must pay $840 for a year, with a high deductible, and you must pay to 20 percent of your health costs, can add up to a few thousands of dollars a year. You may even have to pay for parking on the company's lot if your office is downtown, which can cost you another $360 a year or more. Take a good look at the company's benefit plan. Feel free to phone the employee benefits office and ask exactly what you would have to pay for any benefit you are interested in, and ask yourself whether, if benefits like discounts, supplementary insurance, savings plans, and group travel rates are offered, you would be likely to use them.

Some companies will be very open with you about what range of salaries they pay at each job classes and will even show you graphs of their salary scales at the interview. In other companies the salary scale is a deep, dark secret. Electronic Data Systems even goes so far as to tell you up front that revealing your salary to another company employee is grounds for immediate dismissal. I would assume that this secrecy is needed to cloak the fact that in these companies people doing the same work are receiving widely different salaries. I would be suspect of any organization that makes a big production about this. Other companies, while not expressly forbidding such discussions, have corporate cultures that make discussing your salary a real faux pas. However, you will often find that once you get to be good friends with a coworker in this kind of place salary information is often exchanged.

Once you have a good idea of the salary range open to new hires with your credentials you should probably ask for an amount a little higher than the middle of the range, unless you know you are ir-resistible. In that case, particularly if you don't feel that you just have to get this job, you might ask for a figure at the top of the range.

Besides your starting salary there is another important factor that affects how your salary will grow, and that is the frequency of salary reviews. Usually a new employee is given an appraisal and a salary review anywhere from six months to a year after being hired. The frequency of these reviews in subsequent years varies greatly. In some companies you might continue to be reviewed every six months, but in others you could easily wait eighteen months for your next review. This is important because it is only after a salary review that you generally are eligible for a raise.

In a company with frequent salary reviews a programmer who does a terrific job has more opportunities for raises. Since typical raises in your first years can be anywhere from 5 percent to 19 per-cent of your current salary, getting those reviews on a regular basis means a lot to your salary development.

Find out, too, how long a programmer can be expected to remain at each job class in the company. Most managers will tell you something to the effect that, for example, you should expect to remain at a trainee grade for a year, and then to spend three years at the next level and an additional four years at the level at which you most likely would become a team leader before reaching a manage-ment entry job class.

This information is important because each promotion repre-sents an opportunity to get a larger-than-usual boost in salary. Many companies confer promotion bonuses on top of your usual salary hike that can amount to 5 percent or 10 percent more. A company that has regular merit reviews and steady promotions can provide you with the opportunity for dramatic salary growth and may end up paying you better in the long run than a company that starts you at a higher salary but gives out small raises sparingly thereafter. This is particularly true if you are a dazzling performer.

In one company I know of, where revealing your salary was frowned on, but not completely unknown, a group of programmers discovered in whispered conversations that no matter what salary they had individually started out at, and no matter what their per-formance ratings, they were all making within $1,000 of each other after a few years with the company. The only difference was that those programmers who had started out at lower salaries and received huge raises felt much prouder of themselves than the ones who had started at higher figures and as a result received only modest raises.

An additional word of caution is in order to new hires who are interviewing for positions outside the region of the country they are familiar with. You, in particular, will need to investigate the cost of living where your new job might be. If housing costs are much lower where you currently live than where you are thinking of going, the salary that sounds quite adequate to you now may turn out to be woefully short of what you need to live a middle class life where you are going. Usually salary ranges reflect the cost of living, so be sure that you do not cheat yourself by asking for an amount that is less than what you will need to earn in your new location.

### Your Salary When You Change Jobs

Once you are an experienced programmer there are a few more wrinkles to consider in the salary game.

You should still attempt to figure out what the prevailing ranges are for your geographical area and the kind of business you are working in, but there is a new factor to be added in: your current salary.

If you look in the classified section of your local Sunday paper, at least if you live in an urban area, you will see many advertisements for programmers listing dollar amounts. If you are interested in seeing advertisements for jobs outside of your local region you can find these in the back pages of *Computerworld* and, occasionally, in special professional employment supplements of the *New York Times*. You should take any salaries you see in such ads with a grain of salt, and never assume that you could get the top figures listed when you see a range. These numbers are put in the advertisements most often by headhunters who make them high enough to catch your attention without seeming completely out of line. Generally the salaries mentioned in these ads can give you an idea of the relative salaries paid for different types of experience, and occasionally the actual salary you could command.

However you now face a Catch-22 situation. The sad fact is that in the interview situation everyone will ask you what your current salary is, and everyone will assume that you are lying when you give them an answer. That may be because almost everyone *is* lying when they state their current salaries, but there is good reason for them to: if you don't inflate your salary when asked about it at an interview the interviewer will routinely lop off 10 percent and assume that the diminished figure is your real salary.

The result of this is that if you are an honest soul you might find a job you really like, only to be offered the job at a figure identical to your current salary. The reason behind this is that the person making you the offer assumes he has just given you a whopping 10 percent raise!

I'm not sure what the answer to this situation is. I've tried being completely honest about my salary and received offers lower than the salary I was currently receiving! I've tried inflating the figure too, and concluded that it works better, but I hate having to do things this way. I'll leave it to you to decide, but sometimes I've wished I could just pull out my last paycheck to make my point rather than have to give in to a system based on the assumption that would-be employees are all dishonest.

There is one situation in which you should be extremely careful when asked about your previous salary. And that is if you are relocating to another part of the country. In the previous section I mentioned how you could lose out going to a more affluent part of the country. It also works in reverse. If you are an experienced programmer whose salary has been in the mid-thirties for a few years and move to a region where the economy is weak or where salaries for some other reason are depressed, telling the truth about your salary can result in the rapid termination of the interview. There are places where programmers do not make more than $29,000 a year and if you move to one of them you will have to "exaggerate" your salary downward, or you may not be able to find a job at all.

You face a similar problem if you are trying to go back to work as a corporate employee after having worked as a consultant. Most people in this situation, when asked their previous salary will give their hourly consulting rate, which can be $25 or more. An interviewing manager will usually multiply this out by the number of work-hours in a year and arrive at a figure somewhere upward of $50,000 as your previous salary. Since his own salary is unlikely to be this high, your prospects for being hired are slim.

The smart thing to do in a situation like this is to remember that the figure you should be presenting is your actual net. Calculate how much money you ended up with annually as a consultant after figuring in sick days, holidays, time without work, and after deducting for insurance payments that can easily be more than $3,000 a year. After doing these calculations you probably will have a more modest figure to present a would-be employer. If it is still too high you have some hard thinking to do. Will you really be able to live at the reduced standard of living the corporate job represents? If you can you probably will have to decide what your absolute minimum salary requirement would be and state that you were making about that amount as a contractor. The reason for this is that almost no company will hire you in as a new employee at a salary substantially less than you used to make because they assume that if they did so you would soon quit.

For those of you, by the way, who are wondering, a potential employer cannot call your old company and find out what your salary really was. If you've ever applied for a mortgage you've seen a permission form which must be filled out by an employee before a company will divulge salary information. Without this form an employer, or ex-employer, cannot give out information about what you were paid. However they can if they choose tell someone what your old job class might have been, although many choose not to. Since most managers have a pretty good idea what the salary range should be for each job class, at least in local companies, lying about your salary in a big way will be spotted and probably result in your not being considered for a job.

If you are job hopping and using the services of a headhunter you should be aware that the headhunter will sometimes tell you before an interview that the job pays less than it actually does. This puts them in a position where they can offer you a nice "surprise" if an offer comes through. This might give you the psychological boost that encourages you to take the job. It also keeps you from asking for a too high salary at the interview that will preclude your getting the offer.

---

Do your research about money, but when you sit down and are about to make the decision about what job to accept, don't let money alone shape your decision. If you have absorbed what this book has been saying, you should realize by now that what you are doing is building a long-term career, and the money you are really interested in is long-term money. If you select a job that lets you do something you enjoy doing, with a company whose corporate style is compatible with your own, you are likely to get what you need to be a success in the job, and success within a company will give you the educational opportunities and the contacts which in the long run will make it possible for you to take control of your career. When you are truly in control of your career, money ceases to be a problem. And it is only when you have that feeling of being in control, of having chosen your own direction and having achieved your own objectives that you will have the feelings of contentment and pride in your own accomplishments that characterize the successful person.

# Twenty-Five Questions to Ask at the Interview

The following is a list of 25 sets of related questions that you might want to ask an interviewer when you are being interviewed for a programming job. They are drawn from many different chapters of this book. After each set of questions is the number of the chapter or chapters where topics related to those questions are discussed. If more than one chapter is listed, the first one is the place to start your review.

Browse the list before you go to an interview and try to select the five questions that would be most important to you, given your chosen career direction. Merely by reading these questions and planting them in the back of your mind you are more likely to spot trouble signals and bonuses in a job you are considering.

**Questions for an Interviewer:**

1. What is your position in this organization? (Chapter 8)

2. How many programmers work for the company? In this division? In this department? If relevant: how many systems programmers are there? (Chapters 9 and 3)

3. What kinds of applications does the company have computerized? The division? The department? (Chapters 13 and 9)

4. What kind of courses do you give programmers in-house? At outside training centers? How often? (Chapters 3 and 11)

5. What kind of a machine does your system run on? Does the rest of the company use this hardware too? Are there any plans, if it is not IBM, to do a conversion in the next few years? (Chapter 10)

6. What operating system are you using? If it is VM/CMS do you do any development that runs in VM/CMS itself? If DOS, are there plans to migrate? If non-IBM, does the operating system include its own programming language or does it use COBOL or another standard language? (Chapters 11 and 12)

7. Does the system I will personally be working with use a database? Which one? Will I get classes in it? Does a separate department handle, write, or maintain the database access modules? (Chapters 11 and 9)

8. Am I being hired for a batch or on-line system? If batch does the system have an on-line portion? Does the system process a tape master file? How is testing turnaround? If this is an on-line system what software provides the on-line services? Will I be sent to any classes to learn how to program in the on-line environment? If CICS, does a separate tech support group debug the complex and interesting systems problems? If batch, am I expected to do my own JCL? (Chapters 11 and 9)

9. What will I actually be responsible for on this system? Is this definite or liable to change? What could I evolve toward in this system over a course of years? (Chapters 8 and 3)

10. What does the person who used to do this job do now? If it is a new job, why are you bringing in outsiders? (Chapters 4 and 8)

11. What languages do you use here? If PC based, will I be working with the mainframe system too? In what way? If assembler, will I be writing new code too or just maintaining an old system? If

a 4GL, do you do all your development in this 4GL or do you use some procedural language too? Will I be sent to classes to use this language? (Chapters 12 and 11)

12. If a package from an outside vendor is used, was this package developed only for your company or is it in general use? Will I be sent to outside classes to use it? Are you planning to modify the package here? Has the package been delivered and tested or is it still in development mode? (Chapters 3, 11, 13, and 14)

13. Is this a maintenance phase project? If so, how active is the system: does it require a lot of changes and enhancements or is it fairly stable? (Chapter 14)

14. If this is a development project, how much coding has already taken place? Would a lot of new people come into the project with me right now? If so, why? How much of the actual design will I participate in? Is the specification phase complete? What kind of testing is planned? Will I personally work with the system's users? With systems analysts? (Chapters 14 and 9)

15. Tell me more about the application. Who are the users? Will I work directly with them or through an interface group? What is their level of sophistication as far as computer systems go? Do you encourage programmers to take courses in subjects relating to the application? (Chapter 13, 9, and 15)

16. Will I be on call? How often? Do you give on-call programmers a beeper? Do on-call programmers take home a PC with a modem? If I have my own PC and modem, can I use it from home to work on the system? (Chapter 15)

17. How much overtime will be expected of me in this position? Is that year-round or just during crunch periods? (Chapter 15)

18. If this is an established system, do you have a functional test system? (Chapters 15 and 2)

19. How long has this team been together? How long have you (or the real boss) been with the team? (Chapters 15, 3, and 4)

20. Does the company post job listings? If not, how does a person get a new position within the company? What conditions must be met before a person can apply for a job that is posted? (Chapters 4 and 15)

21. Do you have formalized performance appraisals? Do they go along with salary reviews? How often do you schedule salary reviews? (Chapters 16 and 15)

22. Are certain educational requirements needed for promotion beyond certain job classes on my career path? What are they? Will the company pay for courses needed to improve my academic credentials? (Chapters 1, 3, and 16)

23. Would benefits be effective immediately? If not, how long is the waiting period? Does the company pay my health and other benefits entirely or do I have to pay a portion? How much? (Chapter 16)

24. Who will be my supervisor? May I meet him? Who will be my team members? May I meet them? (Chapters 2, 8, and 15)

25. Is this where I will work? If not where? If downtown, does the company supply parking? How likely is it that I will be transferred to another location in the next two years? Do programmers move from site to site often? (Chapters 4, 9, and 15)


Good Luck!

# Glossary

This glossary is intended as an aid for nontechnical readers. Included are those terms that might need more explanation than that given in the text of the book. In most cases I have tried to document all technical terms where they first appear. As a result you can use the index to locate definitions for many other terms not found below.

**ABEND** See "Bomb" below.

**APPLICATIONS PROGRAMMER** Term used for programmers who develop or maintain programs whose purpose is to address a business need, for example a payroll program, as opposed to those whose responsibility is for programs that are used by programmers, such as program editors or language compilers.

**APPLICATIONS GENERATOR** Programs developed in the hopes of doing away with the need for legions of the above applications programmers. In theory they reduce the amount of coding needed to develop programs and allow less highly trained personnel to create programs.

**ASSEMBLER** The computer language whose instructions closely match the machine operations the computer actually performs.

**BATCH** Applications programs in most DP establishments are broken down into two groups: on-line programs and batch. Batch programs are executed at some scheduled time and create and update files without any use of screens. Batch systems usually are made up of "jobs" which are collections of batch programs run in a predefined order. Historically batch systems predate on-line systems. Batch systems are often perceived as being lower status than on-line although in fact, they can be more complex. Most heavy report writing is done by batch systems as are routine operations that must be applied to thousands, or millions of items. Batch production systems often run at night thus necessitating midnight visits by on-call programmers when they misfunction.

**BOMB** Programmer slang for what happens when a program not only fails but does so in an obvious way, spitting out obscure messages as it dies. A classier term for the same thing is "abend," short for "abnormal end."

**CODE** Programmer term for the statements out of which computer programs are built. Source code is written in languages like COBOL or Assembler. Machine code is that code in the binary form in which it is fed to the computer. Sometimes used as a synonym for "program."

**DP** Data Processing. Term applied to the use of computers to perform business tasks. Typical data processing applications are payroll, inventory, insurance policy processing, and account management. Data processing is distinguished from scientific and engineering use of computers in that it usually involves little "number crunching" or mathematical manipulation of data.

**DATABASE** This word is subject to tremendous abuse. In the PC world familiar to many people who are not DP programmers, it means any system that performs file access and manipulation but usually includes additional features like report writing. In the mainframe world it has a more narrow meaning and refers to a group of highly complex programs that provide sophisticated cross-indexing to file information, which allows the programmer to create custom "views" of his data without affecting the way in which the data is actually stored in the computer. The data is actually stored in a single format, which appears hundreds of different ways to different applications. This feature is very useful when the same data must be accessed for widely different purposes. It is quite possible to have a very complex mainframe application that uses a great number of files and a complex indexing structure that is not considered a "database" application.

ENHANCEMENT A euphemism for maintenance (see below). Since maintenance programming has developed a low-status image in spite of its very real importance, hiring managers have had to create a new term to describe what the vast majority of all programmers do.

HARDCODING Programmers are supposed to use general algorithms (logic patterns) in the construction of programs to handle all situations that might occur. However, when a program does not work right and the programmer cannot trace through the program logic and fix it, he sometimes resorts to putting in very specific logic to bypass the problem without really eliminating it. This is called hardcoding. It is sometimes necessary in a crisis when time is not available for a better fix but it should be removed and replaced with a logic solution.

HARDWARE The machines that programmers work on. To a far greater extent than is realized by most nonprogrammers, hardware is irrelevant to the programmer and is treated as a black box. In spite of this, ignorant personnel interviewers often niggle about the exact computer model that an applicant's experience applies to. It is *software* (computer programs) that a programmer works with and must know the specifics of.

HEXADECIMAL Base 16 number system used to represent the on and off condition of the switches that make up computer storage.

IPL Term used for loading the operating system software into a computer.

JCL Acronym for Job Control Language. JCL statements give the operating system information it needs to know before it can run a batch program, such as where to find data files, where to write output and what program to run.

MAINFRAME A large computer system costing anywhere from $250,000 to $10,000,000, usually used for multi-departmental data processing. IBM's 43XX series computers and 3090 series computers are among the most popular mainframes on the market.

MAINTENANCE The endless and very important task of adapting existing production computer systems to the small changes characteristic of real businesses. Maintenance includes making fixes to programs when errors are found, making small additions of function to existing programs, and reacting to changes in the products that make up the supporting software environment which occasionally make it necessary to change existing programs.

MINICOMPUTER A medium sized computer system costing anywhere from $5,000 to $200,000. Commonly found in companies of all sizes that are not DP-intensive for company-wide data processing. Also used often as departmental stand-alone machines, or networked with large mainframes.

**ON-LINE** Most broadly this term refers to programs that use a CRT screen to communicate with a user. On-line programs typically view or update small amounts of data at one time. See Chapter 11 for more detail. On-line contrasts with batch.

**OPERATIONS** This term refers to the generally lower status personnel who tend the machinery that performs data processing. Operations staff do many tasks from the most menial, such as hanging tapes on tape drives to the most vital, such as fixing abends and JCL problems and taking responsibility for backing up and restoring systems. Any intelligent programmer will treat operations people with tremendous respect since their cooperation is essential in many cases for the successful completion of the programmer's assignments. Contact with operations personnel is most likely in a small- or medium-sized shop. In large shops they are often invisible to the programmer.

**PC** Term used for microcomputers derived from IBM's successful Personal Computer product. Originally developed for the home computer market, PC's are mainly sold now for business use. Very small businesses use PC's for their data processing needs, mainly using off-the-shelf software. Many large businesses originally bought great numbers of PC's as executive perks and status symbols. In these large businesses they are most often used now for word processing and spreadsheet applications, again using off-the-shelf software; however, many companies are currently developing mainframe based applications that communicate with networks of PC's at remote locations.

**PRODUCTION** This term refers to the computer systems that the company uses in its day-to-day operations. These programs are considered "debugged" and are not changed without extensive controls. The fact that they are "debugged" does not, by the way, mean that they do not have bugs. They do, but usually very subtle ones that occur only when odd combinations of hard-to-predict events occur. As a result programmers usually must be "on call" for production systems so that they can fix these bugs when they emerge.

**SOFTWARE** This term most broadly applies to any program that, when loaded into a computer, makes it do something. Sometimes the word software is used to mean a more specialized subset of these programs, those created to be sold, as opposed to programs created to be used in-house. In this capacity it includes the many programs that are used by mainframe programmers in the course of developing in-house programs.

**SYSTEMS PROGRAMMER** Programmer whose responsibility is the installation and maintenance of the software that is used by the applications programmers as tools to create the business programs they work on. Systems programmers also, but only very occasionally, develop these tools, called systems software.

**VENDOR** A company whose business is the supply of software or hardware.

**VENDOR PACKAGES** Software developed by outside software companies and bought by DP departments in the hope that they can avoid the costs of developing the software themselves. Generally developed to provide applications solutions, these packages are usually only successfully implemented when they require almost no customizing and can be used as supplied by the vendor.

# Index